URBAN POLITICAL THEORY AND THE MANAGEMENT OF FISCAL STRESS

Urban Political Theory and the Management of Fiscal Stress

Edited by
MICHAEL GOLDSMITH
Department of Politics and Contemporary History
University of Salford
and
SØREN VILLADSEN
Institute of Political Studies
Copenhagen

Gower

Published by

Gower Publishing Company Limited
Gower House
Croft Road
Aldershot
Hants. GU11 3HR
England.

Reprinted 1989

Gower Publishing Company
Old Post Road
Brookfield
Vermont   05036
U.S.A.

British Library Cataloguing in Publication Data

Urban political theory and the management of
    fiscal stress.
    1. Local government——Great Britain——State
    supervision   2. Municipal government——Great
    Britain   3. Great Britain——Politics and
    government——1979-   4. Local government——
    Denmark——State supervision   5. Municipal
    government——Denmark   6. Denmark——Politics
    and government——1972-
    I. Goldsmith, Michael   II. Villadsen, Soren
    354.4108'3   JS3137

    ISBN 0-566-00835-1

    6003731143

Printed in Great Britain by
Kingprint International, Kingston-Upon-Thames, Surrey

Contents

Tables and Figures   vii

Preface and Acknowledgments   x

Introduction   xi

1. Reflections on the dual politics thesis: the   1
   argument, its origins and its critics.
   Peter Saunders.

2. The dual state and corporatism: reflections in   41
   the light of recent Danish experience.
   Søren Villadsen.

3. Decentralisation in Denmark: towards a new   63
   inequality.
   Frank Bundgaard and Mads Christoffersen.

4. Urban politics, the local state and consumption: 77
   problems in recent social and political theory.
   Rob Flynn.

5. Danish local government: recent trends in   100
   economy and administration.
   Carl-Johan Skovsgaard and Jørgen Søndergaard.

6. Fiscal pressure and central-local relations   123
    in Britain.
    Edward Page.

7. Deconcentration or decentralisation? Local   137
    government and the possibilities for local
    control of local economies.
    Ray Hudson and Viggo Plum.

8. Central and local state relations in U.K. land   161
    supply.
    Gill Whitting.

9. The labour movement, local politics and   179
    spatial sociology: some recent Danish
    experience.
    Jens Chr. Tonboe.

10. The local state and social movements in Denmark.   206
    Kirsten Simonsen.

11. The perceived impact of spending cuts in   224
    Britain, 1980-1984. Social class life cycle
    and sectoral location influences.
    Stephen Edgell and Vic Duke.

12. Protecting the local welfare state: what   256
    can localities do? Some British examples.
    Michael Goldsmith.

Tables and figures

The Dual Politics Thesis   13

Attitudes to increased local autonomy versus   46
equalisation organised by the State, 1981 and 1978

Attitudes towards state control and spending limits   47
by leading local councillors and in the population,
1981.

Citizens' views on local government spending on   48
various sectors, 1981

Increases in taxes v. increases in services: the   50
local politicians' views

Local politicians' spending preferences on various   50
sectors

Local politicians' perceptions of group influences   54

The three elements of the urban question   56

Percentage increase in tax rate and real   108
expenditure, Denmark 1977-83

Current expenditures on selected functions   109

Distribution according to growth of expenditures   113
on selected items, 1978-82, Denmark

Central directors' evaluation of sector strength   114

Strategies for handling fiscal strain in local   116
government

Bureaucratic innovations for handling fiscal strain   118
in local government

The implementation of selected bureaucratic   119
innovations, 1982-83, Denmark

Local government grant, current expenditure and   126
capital expenditure, 1972-83, Britain

Revenue for local governments, 1981 Denmark   151

Current and capital expenditure by central and   152
local government, 1982, Denmark

Index of manufacturing employment in Danish   154
Counties, 1982

Distribution of employment in municipalities,   189
1980, Denmark

Current and capital expenditure per inhabitant   192
in two Danish municipalities, 1978-83

Real increase for current expenditure per   193
inhabitant in two Danish municipalities, 1978-83

Real increase for capital expenditure per inhabitant   193
in two Danish municipalities, 1978-83

Real increase for current and capital expenditure   193
per inhabitant in two Danish municipalities, 1978-83

Employees and salaries in the public sector in   199
Hjørring, 1982

Grassroots participation by sector, Denmark   215

Labourville and Torytown comparisons:1981 Census   228

Labourville and Torytown comparisons: 1981 Census   229

Knowledge of spending cuts in education, health,   232
transport and social services by area

Perception of spending trends and knowledge of   233/4
cuts by area

Actual central government spending trends on eight   236
selected services 1979-83

Actual local authority spending trends on three   237
services 1979-83

Perceived impact of spending cuts on household as   239
consumers and producers by area

Perceived impact on spending cuts on household by   242
social class

Perceived impact of spending cuts on household by   244
life cycle stage

Perceived impact of spending cuts on household by   245
life cycle stage and class

Perceived impact of spending cuts on household   247
by consumption and production sector

Perceived impact of spending cuts on household by   248
sector location and class

Preface and acknowledgments

Like most books, this one owes a debt to a number of people and institutions. Financial support for the meetings of the Anglo-Danish Study Group has been forthcoming from such bodies as the Danish Social Science Research Council, the Danish Association of Municipalities, the British Council, and the Universities of Salford, Copenhagen and Roskilde. The editors have benefited, as has the Study Group, from their association with Pat Dunleavy. Martin Boddy and Edmond Preteceille in an EEC-financed urban studies teaching programme, which has provided further opportunities for the editors to meet and exchange ideas. Spoon, Big Joe, Miles, Mingus and Fessor provided musical support.

Pat Bellotti prepared the typescript, dealing with the peculiarities of Danish spelling and grammar with no more grumbling than usual. Last, but not least, the editors' wives, Lissie and Anne, not only bore the usual difficulties associated with the preparation of books, but also had to cope with additional foreign guests on more than one occasion. They rose to the challenge of accommodating and feeding up to a dozen adults and children without the slightest sign of the upheaval such intrusions no doubt caused. The editors thank all of them with gratitude, though remain responsible for the content in the usually accepted manner.

Mike Goldsmith and Søren Villadsen.
Salford, Copenhagen and Roskilde, 1984/1985.

Introduction

The essays included in this collection are drawn from
contributions made at the first meeting of the Anglo-Danish
Group in Copenhagen in 1983. A second meeting of the Group
took place in May 1985, at which the essay by Edgell and Duke
was presented, though the decision to include it had been
taken some time earlier.

Inevitably the process of publication has been delayed by
the time it has taken to revise and subsequently edit the
various contributions, and of course waiting for the more
tardy contributors. Some of these proved so tardy that they
never arrived, though their contributions to the meeting
greatly assisted our deliberations in the first place.

The Study Group grew out of a chance meeting between the two
editors at a conference in Gilleleje in 1981, when the pair
discovered that not only did they share a common interest in
some of the murkier sides of urban politics and sociology, but
also a love of jazz and good beer. At the time Villadsen was
a member of the large Danish team studying aspects of Danish
local politics: Goldsmith was Research Coordinator for the
ESRC's research initiative on central-local government
relations. In between the beer and the jazz the two
discovered that their two countries were sharing similar
experiences of stress and strain in central-local relations,
both in fiscal and policy terms. Cutbacks which had become
common in Britain were making themselves apparent in the

Danish context, whilst some of the pressures of Danish inner city life and change were echoed in Britain. The two also shared a desire to seek out explanations for what was happening and to attempt such an analysis in a comparative context. And since both were members of extensive networks of researchers working in the area, they were well placed to bring together some of the best people working in the field in their respective countries. Plans were thus laid for a joint meeting to be held, and these finally reached fruition in 1983.

By that time, researchers in Britain had made considerable progress in both theoretical and empirical terms. Since the mid seventies, when Marxist perspectives on the urban had emerged to assume a dominant position in the conceptualisation of many urban problematics, the theoretical literature had blossomed. The work of Castells from France (Castells, 1977; 1978), Offe and Habermas in Germany (Offe, 1975, 1976; Habermas, 1978), and of Pickvance and Dunleavy in Britain (Pickvance, 1976; Dunleavy, 1980) and of people like O'Connor in the United States (O'Connor, 1973) were all examples of work which was influential at the time. In essence much of the stress of this literature was to shift explanations of urban issues away from the locality to the national and international level, and away from overtly political/governmental ones to more structuralist explanations in which the importance of the dominant forms of economic production (in Western Europe and North America predominantly capitalist systems) were paramount. Politics was subordinate to economics: the state subordinate to the capitalist system, the central state superior to the local state... in so far as this distinction was ever made.

Such almost monolithic explanations raised a number of issues, paramount amongst them being the issue of the relative autonomy of the State. There are clearly actions by the State which are clearly not always in the interest of the dominant economic forces. Equally opposition by the local State to actions imposed by the centre have been very much part of the story of relations between central and local government over recent years, especially since the election of the Conservative government under Mrs. Thatcher in 1979. Equally, too, non-marxist theorists began to produce work which challenged the apparent dominance of the Marxist theorists...Rhodes's important work on central-local government relations in Britain (Rhodes, 1981) or Peterson's work in America (Peterson, 1981). One of the major contributions came from the work of Peter Saunders (Saunders 1979; 1981), in which he attempted to build on Marxist theory but fusing it with ideas drawn from a Weberian perspective.

He not only highlighted some of the weaknesses of Marxist work, but also took its strengths and developed them in his own theoretical construction of what has come to be known as the "dual state" model.(1) By the time the study group had come to Copenhagen for its first meeting, a number of criticisms of the dual state model had been forthcoming, which, along with the model itself, were receiving considerable attention both in the United Kingdom and abroad.

Some of the ideas about the nature of corporatism in Britain were to be found in the work of Alan Cawson (Cawson, 1981), a close associate of Peter Saunders (Cawson and Saunders, 1983). What Cawson stressed, along with other writers in the corporatist vein, was the extent to which British politics at national level had become more and more closed...a partnership between government and vested interests which was able effectively to take decisions on policy matters without a great deal of reference to the usual democratic, parliamentary procedures traditionally associated with British politics. The mid-seventies experience of the "social contract" between the unions and the then Labour government was frequently cited as an example of the new corporatist style of British politics, with the operation of the Consultative Council on Local Government Finance in the early seventies being another (Rhodes et al, 1983), and the question of the NFU's influence over agricultural policy being a third. (Self and Storing, 1960). Grant and Marsh's (1979) work on the Confederation of British Industry was yet another example, and despite the many varieties of corporatism which seemed to exist, the phrase appeared a useful way of describing much of the style of British politics up until 1979, and indeed provided Mrs. Thatcher with one element of her platform in the election of that year. Letting government govern, rather than listening to the grinding of axes wielded by vested interests was one of her rallying calls. Reflecting both the experience and the literature of the late seventies, as well as his work with Cawson, Saunders's dual state model has strong corporatist overtones, especially in terms of its characterisation of central/national level political processes concerned with production issues.

But corporatism or corporatist is a word frequently used to describe the Scandinavian model of government, especially that of Sweden, but hardly less apt in Denmark. Not surprisingly then, both Danish and British members of the Study Group were concerned to explore both the "dual state" model, Scandinavian corporatism and other theoretical perspectives on urban issues. The first section of this book thus reflects those discussions and concerns, as the contributions from Saunders, Flynn, Villadsen and Bundgaard and Christofferson demonstrate.

Saunders is particularly concerned in his contribution to review the various criticisms made of the dual state model and to answer them, seeing whether (to use his analogy) the horse is worth at least an each way bet. Not surprisingly, he concludes that it is, something which other writers echo from time to time. For example, whilst Villadsen ends by sketching his own model for understanding local politics, it owes something to Saunders's formulation, and Villadsen himself does not totally reject the dual state model. He is, however, somewhat more critical of the applicability of the corporatist model in the current Danish context. In their different style of review, Bundgaard and Christofferson, together with Flynn,m are concerned to highlight some of the theoretical and methodological limitations of the existing literature and the need for yet still more empirical research.

Much of what lies at the centre of current theoretical debate in the urban field concerns the changing nature of the welfare state and the problems which governments have faced in the light of continuing economic decline since the early seventies. In many countries this decline and the pressures which it has generated to reduce the level of welfare services has been accompanied by a realignment of political forces, often involving the emergence of a government whose political persuasion has been much more right wing than for most of the post war period. Such has been the case in both Britain and Denmark, with the arrival of the Thatcher government in Britain in 1979 and the Schluter government in Denmark in 1981.

Prior to that, the growth of the welfare state in both Denmark and Britain had by and large taken the same form, as it had in other Scandinavian countries. New services were introduced by social democratic governments and passed on to the local government level for the purposes of service delivery. This form of organisation, which leaves the centre with no or little responsibility for the actual delivery of services, results in considerable local discretion when it is linked to a tradition of local self government, which in Scandinavian countries includes some constitutional provision for local autonomy and in Britain permits considerable local discretion to determine both the nature and actual level of local service provision. This local democratic tradition thus results in considerable variation in the nature and level of service provision as and between difference municipalities.

What fuelled the growth in local services above all else was the increase in living standards associated with the expansion of economic activities in most Western countries this century, but particularly after World War 2. Economic growth not only raised people's perceptions and expectations of appropriate private living standards, but also raised their idea of what public services should be provided and to what kind of standards. Until the mid-seventies most people in both Britain and Denmark came to expect ever increasing private and public service standards. Today's luxuries became tomorrow's necessities: washing machines, colour televisions, hi-fi etc. all became the symbols of a new consumer society. And in the public sector people came to expect more and better education for more people; more facilities for leisure and recreation; better public transport, more day care provision, better facilities for the handicapped and so on. The world recession and general economic slowdown which followed the 1973 oil crisis severely affected the public sector's capacity to finance these ever-increasing public services, just as the downturn had its impact on the private sector's activities, particularly in the manufacturing sector. This fiscal crisis, or crisis of late capitalism, as radical writers came to call it, hit Britain in the mid seventies, when the Callaghan government was forced to begin a process of retrenchment and cutback in service provision as a result of the financial crisis it faced in 1976 and as part of the price it had to pay for IMF assistance. The same crisis came shortly afterwards to Denmark, and by the early eighties both countries had right wing governments concerned not only to reduce levels of public expenditure, but also to reduce the form and nature of the welfare state.

As a result of these changes, by 1983 both countries had experienced a considerable period of sustained attempts at reducing local welfare state expenditures. In Britain's case, the Thatcher government had considerably tightened the screw which the previous Labour government under Callaghan had already started to turn as a result of the 1976 financial crisis and the terms imposed by the IMF for assistance to deal with it. By 1983, Britain was in its seventh year of cutbacks. Though Denmark had reached crisis point a year or two after Britain, both the higher level of welfare expenditures and the severity of its own economic crisis meant that in some ways the crisis was more intense and actions to correct the imbalance more severe, and by 1983 Denmark was in the throes of severe cutback.

Not surprisingly, then, perhaps the most important empirical theme dominating the first meeting centred around the financial changes affecting local governments and particularly the way in which they had reacted to loss of central government grant. The paper by Page on British experience and that by Skovsgaard and Søndergaard on changes in Denmark reveal both some of the similar effects which reductions in grant have had in both countries. Whilst Denmark has not as yet progressed as far down the centralist road as has Britain, it is interesting to note that the Danes had their own form of voluntary rate capping (limits on the level of local income tax chargeable) long before it was introduced into England, but that the centre also seems to share some of the same difficulties which British local government has faced in securing local compliance with central guidelines. Skovsgaard and Søndergaard concentrate particularly on the kinds of strategies which Danish municipalities have adopted in order to cope with cutbacks, revealing something of the ingenuity which is also to be found in British local authorities, even if they have not adopted quite the kind of creative accounting practices which have become more commonplace in Britain.

But policy issues other than finance have also been involved in the disputes between centre and locality. Some of these are caught in the contributions by Gill Whitting, Plum and Hudson. Whitting is concerned to examine the consequences for central-local government relations of aspects of the Community Land Act in the late seventies, whilst Hudson and Plum turn their attention to issues of regional policy. In both cases something of the complexity of central-local relations is again caught, as well as the kind of successes and failures which centre and locality have had in tackling their problems. Again local ingenuity is revealed.

The last section is concerned with reactions at the local level to the impact of expenditure reductions. The contributions by Simonsen, Edgell and Duke, Tonboe and Goldsmith look at number of different issues. Simonsen looks at the literature on urban social movements in the light of new youth and women's groups entering onto the local political stage; Edgell and Duke report panel survey data on how expenditure cuts affect people in Greater Manchester, Tonboe looks at some of the new alliances being formed between local labour organisations and local governments in opposition to the centre in Denmark, whilst Goldsmith considers both the conditions under which such local opposition is likely to succeed and reports on two policy areas where local alliances might be built up in Britain.

Whilst Tonboe describes the way in which local unions have become more involved in local politics following the cutbacks in Denmark, he is also concerned with the way in which different localities respond. In other words, he is interested in the way locale plays a role in local politics. Simonsen's concern with such social movements as the young, the greens and women also hints at the importance of locale, but additionally provides evidence of the way new forces are beginning to emerge at the local level, forcing themselves onto the political agenda, getting their voices heard in the council chamber and eventually beginning to be a concern at the centre. In a similar fashion Goldsmith also raises the issue of how important locality is in political processes, reporting as he does the way in which the new kinds of local alliances have grown up around issues concerning local employment and service provision in different municipalities, whilst at the same time highlighting some of the barriers to successful action in the way of such new groupings. Whilst concerned primarily with reporting and explaining popular perceptions of and reactions to spending cuts, Edgell and Duke also focus attention on the issue of local differences, comparing as they do reactions in a Labour controlled town with those from a Conservative controlled one. But another concern of theirs is the difference which exists between producers and consumers in different sectors, particularly the distinction between those mainly concerned with working and consuming in and from the private sector and those predominantly located in the public sector.

All of these pieces are important for two reasons. Together they constitute evidence of the changing nature of local politics and of the importance of locale in political processes generally, and in this they support the work of others who have come to question the overly centralist non-local view of urban politics which had come to dominate work in the field in the late seventies and early eighties. Second, they provide some support for Saunders's view of local politics as essentially more pluralistic and competitive in nature than politics at the centre, though they also reveal the extent to which local level politics has increasingly become concerned with production processes as well as issues concerning the consumption of public, welfare state services. As such they both provide support for elements of the dual state thesis and suggest the need for yet further modification of it. It is out of exchanges and debates such as these that both the quality and quantity of our theoretical and empirical work improves, as does our understanding of the problems facing governments today. Hopefully they also provide some clues as to the practical solutions to those problems, and it is to this end that the work of the Anglo-Danish Study Group will continue.

NOTES

(1) Saunders's dual state model is spelt out more fully in his contribution below

REFERENCES

Castells, M. (1977) The Urban Question, London, Edward Arnold.
Castells, M. (1979) City, Class and Power, London, Macmillan.
Cawson, A. (1981) Corporatism and Welfare, London, Heinemann.
Cawson, A. and Saunders, P. (1983) "Corporatism, competitive politics and class struggle in R. King (ed) Capital and Politics, London, R.K.P.
Dunleavy, P. (1980) Urban Political Analysis, London, Macmillan
Grant, W. and Marsh, D. (1974) The CBI, London,. Hodder and Stoughton.
Habermas, J. (1976) Legitimation Crisis, London, Heinemann.
O'Connor, J. (1973) The Fiscal Crisis of the State, New York, St. Martin's Press.
Offe, C. (1976) Industry and Inequality, London, Hutchinson.
Offe, C. (1975) "The theory of the capitalist state and the problem of policy formation in Lindberg et al. Stress and Contradiction in Modern Capitalism, New York, Lexington.
Peterson, P. (1981) City Limits, Chicago, Chicago University Press.
Pickvance, C. (ed) (1976) Urban Sociology: Critical Essays, London, Tavistock.
Rhodes, R.A.W. (1981) Control and Power in Central-Local Relations, Farnborough, Gower.
Rhodes, R.A.W., Hardy, B. and Pudney, K. (1982) Corporate Bias in Central-Local Relations, University of Essex, mimeo.
Saunders, P. (1979) Urban Politics: a sociological interpretation, London, Hutchinson
Saunders, P. (1981) Sociology and the Urban Question, London, Hutchinson.
Self, P. and Storing, H. (1960) The State and the Farmer, London, Allen and Unwin.

1 Reflections on the dual politics thesis: the argument, its origins and its critics

PETER SAUNDERS
School of Cultural and Community Studies, University of Sussex

The so-called 'dual state' or 'dual politics' thesis has attracted some comment and criticism over the last three or four years. Some of the criticisms have, I believe, been misconceived, but others have indicated some significant problems or weaknesses in the thesis as it stands. In this chapter I shall discuss the various criticisms which have been made in order to come to some conclusions about the theoretical adequacy and empirical applicability of the thesis, and to explore ways in which it may fruitfully be developed.

The chapter is organised in three sections. The first identifies the theoretical origins of the dual politics thesis in various strands and traditions of work which were developing through the 1970s. It is important to remain aware of this intellectual ancestry, not only to understand whence the thesis derived, but also to appreciate the principal problems to which it is addressed. The second section then briefly outlines the basic elements of the thesis itself and the core hypotheses which follow from it. This is a short section, for the thesis has been set out in more detail elsewhere and there is no need here to go into the argument in any great detail. The third, and longest, section then considers some of the main criticisms which have been advanced against the thesis as well as some of the empirical case studies which have employed it. In this way, the chapter arrives at some tentative conclusions regarding the relevance and applicability of the thesis for understanding political processes in different countries in the current period.

THEORETICAL ORIGINS

The dual politics thesis was developed from the late 1970s onwards in response to at least four distinct yet related areas of work which were prominent at that time in western social and political science. As we shall see, each of these areas was developing in relative isolation from the others, yet each had thrown up conceptual or theoretical dichotomies which had certain elements or problems in common.

The debate over corporatism.

It was in 1977, in his working paper on corporatism and environmental planning in Britain, that Alan Cawson first suggested that the division between the monopolistic and competitive sectors of the contemporary capitalist economy had a parallel in the division within the capitalist state between a relatively closed 'corporatist' sector and a more open and pluralistic 'competitive' sector. Cawson then elaborated on this idea in a paper published the following year in **Government and Opposition,** while at the same time, other writers also began to identify much the same sort of political cleavage.

Of particular significance here were two papers by Bob Jessop published in 1978 and 1979 in which he argued, more or less consistently with Cawson that British politics had become 'bifurcated' between a sphere of electoral-democratic politics (the world of parliament, petitions and pressure groups) and a newer sphere of corporatist interest representation in which powerful functional economic interests (i.e. mainly major capitalist firms and federations such as the CBI) were directly represented in policy-making. These ideas then received further support in 1979 when Keith Middlemas published **Politics in Industrial Society** in which he argued that what he called a 'corporate bias' had been developing within the British political system ever since the end of the first world war.

Now it is important to recognise that these various writers differed among themselves over the nature of the corporatist arrangements which they identified. For Cawson, for example, corporatism should not be equated with tripartism, for he insisted that corporatist modes of representation and mediation were not confined either to economic policy (indeed, his main interest was in corporatism and social policy as was demonstrated in his publication in 1982 of **Corporatism and Welfare**) nor to the relations between capital, labour and the state (the professions, for example, were often key actors in corporatist arrangements). Jessop, by contrast, placed his key emphasis on the relation between capital and the state, arguing that organised labour was very much a 'junior partner' in all this, while Middlemas's thesis was that organised labour had come to play a key role in corporatist mediation at the expense of private sector capital.

Despite these differences, however, the similarities in approach of these and other writers at the time were, for our purposes, more important, for they all pointed to the emergence of a distinct corporatist sector of politics co-existing uneasily with more open, democratic state institutions, and they all suggested that power was shifting from the latter to the former. There is no doubt that these ideas were in part influenced by the context in which they were produced - notably the economic and social strategies pursued by the 1974-9 Labour government (especially the 'social contract' and the policy of economic management entailed in the notional commitment to planning agreements, price controls and the National Enterprise Board). However, unlike Jack Winkler, who suggested in two influential papers in 1976 and 1977 that all this was indicative of a transition from a capitalist to a corporatist society, these writers insisted that corporatism referred not to a new system of political economy but to a new way of organising the existing one.

Following Philippe Schmitter (1974), the argument being advanced in the late 1970s was thus that corporatism was a new mode of organising key interests within advanced capitalist countries. It was, to be more precise, a mode of interest mediation which had grown up alongside the liberal-democratic institutions of the state and which enabled certain core functional interests to play a role both in negotiating public policy and in implementing it. Seen in this way, the main questions which arose out of the corporatist literature were (i) which interests came to be represented in corporatist mediation?; (ii) how are they involved and in which kinds of policy areas?; and (iii) how does this corporatist sector of politics relate to the more pluralistic competitive sector? Here, then, was one set of questions which directly informed the development of the dual politics thesis.

The debate over urban politics.

At the time when Alan Cawson was grappling with the problems of corporatism in late capitalism, I was working on an apparently very different body of literature concerned with the explanation of urban-based inequalities. As a postgraduate student in the early 1970s, I had conducted a study of local politics in the London Borough of Croydon which was eventually published in Part Two of my **Urban politics: a sociological interpretation** (1979). The original motivation for this research had been to produce a British 'community power study' which would complement the massive North American community power literature by empirically evaluating the contrasting theories of elitism and pluralism in a British context. Very early on, however, it had become apparent that the concerns of North American researchers could not simply be transferred across the Atlantic, partly because municipal governments in Britain played a more central role in urban policy-making than was the case in the USA, and partly because local autonomy in Britain was much more restricted by higher level authorities than was apparently the case in the United States. The problem to be addressed in urban politics research in Britain, therefore, concerned first the relation between local government and various interest within the local population and, second, the relation between local politics and the central state.

During the 1970s, these problems were explicitly addressed above all in the work of Ray Pahl on 'urban managerialism' (Pahl, 1975, especially chapters 10 and 13). Pahl had originally argued that certain strategically-located individuals, whom he termed 'urban gatekeepers' or 'urban managers', were responsible for allocating crucial urban resources (such as housing or schooling) among different sections of the local population with the result that inequalities generated in the world of work came to be mediated or exacerbated by the distribution of life chances in the local community. However, in response to a growing barrage of both empirically and theoretically informed criticisms, Pahl soon shifted his position from a view of urban managers as the 'independent' sources of urban inequality to one which saw them as 'intervening variables' mediating between the demands of private sector producers and state consumers on the one hand, and between the demands of the central state and of the local population on the other.

This, of course, raised again the question of the degree to which local authorities (for Pahl had by this time limited his definition of urban managers to local state bureaucrats) enjoyed autonomy and discretion vis-a-vis different local sectional interests and higher level state authorities, but Pahl himself never satisfactorily answered this question. Instead, he simply argued that urban managers retained some (unspecified) degree of discretion, and with that he effectively abandoned the concept to its fate while transferring his attentions to the question of corporatism at national level where, it seemed, the power 'really' lay.

The concept which displaced 'urban managerialism' at the heart of academic discussions of urban politics in the latter half of the 1970s was that of the 'local state'. The concept of 'local state' was first introduced by Cynthia Cockburn in a book of that name, published in 1977. In her study, based on research in the London Borough of Lambeth, Cockburn not only dismissed the idea of local autonomy but also argued strongly against analysing urban politics in terms of the goals and values of key individuals such as urban managers. Instead, she drew upon the theories being developed in France and elsewhere by writers such as Nicos Poulantzas (1973) and Manuel Castells (1977) which emphasised the determination of political outcomes by the development of contradictions deep within the structure of a capitalist mode of production. In particular, these writers argued that the role of the capitalist state lay in regulating the class struggles which were generated by the growing contradiction between the accumulation of capital and the reproduction of the social relations of production. For Cockburn, this meant that the 'local state' (by which she seems to have meant little more than local government - see Duncan and Goodwin 1982) could only be understood as part of a unified capitalist state, and that the form of provision of services at the local level reflected the requirements of capital as a whole (i.e. social welfare reproduced cheap and efficient labour-power while also underpinning the legitimacy of existing social arrangements).

Now there is a lot wrong with the argument which we cannot examine here, but for our present purposes the major error lies in the theoretical reduction by which Cockburn equated 'local state' with 'capitalist state' thereby denying any degree of local discretion or autonomy), and 'capitalist state' with 'the interests of capital as a whole' (thereby denying any effective degree of autonomy at the political level). In this way, the problems posed (though not resolved) by Pahl's revised urban managerialism thesis were simply swept away by the broad brush of theoretical generalisation.

Many of those working in the field or urban politics at this time were unhappy with this approach. In a seminar on the local state held in 1980 at the Bristol-based School for

Advanced Urban Studies, for example, Martin Boddy and Colin Fudge argued in their position paper (subsequently published in 1981) that it was necessary in some way to combine the theoretical strengths of such marxist-inspired work with the insights developed in mainstream political science work on central-local government relations which demonstrated that the local level could not be seen merely as the agent of the centre but was rather engaged in negotiation and bargaining with the centre (for an example of such an approach, see Rhodes 1980). This was what I tried to accomplish, both in my book on urban politics, and in a paper given at the 1979 Urban Change and Conflict conference at Nottingham (subsequently published as Saunders, 1981a), in which I argued that the local state had its own specificity such that different types of political determinations were operative at central and at local levels, and that different kinds of theories may therefore be appropriate to the analysis of each.

The argument, basically, was that marxist-inspired 'instrumentalist' state theories (which were in a sense the marxist version of the old elite theories) were more likely to be appropriate to the analysis of national level politics where the interests of capital were necessarily paramount, but that pluralist theories could better explain local political outcomes where diverse interests competed for resources. Urban managers could then be seen, as Pahl had suggested, as mediating between these two political processes, but given the priority of private sector profitability over considerations of social need, and the power imbalance between central and local state agencies, their ability to direct resources towards less privileged groups was necessarily highly limited.

Here, then, was the second element which fed into the dual politics thesis, for the concern with corporatist mediation and its relation to competitive politics now was complemented by a concern with the theoretical distinctiveness of central and local level political processes.

The identification of different state functions.

The third element originated not in Britain, but in intellectual developments in Germany from the 1960s onwards, and particularly in the work of two 'critical theorists', Jurgen Habermas and Claus Offe. From the 1960s onwards, Habermas had been arguing that Marx's political economy was no longer adequate for an understanding of late capitalist societies. In particular, he suggested that the increased significance in the twentieth century of scientific innovation in revolutionising technology as a force of production had undermined the labour theory of value, and that the crucial role of the state in supporting such innovation and in managing the economy meant that a theory of economic determinacy such as that built upon the base-superstructure metaphor was no longer applicable. In his **Legitimation crisis**, published in English in 1976, Habermas brought together many of the themes explored in his earlier works by suggesting that the 'steering problems' in late capitalist societies had been displaced from the economic sphere of the market to the political sphere of the state. The state, in other words, had taken the responsibility upon itself to direct the future development of the society rather than leaving this to free market forces, but in doing so it had undermined the traditional ideologies of laissez-faire capitalism while at the same time creating immense 'rationality problems' as regards how best to manage and direct economic growth. Failure to resolve these problems threatened both the legitimation of the system (which now rested solely on the ability of the state to 'deliver the goods') and the motivation of individuals to participate fully within it.

Habermas's ideas were taken up and explored in the work of Claus Offe (e.g. in his influential 1975 paper and in various of the essays reprinted in Offe, 1984). He distinguished between two aspects of the state's role; the traditional 'allocative' functions (in which the conditions of capital accumulation are maintained in a purely authoritative way through, for example, control of the money supply, regulation of the conditions of labour, and so on), and the newer 'productive' functions (in which the state becomes directly involved by itself producing resources required for capital accumulation - e.g. by nationalising key sectors of the economy or by providing welfare services to support the labour force). Offe argued that while allocative functions could be discharged simply by allowing policies to be determined by the relative political weight of major interests in society, this was not possible in respect of productive functions which had in some way to be insulated from competitive political pressures if they were to achieve their desired ends. Offe discussed various strategies by which such insulation may conceivably be achieved, but concluded that none of them could ensure that productive interventions did in fact accord with the requirements of the system. For him, therefore, the 'rationality problem' of the capitalist state was ultimately irresolvable.

Offe's distinction between allocative and productive state functions, each of which was subject to different determinations, was reflected in various works written outside of Germany through the 1970s, not least of which was James

O'Connor's influential study, **The Fiscal Crisis of the State,**
published in New York in 1973. Like Offe, O'Connor believed
that the primary role of the capitalist state lay in the
support of capital accumulation in the private sector, and
that this was achieved (to the extent that it was possible to
achieve it) by different kinds of interventions. The main
distinction drawn by O'Connor, however, was that between
different types of state expenditure, and here he
differentiated between 'social expenses' (such as spending on
law and order or social security benefits which were necessary
in order to maintain social order and legitimacy but which
represented a drain on private sector profitability) and
'social capital' expenditures which contributed to capital
accumulation either directly (through provision of 'social
investment' which lowered the cost of constant capital) or
indirectly (through provision of 'social consumption' which
lowered the cost of variable capital, i.e. wages). In
O'Connor's view, the escalating demands on all three types of
state spending resulted in a fiscal crisis as the state
attempted in vain to maintain profitability and to suppress
social unrest as the economy slid inexorably into decline.

The legacy of all this work as regards the development of
the dual politics thesis lay in the recognition that the state
in late capitalist societies was engaged in different kinds of
provision serving different kinds of interests in different
kinds of ways. In its earlier versions, the thesis drew
directly on O'Connor's terminology, distinguishing between
'social investment' functions designed to aid capital
accumulation through provision of direct inputs (e.g.
financial aid, physical infrastructure, cheap raw materials)
into private-sector production, and 'social consumption'
functions designed to support the working population and its
dependents through provision of welfare services (e.g.
housing, health care, education) which would otherwise have
had to have been paid for out of household income. However,
it was always a feature of the dual politics thesis that it
rejected the functionalism inherent in O'Connor's approach
(which assumes that <u>all</u> state spending is in some way
necessary to support the interests of capital), arguing
instead that consumption provisions should be seen primarily
as serving interests other than those of private capital. The
logic behind this crucial revision of O'Connor's ideas is
simply that the expansion of the welfare state in most western
countries since the last war has gone far beyond anything that
might be required by capitalist producers. While welfare
spending undoubtedly does contribute in some ways to private
sector profits (both by reducing wage costs and by stimulating
demand for the commodities produced by drug companies,
house-building firms and the like), the primary beneficiaries

have been the consumers of these services and the professional groups (e.g. social workers, teachers and doctors) who have provided them, for these groups have made real gains in their material life chances at the expense of profitability in many parts of the private sector.

In later versions of the dual politics thesis, this fundamental break with functionalist marxism was made more explicitly by dropping O'Connor's terminology in favour of a distinction between the 'politics of production' and the 'politics of consumption', and in this way the key difference between these two aspects of state intervention was seen less in terms of the 'functions' performed, and more in terms of the different interests served. This revision also helped to make explicit the fundamental distinction drawn in the dual politics thesis between a sphere of 'class politics' (corresponding to the politics of production) and a sphere of non-class-based 'sectoral politics', (corresponding to the politics of consumption). This last point can be made clearer, however, if we now consider the fourth strand of work which contributed to the development of the thesis.

The problem of relative autonomy.

I have already noted, in the discussion of the urban politics tradition, the influence achieved by French structuralist marxism during the 1970s. This work derived from the philosophy of Louis Althusser who, like Habermas in Germany, spent much of the 1960s grappling with the problem of economic determinacy in Marxist theory. Unlike Habermas, however, Althusser argued not that Marx's political economy was no redundant, but that it had been misunderstood. In particular, he asserted in various essays published in **For Marx** (English edition 1969) that it was a mistake to see Marx's materialism as a simple 'inversion' of Hegel's idealism;, and that economic determinacy did not imply a base-superstructure determination but rather referred to the way in which economic organisation determined the relative dominance of the economic, political and ideological 'levels' within any given mode of production. For Althusser, these levels developed relatively autonomously of each other, and it was this notion of 'relative autonomy', applied to the political and ideological (or cultural) aspects of social organisation, which was later developed by Poulantzas and others in their theorisation of the capitalist state and of bourgeois ideology.

The theory of relative autonomy is too complex to unravel (still less to evaluate) in the context of this chapter (see Saunders, 1981b chap.6 for a discussion of it). Suffice it to say that the theory attempted to explain how the state was able to respond to interests other than those of the bourgeoisie and yet remain wedded in the long term to the requirements of the capitalist class, and how the dominant ideology in capitalist societies was able to express elements of working class life experience yet still affirm the naturalness of bourgeois social relations. The essence of the explanation which was offered is that it was dualistic: the relative autonomy of politics and ideology was 'explained' as the product of structural determination (i.e. necessary functions) and class practices (i.e. agency), of the needs of the capitalist class and the demands of the working class. The problem with this 'explanation' was that it failed to show how relative autonomy actually worked: how class practices necessarily and inevitably resulted in the fulfilment of system needs, or how the struggles of the working class invariably resulted in the long run in the maintenance of bourgeois domination.

Poulantzas himself seemed to recognise this weakness in an interview he gave to **Marxism Today** in 1979. "The problem still remains", he suggested, "how to find the specificity and the autonomy without falling into the absolute autonomy of politics." The concept of relative autonomy provides us with an elaborate redescription of the problem (for it is undoubtedly true that the capitalist state, for example, does respond to diverse social interests while in the long term safeguarding the interests of the dominant economic class), but no solution. And the reason why it does not and cannot provide a solution lies, in Poulantzas's words, in the inability of marxist theory to recognise the 'absolute autonomy of politics'.

Structuralist marxism set up a problem which it could not resolve given its commitment to a totalistic mode of theorising in which everything was (albeit in 'the last instance') to be understood in the context of the system as a whole and was to be explained in terms of the essential dynamic of class struggle. There was no room in such a theory for the possibility that different outcomes (i.e. policies supportive of capital accumulation and policies supportive of non-capitalist interests) may have their origins in different causes (for class struggle is held to be the universal cause), nor that the observed relative autonomy of the state as a whole may be a product of the fact that different parts of the state system operate in different ways in response to different determinations. Poulantzas's problem, in short, was that the recognition of relative autonomy demanded that he also recognise that the state (and, for that matter, 'ideological apparatuses') is, in some situations 'absolutely autonomous' of economic class interests (for how else can any degree of autonomy be possible? -see Hirst 1977), yet his theory denied such a possibility.

What was needed, yet could never be granted from within structuralist marxism, was the identification of that aspect of politics and of ideology which could be analysed in class terms and which could be explained with reference to the need to maintain capital accumulation, together with the identification of another aspect of political and ideological processes which was not reducible to economic class interests and which was in some way autonomous of determination by the economy. Put another way, it was necessary to recognise the partiality and limited applicability of Marxist political theory - something which could not be recognised given the commitment to a notion of Marxism as a total theory. Such a recognition was only possible by developing some sort of dualistic approach to the analysis of politics involving an attempt to explain different types of state intervention by different kinds of theories. The dual politics thesis was above all an initial attempt at developing one such approach.

The dual politics thesis

The dual politics thesis draws on all four traditions of work discussed in the previous section. From the first tradition it takes the focus on the bifurcation between a corporatist and a competitive mode of interest mediation. From the second it takes the problem of the relation between different levels of the state system. From the third it has developed a concern with the distinction between a class-based "politics of production" and a sector-based "politics of consumption". And from the fourth it takes its core concern in explaining the relative autonomy of politics and of ideology while arguing that this can only be resolved by recognising that different theories which have hitherto been seen as incommensurable may in fact be complementary once different aspects of politics and ideology have been identified.

What welds all this together into a cohesive framework for analysis is the methodology which lies at the heart of the dual politics thesis. I have already noted in the discussion of the problem of structuralist marxism that an holistic theory appears to be self-defeating. I would also argue, following Weber, that such a theory is in any case an impossibility - partly for logical reasons (for it assumes that we know the whole prior to developing an understanding of the parts - the classic problem of Marxist methodology from the **Grundrisse** through Lukacs and Althusser to the current preoccupation with developing a so-called 'realist' epistemology), and partly for ontological reasons (for human history is so vast and social reality so infinite that it seems reasonable to suggest that we can only ever hope to develop partial and inevitably one-sided explanations of the causes of social phenomena).

The methodology of the dual politics thesis is altogether more modest. It does not claim to explain everything; nor does it make any claim to prior knowledge and an epistemologically-privileged insight into the deeper layers of reality lying hidden behind the phenomenal forms of appearances, the distortions of ideology and the confusing melee of contingent events. Rather, it simply involves the construction of partial, one-sided idealised concepts with which one can get a grip on the messy stuff of political reality. The distinctions which it draws and the connections which it posits take the form of Weberian ideal types, and it is on the basis of this typology that hypotheses are developed which are in principle amenable to empirical evaluation by identifying the different aspects of reality which may be explained through different theories. The arguments in favour of such a methodology are discussed elsewhere (Saunders 1983a) and I shall not rehearse them again here. The dual politics thesis itself has also been set out in a number of different publications and has been applied in a number of different contexts. Cawson (1982) discusses it in relation to the problem of corporatism; Saunders (1981, chap.8) outlines it in the context of a discussion of urban social theory; and Saunders (1982 and 1984a) applies it to the question of central-local state relations. The thesis is set out and discussed most explicitly, however, in a paper written jointly by Alan Cawson and myself for a conference in 1981 and which was published two years later under the title "Corporatism, competitive politics and class struggle" (1983). The thesis as outlined there is set out in summary form in Figure 1.

Two points must be emphasised about this framework. The first is that the dual politics thesis does not suggest that the elements identified within each dimension are empirically separate, only that they are analytically distinct and that it is useful to draw such distinctions in oder to facilitate comparative and historical work (by drawing a yardstick for comparison between different places or different periods) and to enable hypotheses to be drawn up and tested. It is obviously the case, for example, that production and consumption are interrelated (e.g. as noted earlier, provision of welfare services can and does aid certain producer interests as well as those who consume such services), that competitive political struggles occur within the constraints established by corporatist bargaining and compromise, that central and local state agencies are engaged in a relationship in which each has some degree of power and some resources at its control, and so on. Furthermore, the dual politics thesis recognises that the various elements identified as

Figure 1: THE DUAL POLITICS THESIS

	POLITICS OF PRODUCTION	POLITICS OF CONSUMPTION
SOCIAL BASE	Class interests	Consumption sector interest
MODE OF INTEREST MEDIATION	Corporatist	Competitive
LEVEL OF INTERVENTION	Central state	Local state
DOMINANT IDEOLOGY	Rights of private property	Rights of citizenship
APPROPRIATE STATE THEORY	Instrumentalism (class theories)	Pluralism (interest group theories)

constituting the 'politics of production' tend to set limits on the elements constituting the 'politics of consumption',for the concern to safeguard capital accumulation tends to take priority over the concern to safeguard capital accumulation tends to take priority over the concern to provide for social need, the corporate bias tends to prevail over demands expressed through democratic institutions, the centre tends to extend its control over the locality, and ideologies of private property tend to take precedence over ideologies of citizenship both in law and in cultural forms. That there is a relationship between the left and right hand columns in Figure 1 is axiomatic; that it is also an unequal relationship is similarly recognised. But if we are to escape the confines of an holistic approach, such analytical distinctions still need to be made, no matter how difficult it may be to draw such rigid dichotomies in looking at empirical reality.

The second point to note is that the dual politics thesis does not posit any necessary correspondence between the two dimensions on the vertical axis. There is no attempt to suggest, for example, that production politics are always and everywhere associated with corporatist initiatives at central level any more than consumption politics are necessarily limited to the competitive sphere of politics at local level. It is obviously the case that class-based organisations may mobilise over consumption issues (e.g. the sporadic involvement of trade unions in community action), that local levels of the state may enjoy some scope for intervening in the organisation of production (e.g. the small-scale attempts in recent years in some parts of Britain to establish municipal enterprise boards and cooperative development agencies), that consumption-based organisations may force their concerns onto the competitive agenda at national level (e.g. the limited success enjoyed by some welfare pressure groups through parliamentary lobbying), and so on. What is being suggested, however, is that there is a <u>tendency</u> for the different elements within each of these <u>two</u> dimensions increasingly to correspond, and that (most crucially) the more they do correspond in practice, the greater will be the applicability of the relevant political theory to understanding and explaining them. What is not being denied, however, is that different countries vary across different times in the way in which these various elements correlate, and that such variations must themselves be explained historically rather than through any general theory.

The point of this framework, therefore, is not to replicate reality (it is not a model) but to render it intelligible. This is achieved through the development of hypotheses which allow for counterfactuality and which are therefore in principle testable. The key hypotheses which have been advanced on the basis of this framework are that (a) the state will operate in the interests of the dominant class or class fraction the more its interventions are directed at the process of production, the more corporatist its organisational forms, the more centralised its operations become and the more those in key positions are predisposed to support the principles of private property rights; and that (b) the state will be more responsive to the weight of popular opinion and articulated demands from different sections of the population the more its interventions involve provision for consumption, the more democratic its organisational forms, the more localised its operations and the more those in key positions are predisposed by their personal values and/or by their training to support the principles embedded in the notion of citizenship.

Although it is possible to develop other subsidiary hypotheses (e.g. regarding the scope of class mobilisation in politics or the limits on local state activity), these are the principal hypotheses by which the dual politics thesis stands or falls, for these represent the attempted solution to the problem of relative autonomy which was the mainspring for the development of the thesis in the first place. If a situation could be found in which productive interventions at central

14

level organised through corporatist initiatives managed by individuals supportive of private property were nevertheless determined by pluralistic political processes, or in which consumption interventions at local level organised through elective or participative agencies and managed by progressive individuals were determined by the influence of dominant economic class interests, then the thesis would be refuted. More likely, of course, is the possibility of finding various 'mixtures' of these elements in which both instrumentalist and pluralist interpretations appear to have some varying degree of validity, and in such cases it should be possible to refine the thesis in order to identify which elements play a more or less significant part in affecting political processes and outcomes (I have made a start in this direction in Saunders, forthcoming, a).

Unfortunately, however, little critical attention has been devoted to the question of the empirical adequacy of the dual politics thesis. Indeed it is something of an irony that the thesis, which was developed in an attempt to escape from the somewhat arid theoretical and conceptual disputes of the 1970s by enabling theoretically-informed empirical research on the state, should itself have attracted so much theoretical and conceptual criticism. Nevertheless, it is to the critics that I now turn.

CRITICISMS AND APPLICATIONS

Eight main sets of criticisms have been made against the dual politics thesis. As we shall see, some are more pertinent than others and some indicate ways in which the thesis may fruitfully be modified or developed, but none in my view necessitate its abandonment.

The elements cannot or should not be separated.

A number of critics have attacked the very notion of a dualistic theory by suggesting that reality cannot be separated out into analytically distinct aspects. The main target for such criticisms has been the distinction which lies at the heart of the dual politics thesis between production and consumption. For Harrington, for example, "The problem with this approach is very simple: that by splitting up the empirical objects of the explanation it draws attention away from any connections between them. For example, the relation between 'production' and 'consumption' emphasised in marxist analysis becomes de-emphasised when using a dualist model" (1983, 215). Similarly, Duncan and Goodwin suggest that "There seems little historical argument for so rigid a

15

separation between production and consumption. Much state activity, in the central concerns of law and social control for instance, are (sic) clearly connected with both" (1982,87).

What is really at issue in such criticisms is the Weberian methodology which forms the basis for such distinctions. What these and other critics seem to be suggesting is that the thesis should be rejected because it is not holistic (which is tantamount in contemporary social science to saying that it is not marxist). It is not, of course, true that, by distinguishing conceptually between production and consumption, the thesis obliterates the relation between them. Harrington, for example, suggests that the dualistic 'model' (his word) leads to the 'nonsensical' conclusion that production and consumption are not connected, but this is simply not the case. For a start, we are dealing here not with a 'model' but with an ideal type – there is no suggestion that production and consumption are rigidly separated in reality. Furthermore, the thesis recognises the interconnections between production and consumption(e.g. the fact, noted by Duncan and Goodwin, that housing may be an important aspect of production) and it even asserts that production is likely to take precedence over consumption. But the crucial point is that, in order to be able to develop such arguments in the first place, it is necessary to develop the distinction conceptually before considering their interrelation empirically. As Weber recognised, but as so few of his critics seem to have understood, we are all obliged to make use of ideal type constructs whether we like it or not. It would therefore seem preferable to do so rigorously.

One further point needs to be made about all this. In social science, it seems to me that we can proceed basically in one of two directions. Either we can assume that we already have the correct theory for understanding society as a totality, in which case we can proceed from the whole to the parts knowing in advance what the interrelation of the parts will be like. This approach, which is characteristic of much of the western marxist tradition, is not only in my view arrogant (in its claim to an epistemologically privileged starting point) and unsupportable (for such a starting point can never be justified other than through mere assertion – e.g. that dialectical materialism is a true science), but it also rules out the need for any empirical research (for if we already know how the world is structured, all that empirical and historical work can achieve is filling in a few details regarding 'contingencies' not covered by the general theory). Alternatively, we can assume that the social world is a very complex place which cannot be known in its totality, in which case we proceed by developing partial understandings of aspects of that world and gradually build up a picture of how the different 'parts' affect each other. If we take this route, then it is essential that we have a clear idea of how the aspects which we are interested in are to be identified and distinguished from other aspects. It also follows that knowledge of the interrelation of the parts will be derived, not from a priori theory, but from empirical research in different places at different times. This is precisely the logic behind the Weberian method of ideal types, and it is this logic which informs the analytical distinction between elements such as production and consumption which characterises the dual politics thesis.

The elements within each dimension do not coincide.

This second set of criticisms is in many ways similar to the first, for while some critics have argued that the two dimensions (the politics of production and the politics of consumption) cannot be separated, others have argued that the elements within each of these dimensions are in fact separated. Both criticisms boil down to the same thing - a rejection (or in some cases a misunderstanding) of the ideal type method.

In some instances, critics have argued that the local level of the state can and does sustain corporatist modes of interest mediation. Villadsen, for example, cites Norwegian and American studies of business and union involvement at the local level in support of his contention that "Corporatism should not be restricted to the analyses of national politics as suggested by the dual state theory" (1983,22); Reade dismisses the link between levels of the state and modes of interest mediation as 'too tidy' and suggests that "Traces of corporatist modes of operating may from time to time be observable in the operations of any governmental agency, and at any level" (1984,104); and Sharpe argues that various forms of 'institutional insulation' have been adopted by local governments in different countries over the years (e.g. the French Prefect system or the British aldermanic system prior to 1972), and that in any case "There may now be emerging something that looks like a corporate dimension at the local level" (1984, 37). Such criticisms, have, furthermore, been bolstered by those who have argued that local democracy is not all it is cracked up to be (Cochrane, for example, attacks the dual politics thesis for developing "a new form of the pluralist and institutionalist myth that local government is more responsive than central government" — 1984,282). In short, the thesis is said by these and other critics to have under-emphasised local corporatism while exaggerating the significance of competitive politics at the local level.

In other instances, critics have argued that the local level is an important site of class struggle and that the local state is crucially involved in the politics of production. Duke and Edgell, for example, agree that "local state issues are frequently consumption based" but nevertheless argue from their research in Greater Manchester that "Political action in response to these issues may involve an important social class component as well as a consumption sectoral component" (1984,196). Cooke goes further on the basis of his research on regional restructuring in South Wales, for although he recognises that "There are genuine difficulties in connecting local, and even some regional, struggles to the available macrotheory since the antagonistic groupings are seldom clearly contesting as classes formed around social relations of production", he nevertheless suggests that the dual politics thesis is flawed because "By allowing that class relations are fundamentally social relations of production but insisting that production issues are the province of the central state apparatus, the local state is divorced from class-based politics by definitional fiat" (1982,188). In Cooke's view, the local arena has often been crucial in generating and sustaining class-based political cultures, and he argues that capital-labour relations produce class struggles at all three levels (national, regional and local) of the state system.

Now much of this work is valid and significant, and neither Alan Cawson nor I would seek to deny either that corporatist initiatives may emerge at local level (indeed, Cawson, forthcoming, discusses precisely this), nor that class relations may surface at this level. The crucial question, however, is whether such patterns are typical, and we would suggest that, in Britain at least, they are not. Indeed, it is our view that when local corporatist initiatives are mounted at local level (e.g. current experiments by various socialist local authorities involving economic intervention in one form or another) they not only prove to be very limited in scope but they also tend to be largely ineffectual in anything other than propaganda terms. Similarly, the history of class mobilisation at local level is generally one of short-term action and highly fragmented organisation as is evidenced by the conspicuous absence of 'urban social movements' in Britain other than the historically peculiar (yet widely cited) examples of Clydeside during the First World War and Poplar during the 1920s (see Saunders 1979, chapter 3). The dual politics thesis does not deny the possibility that elements of the politics of production may appear in the politics of consumption and vice-versa, but it does give both theoretical and empirical grounds for believing that such patterns are not typical and are rarely enduring.

There is, however, one aspect of the thesis which does seem to require some modification, and this concerns the equation of consumption with local levels of the state. While it is certainly true that in Britain the local level is primarily concerned with consumption provision, it is also the case that local responsibility in this field has been eroding for some time, and that the central level is now itself crucially responsible for certain key aspects of social consumption. In particular, as both Sharpe (1984) and Dunleavy (1984) point out, the local consumption function is limited to provision of services in kind (housing, education, welfare services etc.), for central government has taken unto itself the control of transfer payments through the nationalised social security system (although it is worth pointing out that this still tends to be administered through local state offices such as the local branch of the Department of Health and Social Security or local post offices). Thus Dunleavy complains that the dual politics thesis "fudges" this issue by concentrating entirely on collective consumption while ignoring transfer payments, while Sharpe suggests that the thesis should be modified to draw a distinction within the consumption sector between monetary payments (which are easily centralised because of their scale and the low levels of discretion required to administer them) and services (which are less easily centralised because they require high levels of executant discretion given the variations between different localities). I would accept these points and would suggest that such a modification can be made without undermining the fundamental basis of the thesis.

The thesis is eclectic.

There is an explicit commitment in the dual politics thesis to theoretical pluralism - i.e. to the view that no one theory enjoys a monopoly of the truth and that different theories (namely instrumentalism and pluralism) can be applied in a complementary way to the analysis of different aspects of political processes. For some critics, however, this commitment to theoretical pluralism is little more than eclectism. Paris, for example, describes the approach as "unashamedly eclectic" and criticises the way in which it "takes analytic categories out of context from different and mutually contradictory theoretical frameworks" (1983, 225 and 223). Similarly, Kalltorp is critical of the attempt to "unite very different theoretical elements into one single framework", arguing that this "take(s) concepts out of their theoretical contexts" while failing to realise that "these theoretical perspectives to some extent contradict each other if their full ramifications are elaborated" (1984, 63).

Although eclecticism can itself be defended (cf. Goldsmith, 1980), I would in any case deny that the dual politics thesis is eclectic in its theoretical pluralism. Theories are not ripped out of their context and applied, a little bit here and a little bit there; rather, key theoretical arguments from different traditions are held to apply to carefully identified and delimited aspects of reality but not to others. Only if you deny the possibility that different kinds of political processes may be subject to different kinds of social determinations will it make sense to attack the thesis as eclectic. But this, of course, is precisely what many (though not all) marxists do deny through their assertion that one single theory must explain all aspects of the social totality. As I noted earlier in the discussion of the relative autonomy concept, however, such an holistic approach collapses once it is recognised that the same institution seen as a unity (e.g. the state in its entirety) may in fact be engaged in two (or more) different courses of action at the same time, for it then becomes necessary to break the apparent unity down in order to see how different factors are influencing different parts of the system in different ways.

The sort of criticism advanced by Paris and by Kalltorp is simply a shorthand way of saying that they wish to make their marxism undiluted, for armed with their theory of totality, they cannot accept that different perspectives may be complementary rather then contradictory. To accept the dual politics thesis is to accept that Marx was not the fountainhead of all wisdom (equally, it is also to accept that the liberal-democratic tradition is similarly partial in its applicability). Paris and Kalltorp seem wedded to a strict paradigmatic interpretation of the social sciences in which acceptance of one paradigm precludes acceptance of another, yet this is ultimately a recipe for intellectual stagnation and theoretical dead-ends. Some of the most stimulating and influential social theory of this century has come as a product of fusion between traditions rather than of purity within them, and this is as true of broadly marxist work (e.g. the German 'critical theory' tradition with its origins in Weber and Freud as well as Marx) as it is of so-called 'bourgeois' social science (e.g. the early Parsons's attempt to develop a theory of action out of work as diverse as that by Durkheim, Weber and Marshall). The criticism of 'eclecticism' is a thinly-disguised attempt to return us to the theoretical trenches of the 1970s in which different schools of thought were able to seek shelter from their opponents rather than having to engage with alternative ideas which threatened to disturb their precarious ontological security. Therein lies the path to theoretical bankruptcy.

A more sophisticated version of this mode of critique has, however, recently been developed by Pickvance (1982 and 1984) and has been endorsed by Harrington (1983). Pickvance states his position thus: "I have long been an advocate of theoretical pluralism on condition that each theory rests inside the other and addresses questions of differing scales. However, I am not clear that this condition is met in the present case. Each theory is linked to an issue area rather than to a scale of question... I prefer to attempt to specify class interests and allow that within a unitary conception of the capitalist state its capitalist character will be differentially manifest in different policy areas" (1982, 96, emphasis in original). In other words, marxist state theory is to be applied at the macro-level to the state and politics as a whole, but room is to be found at the micro-level for other theories (e.g. urban managerialism) which may be appropriate in explaining problems of a more concrete nature. Marxism, for example, can explain state intervention in respect of both production and consumption, but it may need a different, less abstract, approach to explain particular patterns of allocation in specific policy areas.

There are two related problems with this alluring proposition. The first is that the macro/micro distinction is neither tenable nor useful. It is not tenable because any problem we address will necessarily entail a consideration of the macro and the micro at the same time (this was precisely the lesson drawn by Pahl from the experience of trying to apply the earlier version of his urban managerialist thesis, for he recognised that any explanation of urban resource allocation would need to understand how managers mediate between macro and micro forces). It is not useful because it perpetuates the traditional distinction in social theory between systems and actors, structure and agency, and unless Pickvance specifies how these relate to each other, it will not be possible to hold together theories pitched at one or the other. As Giddens (1979) notes in his theory of structuration, action is constitutive of structures and structures are enabling of action, in which case a macro/micro theoretical distinction would seem to be more of a hindrance than a help.

The second problem with Pickvance's approach is that it is a recipe for theoretical reductionism. Precisely because the macro and the micro cannot be separated in the way he suggests, and given his view that micro-theories 'nest inside' of macro-theories, it follows that in practice any explanation of any phenomenon will be driven back to the umbrella marxist theory of class struggle and the capitalist state. The only way of avoiding such a reduction is to identify those aspects of reality where such a theory does not apply. It is for this reason that I would defend a dualistic approach which rests, not on a distinction between levels of abstraction, but on a distinction between ideal-typical aspects of politics.

The thesis is ethnocentric and ahistorical

Like any ideal type construct, the conceptual framework on which the dual politics thesis rests involves a process of pure generalisation on the basis of specific historical observation. Two points should be emphasised about this.

First, an ideal type is not simply dreamed up in the head of the social scientist but it reflects (albeit in a logically purified form) concrete social phenomena. The dual politics thesis originated in the context of Britain in the late 1970s and, in the form in which it was presented in Cawson and Saunders (1983), made no claim to more general validity and applicability. It was, and is, an 'individual' rather than a 'generic' ideal type (see Burger 1976 for a discussion of this difference) and in this sense it was deliberately and consciously 'ethnocentric'.

Second, ideal types were for Weber the tools whereby historical work could be accomplished, but precisely because they are idealised abstractions frozen in time, they could not themselves be seen as historically dynamic. The point here is that if, like Weber, we see history as a clutter of infinite events, then some pure construct is necessary in order to identify change in any given phenomenon over time. A process of rationalisation for example could only be identified by comparing social life in different periods against a single and logically-pure (yet historically non-existent) type of 'rational action'. Seen in this way, the framework on which the dual politics thesis is based is both ethnocentric and ahistorical.

Here at least, it would seem, I agree with the critics! Paris sees the thesis as "ethnocentric and ahistorical. It is based on English society in the late 1970s (1983, 224), arguing in particular that it does not apply to Australia". Badcock agrees: "A model of central-local relations based on a unitary system of government is not all that relevant to federal systems such as the US and Australia" (1984, 287), and he goes on to argue that in the Australian case, higher levels of government were often supportive of consumption interests while municipal governments were attuned to the needs of capital. A further nail is hammered into the coffin by Kalltorp who suggests that the dual politics thesis "has to be fundamentally changed if applied to the Scandinavian nations" since it reflects "a specific British political organisation" (1984, 63), while Duncan and Goodwin add to this litany of criticism the view that the thesis "encourages a neglect of historical change, change created by people" (1982, 85).

Does all this mean, then, that the dual politics thesis is no more than a framework for analysing politics in one small offshore island during a period somewhere between the 1976 IMF loan and the 1979 election of the Thatcher government? Of course not! To assume that it does is to misunderstand (yet again) what is entailed in an ideal type methodology.

I have already conceded that the framework as set out by Alan Cawson and myself in our joint paper is specific to time and place, but that was because we were trying to explain politics in one country at one period of time. What are not and could not be time and place specific, however, are the elements from which the framework is constructed. Production and consumption, corporatist and competitive mediation, classes and consumption sectors, central state and local state – these are not concepts which are limited in their applicability to any given time or place. Indeed, since these are pure types and do not actually exist in their pure form anywhere or at any time, it would be difficult to claim that they are time or place bound.

What is at issue here is the distinction between the elements in the dual politics thesis and the particular way in which these elements are correlated to construct analytical frameworks appropriate to specific problems. My claim is and always has been that the elements identified in the thesis are generalisable (and thus enable comparative and historical work) while the specific conjuncture of these elements put forward in the joint paper with Alan Cawson is not. The elements are in this sense generic types while the pattern of correlation within the dimensions is, as noted above, an individual type. Just as Weber constructed his individual types (Calvinism, bureaucracy etc.), so too the dual politics thesis can take a number of specific forms through different combinations of general concepts.

To say that the thesis does not apply to Australia or Scandinavia, or that it fails to take account of historical change within any given country, is therefore a nonsense. It is rather like saying that a meteorological system of concepts such as 'rain', 'snow' or heatwave' is ethnocentric and ahistorical because it never snows in Alice Springs and there were never any heatwaves during the British ice age. Indeed, the point can be made still more forcibly by indicating instances where the dual politics thesis has indeed been applied in other countries, modifying the conjuncture of elements as appropriate. I have myself applied the thesis in an analysis of municipal politics in Melbourne (Saunders 1984c) and in a study of different modes of interest mediation in the Australian Capital Territory (Saunders 1984b), and both of these studies should on their own be sufficient to deny the claims of critics such as Paris and Badcock who cite the supposed inapplicability of the thesis in the Australian context. Of all the criticisms made against the dual politics thesis, the charge of ethnocentrism and ahistoricism is perhaps the most galling, for not only does it rest on a fundamental misunderstanding of what is entailed in this approach, but it also ignores the main claim which has consistently been put forward in support of the thesis – namely that it provides the tools to enable us to break out of sterile theoretical argument by developing rigorous comparative and historical research. Nevertheless, there is one feature of this critical literature which does warrant further reflection, and this concerns the question of the rational level of the state.

A number of critics have pointed to the problems entailed in applying a framework derived from a unitary state system where the regional level is weak to a federal state system where the regional level (i.e. state legislatures and so on) is strong. This is a valid criticism for it points to a weakness in the conceptual elements themselves (e.g. in Cawson and Saunders 1983, we simply elided the regional with the central level, yet this is inadequate even in the British context where bodies such as the Regional Health and Water Authorities and the regional offices of the Manpower Services Commission enjoy considerable autonomy from the centre, and it is clearly unhelpful when it comes to analysing federal systems with a tradition of high state autonomy). Here, then, can be identified a problem which requires some modification of the original thesis, and in recent work I have attempted to develop the framework so as to take account of a distinct regional element (see Saunders, forthcoming, b). As with the modification in the concept of consumption to take account of the division between monetary and service provision, so too in this case, the change which is required can, I believe, be accommodated within the base approach without any fundamental revisions.

Functionalism

In the history of social scientific mutual criticism, the charge of ahistoricism has often gone hand in hand with that of functionalism, and so it has been with the dual politics thesis. Duncan and Goodwin, for example, describe it as a "classificatory, functional analysis" which is content simply to label "functions of the state for capital, with only a very generalised and almost asocial account of how these functions have emerged and changed over time" (1982, 85). Similarly, Harrington takes issue with the "emphasis on the functional nature of policy" in which "intervention is said to occur for a particular purpose - to alleviate market failure (1983, 209). And both Duncan and Goodwin and Harrington claim to find in the dual politics thesis echoes of functionalist marxism, for while the former see the thesis as repeating "only less explicitly and to a greater extent, the deficiencies of structuralist versions of the relatively autonomous state" (1982, 85), the latter suggests in a footnote that it "typifies marxist analyses of state intervention and emphasises the debt...to a "functionalist" interpretation of state intervention" (1983, 209n).

Not for the first time, we encounter a certain irony in these criticisms, for the dual politics thesis emerged out of a dissatisfaction with the functionalism, inherent in the work of writers such as Poulantzas, and it explicitly distanced itself from the notion found in O'Connor that everything the state does is in some way in the interests of capital, and hence of the system as a whole.

Clearly the charge of functionalism cannot be said to apply to the analysis of the politics of consumption, for here it is clearly argued that the state responds to a variety of different interests and intervenes in such a way that capital accumulation is likely to be harmed more than it is helped. In respect of the politics of production, however, we do suggest that the tendency will be for state intervention to support capital accumulation and hence, if you like, to serve the "needs" of the system. But does this analysis lead us into the pitfalls of functionalism?

The major problem confronted by functionalist analysis in the social sciences concerns teleology. There is nothing wrong with pointing to the functions that some phenomenon may perform within a society (e.g. the functional character of religion in maintaining social cohesion or in providing explanations for otherwise inexplicable events). The problem arises when this function is said to explain the origins or perpetuation of the phenomenon in question (as in the argument that religion arose in order to bind society together or to provide the explanations which people crave). Functionalism, in other words, is illegitimate as a mode of _explanation_ in that it rests on a teleological form of reasoning - the assumption that there is some purposeful agent creating functional institutions to carry out system needs. Put another way, the question of functions should never be confused with the issue of causality, for while functions refer to consequences (whether intended or not), causality refers to antecedent conditions.

Seen in this way, the charge of functionalism levelled against the dual politics thesis is invalid, for the analysis of the politics of production does not explain state intervention in terms of the functions it performs, but rather seeks the causes in the control of and influence over key state institutions by agents intent on safeguarding the interests of capital. More specifically, the explanation for why the interests of capital will tend to be pursued at the central level of the state is found in (i) the fact that key individuals and groups will recognise that primacy must be accorded to capital accumulation in order to maintain all other state activity; (ii) the fact that capitalist interests will often achieve direct access to policy-making through exclusive corporatist arrangements, and (iii) the fact that most state personnel in key positions at this level will be ideologically predisposed to support the rights of private property. These three factors are not original to the dual politics thesis - they reflect exactly the threefold explanation offered by Miliband (1977) in his instrumentalist theory of the state. And like pluralist theory (but unlike marxist structuralism), instrumentalist theory is not a functionalist mode of explanation - which is precisely why these two theories were employed in the dual politics thesis in the first place.

One further point needs to be added. We see a tendency for the politics of production to result in interventions supportive of capital accumulation, but this is only a tendency. Given that we locate the explanation for this in the purposive actions of key agents, and that human purposes have a nasty habit of producing unintended and undesired consequences, it follows that such interventions may, and perhaps often will, 'go wrong'. Like Habermas and Offe, we recognise that the "rationality" problem confronting the centralised interventionist state is enormous and that a corporatist strategy is no cast-iron safeguard against failure. And like Hayek (1960) we appreciate that, when it comes to directing state power, the best of intentions may turn out to have the worst of consequences. Not only, therefore, is our analysis not functionalist in its method of explanation, but nor is it necessarily functionalist in its expectations regarding policy outcomes.

Reductionism

Unlike the charge of functionalism, the critique of the dual politics thesis as "reductionist" does have some substance. It will be recalled that, in distinguishing a sphere of "class politics" from a sphere of "consumption sector politics", the thesis sought to escape the class reductionism of so much marxist political analysis. However, a mere limitation of the scope of class analysis does not by itself resolve the problem as is demonstrated by two recent criticisms of the consumption sector concept.

It should be noted at the outset that neither of these critics addresses the specific charge of reductionism to the dual politics thesis as such; rather, they direct their comments to Dunleavy who originated the idea of consumption sectors (see Dunleavy 1979) and who, paradoxically, is himself a critic of the dual politics thesis in another context. It should also be noted that Dunleavy's treatment of this concept is rather different from that in the dual politics thesis where it appears as a basis of political alignment distinct from class; for Dunleavy, by contrast, consumption location is only partially autonomous of class and is significant more for its ideological effects in blurring class identities than as a separate material basis for political cleavages. Despite these differences, however, the problem of reductionism posed in relation to Dunleavy's work would also seem pertinent to an evaluation of the dual politics thesis.

The critics in question differ between themselves over the question of the utility of the concept of consumption sectors for political analysis. Where Franklin and Page (1983) describe this mode of analysis as a 'heresy' and try to demonstrate its lack of empirical utility through analysis of 1979 general election date (though see Duke and Edgell, 1984, for an alternative empirical confirmation based on survey date), Flynn (in his chapter in this volume) seems more supportive and suggests only that "consumption sector theory is still emergent and tentative" and that the problem of reductionism is a "gap" which should be closed through future research. Where both sets of critics agree, however, is that a consumption sector theory of politics (like a class theory of politics) must avoid any mechanistic reduction of political action to an objectively-defined social base. The problem, in other words, is that there is a tendency to assume that

27

sectoral interests are automatically "reflected" in political cleavages when what is required is an explanation of how sectoral cleavages are mediated through political consciousness to generate political alignments.

In some ways this is perhaps a peripheral problem for the dual politics thesis for it points, not to a problem in the approach as such, but to a neglected question in its application. To address this question, it is necessary to return to the issues raised some years ago by Pickvance (1977) regarding the ways in which a "social base" may or may not be translated into a "social force", as well as to the familiar problems of ideology and political socialisation. However, these criticisms should also alert us to the problem of defining the social base in the first place, for it is apparent that, if the whole of politics cannot be reduced to class interests, it cannot be reduced to a combination of class and sectoral interests either.

All of this is important in affirming three basic tenets of Weberian social science. The first is that we cannot explain action (in this case, political action) without understanding the subjective meaning of that action for those involved; we need, in other words, to develop an appreciation of how people themselves identify their interests as workers, consumers or whatever. The second is that we must never lose sight of the multidimensional character of domination in the contemporary period; we need, that is, to bear in mind that power relations are not organised solely along just one or two axes and that political struggles may thus develop around one or several of a variety of different and analytically distinct bases of which class and sector are only two. The third, following on from this, is that any analysis will always be partial; the dual politics thesis may be broader than most marxist political theories in that it recognises a basis other than class for political action, but it is still narrow and inevitably incomplete in that it fails to take account of the political significance of other factors such as gender status, ethnic status, moral values such as those of religious communities, nationality or party in generating relations of political domination and conflict. Seen in this way, both structuralist marxism and the dual politics thesis are incomplete theories focusing on specific aspects of political reality. The difference, however, is that the latter recognises this while the former does not.

External and internal influences

The dual politics thesis was not a one-off creation. It evolved over a period of years, both through Alan Cawson's work on corporatism and through my interest in urban politics and the local state, and it continues to evolve today. Inevitably, therefore, some of the criticisms made against the earlier versions of the thesis will no longer be applicable, and this is particularly the case in respect of those critics who take issue with the thesis for overemphasising the independence of the state.

In some of its earlier versions, the dual politics thesis closely followed Offe (1975) in distinguishing a sphere of state activity which functioned autonomously of outside pressures (Offe's "productive" functions) and a sphere which was more open to such pressures (Offe's "allocative" functions). As Harrington (1983) points out, this was therefore a dualistic analysis involving an internal/external dichotomy, and he devotes much of his paper to attacking such a formulation by arguing that "internal arrangements today are simply the product of 'external' pressures in the past". In similar vein, Duncan and Goodwin (1982) attack what they see as the "fetishism" of the state in the thesis: "It...tends to reify the state. "The state" is seen to do this or that, to carry out this or that function; it is implicitly viewed as an independent organism... In this procedure, the national state, concerned with production, displays mediation and co-option – a sanitised non-politics" (1982, 86).

I would broadly accept such criticisms as they apply to the earliest versions of the thesis (although even here it was never suggested that one part of the state operated independently or autonomously of any outside pressures – see, for example, Saunders, 1979, 188). However, the thesis has changed. It is no longer an "internal/external" model, for the two sides of the dualism refer to two different kinds of pressures from outside – namely, class interests expresses through corporatist mediation at central level, and sectoral interests expressed through competitive politics at local level. The discussion of corporatism at central level does not imply a notion of an independent, directive state such as is found in Winkler's work, but refers instead to a distinctive mode of interest mediation and representation.

This change in the thesis occurred fairly early on. It was certainly evident from 1981 onwards, both in my own work and in the joint paper with Alan Cawson which, though published in 1983, was available in manuscript form two years earlier. It is therefore distressing that critics such as Harrington should still be going into print in 1983 arguing against the dual politics thesis as it then stood by attacking a much earlier formulation. Harrington was evidently aware of the change, but chose simply to ignore its significance, for tucked away in a footnote to his paper is the comment that the changes are merely terminological: "These changes are not significant in terms of the arguments we are developing. The distinction between 'corporate' and 'pluralist' modes in (the) new formulation coincides with the division between independent and responsive conceptions of state policy formation" (1983, 207n). This is not only wrong; it seems almost to be the product of a wilful misinterpretation which was necessary in order for the main thrust of the critique to be sustained.

More positive are Harrington's comments towards the end of his paper in which he discusses the problem of reconciling an analysis of external pressures with a recognition of some degree of internal autonomy within the state itself. While suggesting that professional interests within the state system will not be able to act independently of external demands and pressures, he concludes that "The influence of external forces will to some extent be modified by the attempt of professional groups within the state to assert their own interests" (1983, 214).

This problem of how to deal with the influence of the professions within the state system has, paradoxically, given rise to a new set of criticisms of the dual politics thesis, for while critics of earlier versions of the thesis complained that it accorded too much independence to state agencies, critics of later versions complain that it underemphasises such internal factors. In his chapter in this volume, for example, Flynn suggests that "The internal structure of the state and the policy-making process...are often only superficially discussed and/or regarded as epiphenomenal... I would argue that even adopting the ideal type we still require deeper understanding of resource allocation, modes of provision, service delivery and bureaucratic discretion in the administration of collective consumption or state welfare policies". Now this is fair enough - up to a point. It is true that the dual politics thesis is primarily addressed to the problem of the relation between the state and interests in civil society and as such does not explicitly address the question of how bureaucratic and professional interests are organised within state agencies. However, it is not the case that these 'internal' issues are entirely neglected, nor even that they are regarded as "epiphenomenal".

For a start, there is an entire section in Cawson and Saunders (1983) devoted to a discussion of different modes of resource allocation and provision in which a statist or bureaucratic mode figures prominently. More significantly, however, Alan Cawson spends a lot of time in **Corporatism and Welfare** discussing precisely the issue of professional influence within state policy-making and arguing that professional interests such as those of the doctors within the National Health Service enjoy a key role in corporatist arrangements by virtue of their significance as service producers. This argument is entirely consistent with the dual politics thesis in that it extends the analysis of producer interests from the private to the public sectors and shows how in both cases, producer interests tend to operate within corporatist arrangements organised away from the local level (e.g. in national-level quangos or in non-elected regional bodies such as the Regional Health Authorities).

None of this, however, seems enough to satisfy the critics of the thesis. Dunleavy in particular is unimpressed: "Efforts have been made by proponents of the dual state thesis to analyse professionalised policy systems as examples of a kind of corporatism. The conventional models of external interest group co-optation into the achievement of state objectives are here extended to include the professions working within the state apparatus...But it is in terms of originating, disseminating and implementing new ideas, technologies and innovations that professional influence has been greatest. This distinctive influence requires separate analysis" (1984, 77). In other words, the influence of the professions within the state is not simply a matter of their mobilisation as a corporate producer interest (although Dunleavy accepts that this is important), but is also a function of their ability to impose a hegemonic control over the generation of ideas.

Dunleavy is undoubtedly right to draw our attention to this aspect of "internal" professional influence and control, for the evidence of how professional world views come to dominate policy-making agendas within state agencies is clear in many fields of state activity. His own research on high-rise housing policy is one case in point (Dunleavy, 1981), while my recent work on health and water services has similarly indicated the ideological importance of groups such as hospital consultants within the NHS and of professional engineers in the water industry (see Saunders, 1983b) for a review of the literature on this). But having said all this, does it necessarily follow, as Dunleavy suggests, that the dual politics thesis cannot deal with these issues and that a "separate analysis" is required?

In my view, this criticism rests on too narrow a conception of the thesis. In particular, it overlooks the crucial ideological dimension within the thesis - i.e. the distinction between ideologies stressing the rights of private property and those emphasising rights of citizenship - for as I have already noted earlier in this paper, the disposition of strategically located individuals and groups within the state system towards one or other of these ideologies will play an important part in determining policy outcomes.

This argument can, however, be taken further, for it is consistent with the dual politics thesis to suggest that ideologies of private property rights will achieve greater prominence in state agencies at central level dealing with production questions, while ideologies stressing rights of citizenship and the alleviation of social need will be more prominent at local level in respect of consumption-oriented interventions. Professional hegemony, in other words, may be different in respect of different areas of state activity. Furthermore, professional hegemony (even where it is consistent across different types and levels of state intervention) may be expected to have different effects in mediating external pressures according to whether it appears in production or consumption oriented agencies. In my work on the regional state level, for example, I have suggested that professional ideologies in production agencies (e.g. the water authorities) tend either to be consistent with the interests of significant outside producer interests such as major industrial and agricultural users or to be subordinated to them, while professional ideologies in consumption agencies (e.g. the health authorities) tend to take on much greater independent significance (see Saunders 1983b and forthcoming, b).

When considering the problem of the "internal" organisation of the state and the role of professional interests and ideologies in shaping policy outcomes, it is therefore clear, not only that the dual politics thesis can deal with the issues involved, but also that it helps to resolve them. As in its other applications, the thesis enables us to break the problem down and hence to escape from crude generalities, for it is clear to me that any serious analysis of the role of the professions within the state will need to go beyond all-encompassing categories such as "state employees" or "state bureaucrats" or "professional interests" or "urban managers" and to recognise that professional domination may take different forms, and be mediated in different ways, in different types and levels of state agencies. While our understanding of this is certainly in its infancy, there are no grounds for supposing that the dual politics thesis may not prove helpful in bringing it to maturity.

Problems of empirical application

I noted at the end of the second section of this chapter that, although the dual politics thesis had been developed with a view to developing empirical research, most of the criticisms made against it have been theoretical or conceptual rather than empirically-based. However, there have been some attempts to use the thesis empirically, and some critics have addressed themselves to the problems entailed in its application to research.

Most of the attempts to apply the thesis in empirical research have come, not surprisingly, from its authors! I have myself used it as the basis for research on topics as diverse as the sacking of the Melbourne City Council (Saunders, 1984c), the question of self-government in the Australian Capital Territory (Saunders, 1984b) and the activities of regional state agencies in England (Saunders, forthcoming, b), and while I have plans to employ it in an analysis of privatisation in Britain, Alan Cawson will shortly be applying it to an analysis of local level corporatist initiatives in London and elsewhere. Whether or not the thesis proves its worth through these studies is a judgement which modesty dictates must be left to others to determine.

It is also worth noting at this point that the thesis has, in a sense, been applied to empirical work retrospectively. Perhaps the most ingenious attempt to do this can be found in Harrington's paper where he takes my own earlier case study of politics in Croydon as evidence against the thesis, arguing that my own evidence on the town centre redevelopment policy indicates the way in which the local state operated in the interests of local economically and politically dominant classes. Harrington uses this argument in support of his critique of the notion of internal state autonomy, but as noted earlier, the dual politics thesis no longer rests on such an assumption, if indeed it ever really did. However, such evidence could also be used to criticise the amended thesis in that it seems to suggest that a pluralist, non-class theory of the local state is inappropriate. This is at least implied by Duncan and Goodwin (1982, 94) who cite the Croydon case as an example of a "bourgeois" local state dominated by the Chamber of Commerce and the Rotary Club. Such a characterisation is, however, grossly misleading, for it fails to recognise the fragmentation between different capitalist interests, the issue-specificity of big business influence and the importance of other interests (e.g. domestic ratepayers, community groups etc.) in other aspects of local policy, all of which is discussed in the book and all of which would seem (in retrospect!) to support a theory of the local state as an arena of imperfect pluralism in which business interests had achieved dominance over particular issues of direct relevance to them. As Sharpe suggested in his review of **Urban Politics,** the evidence in the book cannot support a class, instrumentalist interpretation of the local state because "Although he (Saunders) talks a lot about the exclusion of the Croydon working class from the levers of power in general terms, the actual examples of power conflicts he places before the reader are all conflicts within the capitalist class and, moreover, they suggest that far from revealing the political elite as being insulated from majority or group wishes, it was responsive, if rather grudgingly, to them" (1979, 120).

It was precisely my unease with the theoretical explanation I had offered for the pattern of political influence I had found in Croydon that led me to revise the rudimentary notion of a dual state worked out there in later work. Seen in this way, it was the evidence from Croydon that eventually (after one or two false starts) led me to my current position on the local state, for if Croydon cannot sustain a class theory of politics, no local area can. Rather then refuting the dual politics thesis, as Harrington suggests, the Croydon study therefore can be said to have helped inspire it!

The only other major application or test of the dual politics thesis of which I am aware is Blowers's recent study of the battle between the London Brick Company and environmentalists in Bedfordshire over a proposal to redevelop a brickworks in the Marston Vale. Writing as an "insider" as well as an academic observer, Blowers found considerable evidence in this issue in support of the dual politics thesis. In particular, he found that the company was able to represent its interests through corporatist-type channels while the environmentalists were limited to the sphere of competitive politics, and he found that this difference was related to their respective interests in production and consumption (this, incidentally, would seem to be consistent with other studies of local planning such as Flynn's work on a county structure plan which similarly revealed the way in which producer interests were accommodated through corporatist initiatives - see Flynn, 1983). Blowers also found that the environmentalists were limited to the local arena while the company was able to pursue its interests at higher levels of the state as well as through its relationship with local planners. Although Blowers concludes that the dual politics thesis may need to be revised to take account of the way in which producer interests are able to utilise corporatist arrangements at all levels of the state, it seems that this study provides considerable support for the overall arguments contained in the thesis.

What Blowers's study also indicates is that the dual politics thesis does indeed lend itself to empirical evaluation, and this, it will be recalled, was one of the major objectives for its initial development. This is not to deny that there may still be problems in devising rigorous tests of the thesis, but it does suggest that such problems are not insurmountable.

One set of problems which I shall not discuss here relates to the epistemological issues raised by any attempt to "test" a theory empirically. I have discussed these issues elsewhere (Saunders 1981b, appendix) and would still stand by the argument advanced there that theories can and should be tested against criteria of adequacy which they themselves identify.

There are, however, other more "technical" problems with testing the thesis which need to be mentioned. Two in particular have been highlighted in the secondary literature. The first, discussed by Flynn (this volume) and Dunleavy (1984), concerns the attribution of causal direction. The problem here lies in determining which if any of the elements identified in the thesis has causal primacy. This is indeed a key issue, but in a recent paper I have suggested on the basis of a comparison of several different empirical cases that the primary determinant appears to be the distinction between producer and consumer interests while the other elements have important mediating effects (Saunders, forthcoming, a). My tentative response to Flynn and Dunleavy, therefore, would be that it is the saliency of a given policy area for producer interests which above all else explains the level at which it is resolved, the form of interest mediation adopted, and the prevailing ideological dispositions of those involved.

The second problem, also identified by Flynn and Dunleavy, concerns the difficulty in moving from ideal type constructs to empirically-operational variables. In particular, since most state policies will involve some relevance for both production and consumption, it can be difficult to disentangle the two and to distinguish empirically between primarily production-oriented and primarily consumption-oriented interventions. Yet, as Pickvance (1982,96) points out, if a clear distinction is not drawn, then the identification of counterfactual conditions which is required if the theory is in principle to be falsifiable cannot be achieved.

Both Alan Cawson and I have always recognised this difficulty - especially in areas such as transport policy where it is virtually impossible to determine whether, say, investment in roads and railways is of greater significance for producer than consumer interests of vice-versa. However, few policy areas are quite a problematic, and I see no reason in principle why an inventory should not be constructed on which most researchers could agree by which most aspects of state policy could be allocated to one or other type without too much difficulty (indeed, Dunleavy himself makes a start on this in his 1984 paper; see also Saunders 1979, 147-8 for an attempt at a taxonomy limited to local state functions). Like the question of causal primacy, however, the issue of how to generate a taxonomy out of the typology is one to which further attention must be paid in the future.

CONCLUSIONS

The dual politics thesis is not without its problems. We have seen that it may be in need of some minor revisions (e.g. by distinguishing within the consumption category between cash payments and services in kind: by building a regional dimension more explicitly into the framework; by further work on the "internal" problem of bureaucratic and professional interests; by establishing causal primacy more clearly; and by elaborating a taxonomy by which to translate the ideal typical elements into empirically manageable variables). There is also the suggestion that some attempt needs to be made to build temporal and spatial dimensions into the these (see Blowers 1984; also Flynn, this volume).

Many of these issues are already under discussion in papers which have recently been published or which are forthcoming, and Alan Cawson and I hope in due course to produce a further joint paper in which we shall attempt to integrate these revisions and amendments while at the same time resolving the differences which continue to separate us (for although we agree broadly over the basic outlines of the thesis, we still have some debate between ourselves over certain aspects of its application).

That, however, is for the future. For the present, it seems reasonable to suggest that the thesis has stood up fairly well both to theoretical criticism and empirical evidence. There is a disturbing tendency in contemporary social science to dismiss ideas and approaches before they have had a chance to develop their full potential (the fate of urban managerialism in urban sociology is a good example), and while I would not wish to use this as an excuse for ducking further criticism (which is of course essential for the continued vibrancy of any perspective), I do feel that the dual politics thesis has, in a sense, "proved itself" sufficiently to warrant further exploration, elaboration and application.

It was, perhaps, rather slow coming out of the stalls, and it undoubtedly stumbled once or twice on the early going, but it has also cleared some significant hurdles along the way and appears now to be into its stride. Rather than devoting our attention to nobbling it, we should perhaps now allow it its head and see just how well it can run and whether or not it can stay the distance. It may even be worth a small wager -each way, naturally!

REFERENCES

Althusser, L. (1969) For Marx, London, Allen Lane
Badcock, B. (1984)Unfairly structured cities, Oxford, Basil Blackwell
Blowers, A. (1984) Something in the air: corporate power and the environment London, Harper & Row
Boddy, M. and Fudge, C. "The local state: theory and practice", (1981) University of Bristol, School for Advanced Urban Studies Working Paper, number
Burger, T. (1976) Max Weber's theory of concept formation, Chapel Hill (North Carolina), Duke University Press.
Castells, M. (1977) The urban question London, Edward Arnold
Cawson, A. (1977) "Environmental planning and the politics of corporatism", University of Sussex, Urban and Regional Studies Working Paper, no. 7
Cawson, A. (1978) "Pluralism, corporatism and the role of the state", Government and Opposition, vol.13, 178-98
Cawson, A. (1982) Corporatism and welfare, London, Heinemann
Cawson, A. (forthcoming) "Corporatism and local politics" in W. Grant (ed) The Political Economy of Corporatism, London, Macmillan
Cawson, A. and Saunders P. (1983)"Corporatism, competitive politics and class struggle" in R. King (ed), Capital and politics London, Routledge & Kegan Paul
Cochrane, C. (1977) Review of Cawson, "Corporatism and welfare", International Journal of Urban & Regional Research, vol. 8, 281-2
Cockburn, C. (1977) The local state: management of cities and people London, Pluto Press

Cooke, P. (1982) "Class interests, regional restructuring and state formation in Wales", International Journal of Urban and Regional Research, vol.6, 187-104.

Duke, V. and Edgell, S. (1984) "Public expenditure cuts in Britain and consumption sectoral cleavages", International Journal of Urban and Regional Research vol.8, 177-201

Duncan, S. and Goodwin, M. (1982) "The local state: functionalism, autonomy and class relations in Cockburn and Saunders" Political Geography Quarterly vol.1, 77-96

Dunleavy, P. (1979) "The urban bases of political alignment", British journal of Political Science, vol.9, 409-443

Dunleavy, P. (1981) The politics of mass housing in Britain, London, Oxford University Press

Dunleavy, P. (1984) "The limits to local government", in M. Boddy and C. Fudge (eds) Local Socialism? London, Macmillan

Flynn, R. (1983) "Co-optation and strategic planning in the local state" in R. King (ed), Capital and politics, London, Routledge & Kegan Paul

Franklin, M. and Page, E. (1983)"The consumption cleavage heresy in British voting studies" University of Strathclyde, Papers on Government and Politics, no.10

Giddens, A. (1979) Central problems in social theory, London, Macmillan

Goldsmith, M. (1980) Politics, planning and the city, London, Hutchinson

Habermas, J. (1976) Legitimation crisis London, Heinemann

Harrington, T. (1983) "Explaining state policy-making: a critique of some recent 'dualist' models, International Journal of Urban and Regional Research, vol.7, 202-218

Hayek, F. (1960) The constitution of liberty, London, Routledge

Hirst, P. (1977) "Economic classes and politics" in A. Hunt (ed), Class and class structure, London, Lawrence & Wishart

Jessop, B. (1978) "Capitalism and democracy: the best possible political shell?" in G. Littlejohn (ed), Power and the State, London, Croom Helm

Jessop, O. (1984) "Corporatism, parliamentarism and social democracy" in P. Schmitter and G. Lehmbruch (eds), Trends toward corporatist intermediation London, Sage

Kalltorp, O. (1984) Review of Saunders, "Social theory and the urban question", Scandinavian Housing and Planning Research, vol.1, 61-64

Middlemas, K. (1979) Politics in industrial society, London, Andre Deutsch

Miliband, R. (1977) Marxism and politics, London, O.U.P.

O'Connor, J. (1973) The fiscal crisis of the state, New York, St. Martin's Press

Offe, C. (1975) "The theory of the capitalist state and the problem of policy formation" in L. Lindberg (ed), Stress and contradiction in modern capitalism, London, Lexington Books.

Offe, C. (1984) Contradictions of the welfare state, London, Macmillan

Pahl, R. (1975) Whose city? (second edition) Harmondsworth, Penguin

Paris, C. (1983) "Whatever happened to urban sociology? Society and Space, vol.1, 217-225

Pickvance, C. (1977) "From social base to social force: some analytical issues in the study of urban protest" in M. Harloe (ed) Captive cities, London, Wiley

Pickvance, C. (1982) Review of Saunders, "Social theory and the urban question" and of Harloe and Lebas, "City, class and capital", Critical Social Policy, vol.2, 94-98

Pickvance, C. (1984) "The structuralist critique in urban studies" in M. Smith (ed), Cities in transformation: class, capital and the state, London, Sage.

Poulantzas, N. (1973) Political power and social classes, London, New Left Books

Reade, E. (1984) "Town and country planning" in M. Harrison (ed), Corporatism and the welfare state, Aldershot (Hampshire), Gower

Rhodes, R. (1980) "Analysing intergovernmental relations", European Journal of Political Research, vol.8, 289-322

Saunders, P. (1979) Urban politics: a sociological interpretation London, Hutchinson

Saunders, P. (1981a) "Community power, urban managerialism and the local state", in M. Harloe (ed) New perspectives on urban change and conflict, London. Heinemann

Saunders, P. (1981b) Social theory and the urban question, London, Hutchinson

Saunders, P. (1982) "Why study central-local relations?" Local Government Studies, vol.8, 55-66

Saunders, P. (1983a) "On the shoulders of which giant? The case for Weberian political analysis" in P. Williams (ed) Social process and the city. Sydney, Allen & Unwin

Saunders, P. (1983b) "The regional state: a review of the literature and agenda for research", University of Sussex, Urban & Regional Studies Working paper no.35

Saunders, P. (1984a) "Rethinking local politics" in M. Boddy and C. Fudge (eds), Local socialism?, London, Macmillan

Saunders, P. (1984b) "The Canberra tea party: bureaucracy, corporatism and pluralism in the administration of the Australian Capital Territory" in P. Williams (ed) Policy, politics and the city, Sydney, Allen and Unwin

Saunders, P. "Corporatism and urban service provision" in W. (forthcoming, a) Grant (ed), The Political Economy of Corporatism, London, Macmillan

Saunders, P. "The forgotten dimension of central-local (forthcoming, b) relations: theorising the regional state", Government and Policy

Schmitter, P. (1974) "Still the century of corporatism?" Review of Politics vol.36, 85-131

Sharpe, J. (1979) "Croydon and the capital holders", Municipal Review, August, 120

Sharpe, J. (1984) "Functional allocation in the welfare state", Local Government Studies, vol.10, 27-45

Villadsen, S. (1983) "Urban politics: Central control versus local demands" University of Copenhagen, Institute of Political Studies, Central control, local communities and local politics report, no.10

Winkler, J. (1976) "Corporatism", European Journal of Sociology vol.17, 100-36

Winkler, J. (1977) "The corporate economy: theory and administration" in R. Scase (ed), Industrial society: class, cleavage and control, London, Allen & Unwin

2 The dual state and corporatism: reflections in the light of recent Danish experience

SØREN VILLADSEN
Institute of Political Studies, Copenhagen

INTRODUCTION

This chapter is an attempt to combine results from research on a number of urban political activities with the recent debate on urban political theory, and especially with discussion about the dual state and the development of local corporatism. These developments are to be seen in relation to empirical evidence of changes in the complex patterns of urban politics.

The first section of the chapter deals with aspects of central control of local government and reactions towards this in Danish communities. The following section discusses varieties of urban, political theory. A final section gives a brief account of an alternative theoretical position which is considered more fruitful for the analysis of local level, urban politics compared with the currently dominant theories.

The results presented in the first section are from a Danish research project covering most phases of local policy processes and politics. A few theoretical considerations, developed in much greater detail elsewhere, are outlined here as well Villadsen, 1983). They deal with conflicts between central control and local interests and may be seen as an attempt to understand the role and importance of localism under changed political and economic conditions.

The question to be examined concerns reactions at the local level to cuts in the local government welfare system. To examine this topic we must deal with collective consumption and its organisation. The concept of the local state, which has come into use to describe recent restructuring of the welfare state, does not seem to lead to a sufficient understanding of **either** politics at the local level **or** central-local relations.

So the question of localism and decentralisation are dealt with briefly to achieve a better understanding of the reactions by municipalities to state initiated cuts in collective consumption sectors in the local authorities, cuts that are themselves supported by some municipalities.

The empirical material for this paper is based on a survey of all major organisations in four districts (N=87). Furthermore, some results are incorporated from two surveys conducted in connection with the two most recent local elections in 1978 and 1981, together with those from a questionnaire administered to leading local councillors in a representative sample of 40 of the 275 local councils in Denmark.

Although the results are recent, the development of central-local relations has been rapid and dramatic. Proposed cuts in block grants from the late Social Democratic minority government have been taken over by the new Conservative four-party minority government, which has also increased the level of cuts considerably. The present local income tax level will be frozen as well, resulting in considerable unemployment among public employees working in collective consumption services. This development is so recent that it is difficult to foresee the consequences for local government in any detail. What has happened already is some increase in local income taxes and a reduction in public services and rising unemployment, especially in the day-care sector. With the proposed income tax ceiling, consequences for the employed are expected to be aggravated.

So, problems of fiscal squeeze take on new dimensions and grow in importance. The problems raised were best introduced by Claus Offe some years ago (Offe, 1975). Local government has been considered relatively legitimate, although signs of a growing urban crisis are apparent. Its efficiency and ability to meet local demands decreased, however, and the combination of declining efficiency and legitimation are of great significance for understanding the changing role of localism.

The ideology of public service cuts has been put forward with enormous drive in Denmark. Many local councillors repeat the message, partly because they accept national party ideology, and partly because the situation in many local authorities points to substantial and unpopular increases in local income tax rates. Local councillors are very sensitive to the level of local taxation, a fact that cannot be explained by a similar awareness amongst the public over this matter. A new aspect of this issue in Denmark is the proposed plan to develop sanctions against local governments who increase income tax levels beyond centrally specified levels

Local income tax is proportionate and varies between rich and poor communities, and between high and low level service local authorities. Low income wage earners in relatively poor communities are thus hit twice: first, by their relative deprivation, and second by a relatively heavy tax burden accentuated by the fact that low income communities demand public services that have to be provided on the basis of a relatively small aggregate income. There are state subsidies to local governments in low income areas (block grants and special grants to the poorest communities), and rich local authorities have to pay some equalisation subsidies to low income authorities, but a complete equalisation would mean interventions in the traditional autonomy of local government, despite the vagueness of the constitution on this point.

The present situation facing local government may thus be described in terms of squeezes, tensions and conflicts. Increases in needs and demands for local policies organising collective consumption contrast with large state cuts in block grants, the introduction of spending limits, and increased state control on spending in various sectors. Important aspects of party politics integrating state and local level politics are opposed to localism and local movements, and demands for decentralisation are opposed by new schemes for central control and equalisation. Before we come to some empirical illustrations of these conflict dimensions, however, a description of the formal setting of local government in Denmark is appropriate.

Local government Reform.

Legal, organisational and socio-economic conditions for local government in Denmark have changed radically in the last 10 to 15 years. By 1970, the old structure of local government had proved to be quite inadequate in meeting demands for efficiency in administrative work and planning, especially in small rural districts, where the practice was to have only one or two administrative staff in each local government.

Amalgamations were the first step in what turned out to be one of the most comprehensive reforms of public administration in Denmark. In the early seventies some 1,300 authorities were amalgamated into 275, and 25 regional authorities into 14.

Financial reform followed, with less emphasis on automatic refunding from the state and the introduction of block grants given according to objective criteria. In the heavy cost areas of social policies such as pensions an automatic refunding of local spending, which is strictly regulated, still occurs.

There was also a functional reform transferring various functions from local state agencies to local government control, especially in social policy fields, and education.

Changes in the local regime also occurred, with the introduction of a single legal framework for all local authorities, (with minor exceptions but excluding the largest cities such as Copenhagen.) A full time mayor in district and regional authorities was introduced, together with obligatory standing committees. Membership of local councils is fixed according to the number of inhabitants in the district/county. District. councils have about 20 members, the mayor being elected from the majority group or coalition.

Following these reforms, other important changes were introduced during the late seventies. The most debated of these were the national, regional, and local planning acts introducing hearings and public participation on alternative planning proposals put forward for public debate. Although the planning reforms were very conspicious, social reforms and the subsequent development of social policies at the local level have been of greater significance for the enormous growth of both local administration and expenditure. Professionalisation of the local bureaucracy and collective consumption organized within local government have also been characteristic features of political developments at the local level.

Today, public participation plays a much less prominent role. Participation was institutionalised in planning, kindergartens and day care centers, schools and in other fields. In the view of local state theory, participation has been introduced to legitimise state intervention in the sphere of private households. It is not always clear whether this process of legitimation is seen as an unconscious, system functional process, or rather a conscious, conspiratorial process initiated by the professional gatekeepers and power holders. However, the experience with institutionalized participation in Denmark confirms legitimation theory only to a certain degree. Participation often leads to both increased political awareness and demands for the decentralization of powers from local government to the body in question. For instance, participation in regional planning (where citizens' participation is most explicit) has resulted in overall demands for decentralized development, which was not foreseen by many of the regional authorities who now seek to reduce participation.

Reactions to New State Control Systems and Demands for Decentralization.

Much of the control and steering of local authorities at district level is negotiated between the Association of Local Governments and relevant departments and ministers. The central control system today is quite confused. One of the leading principles of local government reform was supposed to be decentralization, although amalgamations meant a considerable concentration outside bigger towns and cities. In actual fact, local councillors tend to be very sceptical about the fulfilment of this program. Furthermore, the present economic conditions tend to influence local councillors into accepting the limits set by the state, at least as far as spending is concerned and especially by councillors from the bourgeois parties.

Legitimation may then be seen as working in yet another direction. Local councils need a legitimate basis for a restrictive policy towards local demands for increased expenditure and services. Strict economic control and cutbacks make it very difficult for local governments to meet outspoken demands for both decentralisation and increases in or stabilisation of public services. The first results to be shown touch upon these dilemmas.

To understand Table 1 it is important to remember that increases in local income tax is the means by which increased activity by local governments in Denmark is favoured. Taxes on land play a minor role, but are a matter of great political controversy. Interestingly people have moved in the direction of decentralized action in recent years.

Table 1   Attitudes to increased local autonomy versus equalisation organised by the state. 1981 and 1978

		Pct. agree	
		1981	1978
Item A	The state should ensure that there are not going to be greater differences between services and taxes in local authorities than we have today	28	35
Item B	It is for the voters in any district to decide how much social service they are going to pay for via local taxes	53	49
Disagree with both		6	6
Don't know		12	10

N = 1500 and 1856

The demands for decentralisation and local autonomy are obvious and can be seen from many other items as well. But demands for decentralisation do not automatically point to demands for better local, public services: it might be the other way round, namely that people might want to set very low local standards in opposition to central state equalisation. This seems not to be the case generally, but to a certain degree can be found in small, rural districts and amongst right-wing voters. A number of other items confirm that there is a strong demand for decentralisation and a dislike for state control of local government especially in smaller and less urbanised areas. In the bigger towns and cities the main problem is not decentralisation but growing social needs. People here support equalisation (Item A) considerably more than the national average.

Local politicians are often very sceptical about demands from various social groups, movements and organisations for decentralisation because they feel that such a development would undermine their own position in a representational democratic system.   The Danish Association of Local Authorities has been opposed to institutionalised participation at the local level, which in some cases has been forced upon them by the state. Local authorities see this "controlled" participation as a subtle control. Both the population and the councillors thus favour decentralisation, but whereas local councillors generally want to stop decentralisation at the town hall, citizens point to lower levels of political influence.

It is interesting to note that socio-spatial differences seem to play a more decisive role in these matters than party politics. The least urbanised areas are characterised by the strongest demands for decentralisation, whereas big city areas put greater emphasis on the demands for collectivised consumption combined with a certain equalisation between local governments. However, demands for political decentralisation are also found here, regardless of party identification.

The spending limits agreement between the state and local authorities was forced upon the local governments by the state three years ago and are now at fixed 0%. On top of that came very substantial reductions in block grant, so that the net result is a strongly felt decrease in revenue. The following table shows an interesting and rather surprising pattern.

Table 2   Attitudes towards state control and spending limits by leading local councillors and in the population, 1981

Local councillors' perception of spending limits "agreement", pct. (N=199)

Supporters	Opponents	Neutral	Total
58	32	10	100%

% agreeing with the statement: "The state must control local government effectively".

Agree	Disagree	Neutral & d.k.	Total
31	42	27	100%

Note: 298 leading councillors from 40 district councils were interviewed. The questionnaire was conducted immediately before the local elections Nov. '81. The mass survey was conducted immediately after the election.

It is interesting to note that the leading councillors, who all have a seat on the financial committees or are chairmen of the standing committees, do not oppose the limitations introduced by the state on their activity more vigorously than the figures for all councillors in Table 2 show. One explanation for this might be that local councillors prefer the "agreement" to the legislation which was threatened if local governments did not accept spending limits. However, a better explanation probably lies in the fact that there are parallel interests between central and local government in keeping to the spending limits, mostly because of the economic crisis, but also because of ideological state integration. The growth of local government functions and in local expenditure and taxes seem to worry not only most Conservative/Liberal local councillors, but also concerns Labour members to a certain degree. Much to the dislike also of bourgeois councillors a new intervention has been the requirement that local governments keep a certain level of savings in the central bank.

The answers from citizens to the question about restrictions on local government confirm the trend already described in Table 1. The question is broader than the one put to local councillors, but points not only to a very outspoken opposition to centrally controlled local government finance, but also to the very dubious character of the idea of decentralisation.

To illustrate the interests of citizens on local government spending, the following questions were put in the mass survey.

Table 3. Citizens' view on local government spending on various sectors, 1981, %.

	Too little	Adequate	Too much	Don't know
Schools	14	47	8	29
Day care centres	22	33	10	35
Social security	11	28	23	37
Sports facilities	13	56	9	20
Libraries	8	61	8	22
Traffic regulation of local roads	29	44	3	23
Public transport, green areas etc.	24	48	7	21
Urban renewal	8	36	8	46
Employment programmes	42	20	4	34

N = 1500 (weighted)

As can be seen from Columns one and three, there is only one area where more people think that too much money rather than too little is being spent, and this has a very specific political background of a national character. Generally more people think that more money should be spent than think cutbacks should be introduced. This result is extraordinary,

48

given the vigorous campaigns against growth in public sector expenditure and given that people have to pay for increases in local government spending through increased local income taxes. Again, important socio-spatial and political differences must be emphasised. The "spenders" generally live in cities or towns and are more left-wing than the "saving-decentralists" from more rural areas.

Employment programmes are by far the most popular interventions. They are not specific to any category of age, and unemployment is very much of a general nature, whereas the opposite is the case for day care, traffic regulation and to a certain extent public transport. It is apparent that demands for increased local government services are most outspoken in these areas. It is interesting to note that while central government has introduced substantial cuts in and barriers against local employment programmes, many local governments try to keep such programmes going. The issue is politically very controversial. Although it is difficult to compare English and Danish conditions because of differences in the system of taxation, an opinion poll carried out in Islington (Game, 1982) shows a striking parallel to the Danish results, which are representative of all local authorities. In Islington there was also a strongly felt interest in the maintenance or expansion of local, public services.

These observations demonstrate some of the complexity of urban politics: municipalities squeezed from all angles and by different economic and political principles; state control market economy on the one side, social demands on the other, with decentralisation to local governments as a third major principle. This battle inside the framework of a late capitalist and welfare state state illustrates some of the major controversies in recent urban, political theory and points to the alternative model presented in the final section of the chapter.

The relationship to urban, political theory

In this section the theoretical debate on the role of local organisations and the development of a dual state form is continued, so that the dilemma between central control, cuts and local demands for collective consumption can be discussed at a more general level. The questions of local corporatism and cuts in collective consumption are illustrated with empirical observations.

49

There is a considerable distance between local politicians and citizens when it comes to the question of interests in the various sectors of collectivised consumption. Politicians are very reluctant to increase standards if the consequence is higher local income taxes - an attitude that is not shared by the majority of citizens. We can see this from the following two tables.

Table 4: Do local politicians want to increase standards of local government service if local income tax has to be increased as well? (N = 233 local councillors in 40 districts (communes), Nov. 1981) Pct.

Yes	No	Don't know
22%	73%	6%

Danish local authorities thus do not appear to reflect the demands of local organisations and citizens, or at least only to a certain degree. Table 5 shows that preferences vary between citizens and local politicians on vital questions in the urban, political sphere. Large groups of citizens favour expansion of social policies, whereas the opposite is the case for many of the politicians.

Table 5: Local politicians' spending preferences on various sectors (N = 217)

	Too much spending	Adequate	Too little spending	Don't know
Schools	22	67	11	0 %
Day care	23	61	15	1
Care for elderly	1	69	28	1
Social security (1)	49	32	5	15
Social advice and guidance	15	53	21	12
Sports, culture, leisure	7	71	20	1
Libraries	21	63	16	1
Roads	7	55	36	1
Public transport	32	49	12	7
Gas, water, heating electricity etc.	5	79	4	12
Employment	27	44	24	5

(1) By means of cash payments in case of "social events".

These results reflect some of the hierarchical control elements described above: market economy, ideology, dominance by smaller local authorities. But they also show that the central government's desire to introduce large cuts in local budgets are strongly modified by local forces. Does this lead on to an acceptance of the dual state theory?

The Dual State Thesis and Local Organisations

The dual state thesis deals first with the combined effect of internal contradictions between central and local levels of the state apparatus and differences in relations between outside forces at central and local levels. It suggests that different state forms exist at the two levels so that the political processes taking place are of a different nature. Thereby the relations between the two levels may be contradictory, especially so when socio-economic conditions favour conflicts between their basic interests.

In a way, dual state theory has in a way been represented in each of the "major schools of thought" of urban political theory, namely the German state theorists, the French urban sociologists and the English urban political researchers. So, Saunders has developed a concept that has been implicitly present in different shapes in the latest decade's literature on urban politics, most explicitly in recent contributions by some French urban sociologists. In the German case the idea is expressed as a question of a functional division of labour inside the state apparatus, whereas many French urban sociologists heavily stress the importance of local struggles over and across the boundaries of collective consumption.

The idea of <u>local corporatism</u> stresses the importance of the role local organisations play in policy making at the local level, but also in the battle of interests between the central state and local government (Hernes, 1979; Slagstad, 1978). The Norwegian theory of local corporatism resembles in some ways the better-known discussion in the English-speaking world about corporatism formulated by Pahl, among others (Pahl, 1975; 1977). Here, key actors at the local level are seen as having a considerable influence on the distribution of "urban values" (Saunders, 1979, 1981; Villadsen, 1983).

We shall now examine these two theories further, since both of them stress the importance of local level politics.

The question of local corporatism

The main trends of new urban political theory do not point to corporatism as a central aspect in local politics. There are, however, two central exceptions from this main trend, which must be dealt with here in order to understand the role of organisations in the new patterns of local government in Denmark.

The first school of thought sees local corporatism as an important new feature of public intervention in the sphere of private production. In one sense it is a theory of state intervention, specifically at the local level, and highlights the growing need for specialised intervention in local production to secure employment in communities, including urban areas. Local government intervention may be seen both as a defensive and offensive strategy, depending on whether it is interpreted in terms of German critical theory, or in the terms of the more corporatist line associated with Norwegian theorists.

Urban politics may typically be seen as the politics of social reproduction organized by local government as collective consumption. If this definition is accepted, then local corporatism is restricted to the traditional, urban political field and does not encompass the controversial field of intervention in production associated with capitalist countries. It is, however, a crucial question whether it is relevant to use the term local corporatism in connection with the traditional urban, political field. Local politics is very much a question of organized integration between households, consumers, parents etc. on the one hand and local political institutions on the other, with in some cases employees' representatives as a third party. This interplay may be looked upon as controlled politicisation and participation rather than local corporatism.

At the local level it might be suggested that the well known distinction by Schmitter between state (in this case: local state) corporatism and societal (community) corporatism only partly fits the latest development of politics at local level (Schmitter, 1974). Though the organized and structured participation of two or three different categories of interests typically staged by the central or local state may resemble state corporatism in Schmitter's sense, they do not have the authoritarian features of state corporatism. On the other hand, the three parties do not resemble the labour-capital-state triangle in "real" neo-corporatist tri-partisanism or in the "Liberal" character of societal corporatism.

The second tradition in corporatist theories in relation to urban politics is embedded in the pluralist, corporate tradition, for example James Simmie's work (Simmie, 1982), whilst a different version of this type of theory is also found in Patrick Dunleavy's Urban Political Analysis, (Dunleavy, 1981) which deals with other, very broad topics in urban politics as well.

In Simmie and Dunleavy's versions, corporate processes at the local level are reflections of general, societal developments and may be incorporated into these general patterns of structured influence. In this version, corporatism serves to integrate local institutions, interests and actors into general processes dominated by relatively few organizations or by an ideological corporatism penetrating the urban level (Dunleavy, 1981).

Whereas the questions of local autonomy and conflicts between central and local governments more or less disappear because the topics concerning level and specificity are ruled out in Simmie's analysis, according to Hernes and Selvik local corporatism accentuates structural conflicts between central and local governments and between various local governments as a direct result of late welfare state intervention in the private economy at the local level. As Urry (1981) notes, "There will at times be strong demands from different groupings for functional representation within the state in a manner which transcends the limited effectiveness of the parliamentary representation". If and when local governments are capable of intervening in the private economy, it is a logical assumption that local corporatism must be the consequence. Then Urry's statement could be expanded with consequences for central government and local capital.

According to Hernes and Selvik local corporatism rests on five main arguments. First, demands for industrial consultation and representation on various public/private boards leads to an expansion of the local state apparatus.

Second, there are increased demands for corporatist representation in local administration, which again leads to apathy among the voters because of the depoliticisation of elected bodies. Another consequence might be the development of local grass-roots protest movements.

Third, the creation of a local apparatus for industrial policies implies a potential source of conflict with the central administrative apparatus of the state, they may represent counter-expertise to that at the national level.

Fourth, the recruitment of experts to local government bodies leads to pressure from the local bureaucracy for more selective incentives from the central state.

Fifth, increasing competition is likely to take place between local authorities with the purpose of attracting industrial activity, an observation made in other countries as well, but refuted in an English study by Martin Boddy (1982).

As far as decentralisation and cuts are concerned, the pressure from organisations is of particular interest. One possible way to mediate these interests is by way of direct representation from such organisations onto local councils. Another way is to create corporate bodies with representation from the relevant parties. But very often a "structural anticipation" by local councils of the needs of local capital or other local interests may be at work, in so far as the local councils have legal or financial powers to implement the policy.

Table 6. Answers by local politicians to the following question: " Do you think that the following groups and organizations have increased or decreased their activity to influence local government's priorities and budgets lately?"

	More active	No changes	Less active	Don't know
Loc. gov. employees	32	56	4	8
Business	26	61	7	6
Trade unions	36	56	5	4
Culture, sport etc.	46	47	4	3
Citizens' groups grass roots etc.	45	44	6	4
Local party orgn	33	63	2	2
Persons	18	70	7	5

Note: N =294 Local Councillors Survey, Oct. 1981.

The role of local organizations is discussed in the light of observations from our Danish research project covering more than 400 organisations, groups etc. in our sample of 40 communes. It is generally accepted that central state organizations have increased their pressure on local amenities. But what is the role of different types of organizations in local politics? The above table shows how leading politicians perceive the pressure laid upon them from various groups in the locality.

The table shows that pressure from organizations of a new, "urban" type is strongly felt by councillors, compared to the pressure from individuals or their own party organizations.

Most noticeably, pressure is felt in the urban, political areas where interests and priorities differ between citizens and local politicians. This situation does not point to an encompassing and integrating pattern of local corporatism of the type suggested above. Our survey of organizations does not point to a closely knit pattern of relations between organizations where increases in pressure are not much felt by local politicians. It should be added, however, that the distinction between integration/cooptation and pressure is important. Conservative councillors do not find that private business has increased its activities in any way. They think that trade unions have increased their activities, however, even though they have no contacts with this kind of organisation. The opposite is the case with Labour councillors.

Though there are some patterns of local corporatism type in larger cities, for most local authorities the trend towards controlled politics seems to be of greater importance. So, theories of local corporatism only reflect aspects of urban politics in the bigger Danish cities: in smaller districts, such theories are inappropriate.

Dual state theory and central control.

As a reaction against the very functionalist local state theories, the concept of the dual state stresses the complexity of politics at the local, urban level. Saunders neatly summarizes what the dual state theory is about and what are the consequences for urban political analysis.

Saunders suggests that national or state politics and urban politics should not be analysed in the same terms because different processes dominate at national and local level (Saunders, 1981). In brief, Saunders rejects the idea that corporatism has penetrated local level politics. On the contrary, in his view competition, local conflicts and pluralism are characteristics of urban politics.

Table 6. The three elements of the urban question

Conceptual criterion	Urban aspect	Relational aspect	Principal tension
Primary function	Social consumption	Social investment	Economic management v. social provision
Mode of interest mediation	Competitive politics	Corporatist politics	Planning v. Democratic accountability
Level of administration	Local government	Regional national government	Centralisation v. peripheral autonomy

Source: Peter Saunders: Social Theory and the Urban Question, London 1981.

In view of the present cuts and controls imposed on local governments by the central state, the Hernes-Selvik argument seems optimistic. On the other hand the economic crisis does point to local authorities as important agencies for households, local firms and local organisations as purveyors of services and subsidies. By contrast, Simmie's analysis does not take the intensity and scope of local politics into consideration: he holds a point of view which ends up being very similar to a number of other local state theories from Germany, England and France (Grauhan, 1975). In contrast to Simmie, these studies are often heavily influenced by functionalist schemes of thought, so corporatist developments are not used as explanatory factors. The role of the local state is seen as performing certain functions in the total state apparatus, such as legitimising functions, filling out infrastructural gaps, increasing state output, pacifying competing capitals at the local level and creating social order.

Except for the local corporatist theory of Hernes and Selvik and for dual state theories, all local state urban politics theories described here are universal theories, which means that they are general theories of society or of the political system. It is our hypothesis that the pattern of urban politics is much more complex than that suggested by most local state research and urban political analyses. That is why Saunders's work is of considerable importance. But only when taken together with elements from other theories can it contribute partial explanations of the very intricate patterns which comprise urban politics today.

However, in the main body of local state theories, local authorities are seen as integrated elements of "a national, local government system" (Dunleavy 1981), or as functional parts of a single control system working on behalf of demands for capital accumulation (Grauhan, 1975). That local authorities are subdued is not taken as a sign of conflicting interests, but rather as the successful integration of a decentralised, political level that at times may be growing, at other times restricted, according to needs and goals mediated by the central state from the economic sphere.

In some studies local authorities are seen as instrumental in the hands of a single, coherent body, namely the state (Friedland, 1982). In others, local authorities are not so much seen as subject to a conscious strategy as they are seen as functionally integrated into an overall state policy. This point, however, is not always clear, and raises a whole range of questions connected with functional state theories.

According to dual state theories, local governments may also be instrumental, but rather in the hands of local organisations and only inside a framework of central state control. This situation may of course itself be the source of conflicts between local and central levels of the state apparatus.

Dual state theory thus offers some promising explanations of recent development in local government activities and central control in Denmark. Like many tempting theories, however, it tends to over-simplify matters and to overlook some important features of urban political development. What are the problems, and why is it that dual state theory explains only part of what is happening in the urban political field?

Five arguments against the dual state theory

The following five arguments against dual state theory are not put forward because the theory is considered irrelevant -on the contrary. But the theory as such poses the following problem: why is it that political processes at the local level concerning collective consumption display very specific features? The classical dichotomies, community versus mass society, state versus locality, rural versus urban, state/mass politics versus localism etc. are reflected once again in the dual state thesis, because they stress differences between types of political communities at the general and local levels. But in the classical theories the dichotomies reflected the starting and finishing points of a one-dimensional societal development, where dual state theories build upon an understanding of the economy as 'dual' as well, itself with both local and corporate characteristics (Cawson 1982).

First, then, should state and national politics be of a different nature compared to local level politics? Whereas the main trend in community sociology and in local state theories points to the total disappearance of local politics, dual state theory has perhaps created an artificial antagonism between political forms at the two levels. It would be more realistic to avoid the classical dichotomy altogether by conceiving urban politics as a battlefield for all kinds of politics. In this way urban politics is to be seen as an aspect of this general form of politics, and not a specific and dichotomous political form in itself. The hierarchical control patterns described above are too easily forgotten when analysed in dual state terms.

Second, corporatism should not be restricted to the analysis of national politics, as suggested by dual state theory. As proposed by the Norwegian researchers, local corporatism may also develop, or alternatively, as Roger Friedland suggests, the locality may provide an important setting for the influence of big corporations and unions (Friedland, 1982).

So local conditions and local branches of national organisations interact in ways that are neither general/national corporatism nor local corporatism – but may be specifically urban. The principle of controlled participation may thus at times resemble some form of corporatism.

Third, local parties are not adequately dealt with by Saunders but are on the other hand they are very much the focus of other studies, for example in Dunleavy's Urban Political Analysis (Dunleavy, 1981). But Dunleavy's analysis is part of the dominating trend in urban political theory, encompassing many of the central elements of local state research, although greater emphasis is put on organisational and ideological matters than is often the case.

Fourth, considering the restructuring processes of local government in the last decade and taking into consideration the economic crisis, it is amazing how smoothly changes have been accepted by local governments and by their representative organisations. This situation, however, has been changed with

the introduction of the latest cuts in block grants combined
with a regional redistribution of moneys and continued
conflicts between some local and regional authorities and the
central government. Local governments in the greater
Copenhagen area had decided to withdraw from the local
government association by 1985 in protest against this
redistribution and their organisation's acceptance of it, but
they were calmed down by means of a reconstruction of the
Association of Local Governments. Furthermore, especially in
the urban areas, local authorities have been so badly hit by
cuts in block grants that protests inside party organisations
and in public are now very outspoken. A number of strikes
among local employees illustrate this new situation. The
smooth integration view gives credence to local state
theories: the conflicts do not.

Fifth and last, dual state theory seems to generalise a
problem that is rather diversified by processes of
segregation. The consequences of social segregation between
communities is political segregation and vice versa, so there
is no unified pattern of local politics, but rather specific
sets of political processes according to the type of
community. Dual state processes may be one type of pattern;
local corporatism may typically be present in the big cities,
whilst the "local state" may be a good description of politics
in many developing districts.

It would be very strange indeed if the great socio-economic
diversity between different types of communities and districts
were totally reduced to an organisational pattern of relations
between central and local levels of public administration
(i.e. one of state control, party influence, and corporate
influence). The local, political situation is very different
in the diversified types of communities that exist in
industrialised societies such as Denmark and Britain.
Segregation and local class patterns play an important role
here and are underestimated in the dual state analysis.

Conclusion: A new conception of urban politics

Research in Danish and British local, urban politics seems to
point to a number of different and even conflicting political
forces or principles at work. Instead of local state, local
corporatism or dual state theory, we suggest another model for
understanding urban politics; the-field-of-tension model. At
this stage we only suggest a few concepts and guidelines for
further analyses (Villadsen, 1983). The main principle of
this model is that political processes at the local level
should be looked upon as series of inherent or explicit

conflicts between hierarchical control processes performed by
the state, corporations, national parties and organisations
etc. and local, spatially-oriented forces created by the
segregation of localities/communities into specific,
socio-economic areas. These local or spatially-oriented forces
may be found within some local branches of the above-mentioned
hierarchically structured types of organisations, or they may
be of a specific, local cultural or issue-oriented nature. Of
importance here is especially the local social and class
composition as a base for local mobilisation.

If we accept that urban politics are the politics of
everyday life, a number of other aspects of the urban,
political problematic follow. Politicisation of "private"
households' functions means that different forms of collective
consumption structure social relations in communities and at
the same time create new types of relations between local
authorities, organised interests and the state.

These new types of relations could perhaps be described as
local corporatism, but may rather be understood as a form of
state-controlled politicisation and participation, because
neither societal nor authoritarian types of corporatism
resemble this new type of local polity.

In Cawson's and Saunders's conceptions of duality, the
provision of social services is very much a question of
competition among various groups of "consumers" in the
localities (Cawson 1982). But the pattern of urban politics
is more than a market place for provision of social services
by local governments. The analogy of competition in the
market-place is an insufficient conceptualisation of urban
politics because a number of structures and constraints are at
work both inside each district and between communities,
districts and regions. The market-place is replaced by
politics and bureaucracy. Also, the "logic" of these
processes emanating from a rapidly changing labour market and
social structure will be underestimated by this approach.

Various structures cut across the local area reflecting
socio-spatial forces, political organisations and movements of
both a general and more specific nature and of different
organisations and corporations. All these structures and
forces combine in specific, segregated areas of local
government. The pattern of segregation is caused by a
socio-economic development that may be strengthened by local
planning and social policies. So communities differ according
to class structure, economic structure and population, from
which specific urban political patterns develop. Important
aspects of these political patterns are the complex relations

between local and non-local political agents, such as those between state agents, political parties and ideological institutions.

Thus, segregation is not a question of closed social systems as they were perceived by traditional community studies. On the contrary, the segregated local setting is an arena of complex but specific forces. Uneven economic and urban development lies behind this pattern and creates the setting for urban politics as a field of tension.

The point is that the combination of influences is determined by the character of the local setting: the class setting, geography, tradition, organisational pattern of a locality. Urban politics must be seen as an aspect of political and other relational processes in general, at once inside the overall political universe and something important and characteristic in itself. The character of hierarchical and local/spatially conflicting political processes is in other words specified by segregation processes creating a "field of tension". The local economic and social class settings are important conditions for the local "reception" of overall political and ideological forces.

This is why none of the prevalent theories of urban politics and state-local government relations are adequate, but are only partial analyses of politics at the local level. Most often conflicts and tensions are between levels, between social groupings and between political movements not integrated into the central concepts of these theories. Though the present concept, urban politics as a field of tensions, leaves some matters to be further developed, it does at least avoid some of the problems facing urban political theory today.

REFERENCES

Andersen, B. et al (1979) Lokalpolitik og kummunestyre, Roskilde University.
Boddy, M. (1982) Local Government and Industrial Development, S.A.U.S., Bristol
Cawson, A. (1982) Corporatism and Welfare, London, Heinemann
Dunleavy, P. (1981) Urban Political Analysis, London, Macmillan
Friedland, R. (1982) Power and Crisis in the City, London, Macmillan
Game, C. (1982) "Budget Making by Opinion Poll: Must Services Always Suffer?"Local Government Studies (New Series) Vol.8, no.2 pp.11-18.

Grauhan, R. R. (ed) (1975) Lokale Politikforschung, 1 and 2, Frankfurt-Main.

Hernes, G. (1979) "Local Corporatism in Norway", Scandinavian Political Studies Vol.3

Pahl, R. (1977) "Managers, Technical Experts and the State in Harloe, M. (ed), Captive Cities, London.

Saunders, P. (1979) Urban Politics: a Sociological Interpretation, London, Hutchinson.

Saunders, P. (1981) Social Theory and the Urban Question, London, Hutchinson

Schmitter, P. C. (1974) "Still the Century of Corporatism?" The Review of Politics

Simmie, J. (1982), Power, Property and Corporatism, London, Macmillan

Slagstad, R. (1979) Om Staten, Oslo

Urry, J. (1981) The Anatomy of Capitalist Societies, London

Villadsen, S. (1983) Byblitik, Copenhagen

Villadsen, S. (1983) Central-Local Political Relations: Politicisation or Relative Autonomy? Copenhagen Occasional Paper, Institute of Political Studies, Copenhagen University

3 Decentralisation in Denmark: towards a new inequality

FRANK BUNDGAARD AND MADS CHRISTOFFERSON
University of Copenhagen

As is the case in other European countries, decentralisation has also been on the political agenda in Denmark since the late 60s.

In this chapter we shall argue that the social meaning and content of the decentralisation trend in Denmark has been subject to a fundamental change in recent years.

In the seventies a process of decentralisation or "municipalisation" of important infrastructural and reproductive functions took place. The system built up in those years was characterised by the fact that no particular group of municipalities was favoured. However, this picture has changed drastically as a consequence of the processes of political, economic and social crisis management.

After a brief introduction we shall give a few concrete examples of how this shift in such central areas of urban politics as physical planning, environment protection, and government grants to local authorities, has occurred.

INTRODUCTION

If we consider the relationship between the central state, the local authorities and citizens in post-war Denmark, four characteristic trends can be identified:

First, a very important expansion of the public sector intervening in a long range of infrastructural and, especially, reproductive areas (education, health, social welfare etc.) has taken place.

Second, responsibility for these functions has increasingly been transferred to the regional authorities and - more important - to the municipalities.

Third, a process of disengagement of the public sector has started. The state's efforts to "cut down" and "reprivatise" the welfare state are mainly centred around functions related to the reproduction of the labour force.

Fourth, we can also identify in the same period a dislocation of central state policy concerning the management of local authorities. Former crucial political questions concerning the establishment of common norms and standards for public services, of planning by the local authorities, the question of establishing an equal financial background for the municipalities have all been abandoned. Instead, the state has increasingly concentrated on controlling the total spending of local authorities. The political slogans accompanying this transformation of central/local authority relations are those of "modernisation", "efficiency" and "decentralisation".

These trends have replaced the two, earlier tendencies. It is already obvious that recent austerity programmes have focused mainly on the reproductive functions and have thus reduced the social wage. But there is more to it than that.

Several of the austerity programmes are not just cost-cutting programmes. An inherent feature in the way the retrenchments have been carried out lies in important changes in central-local relations and in the relations between the municipalities; changes that will probably result in the development of new social inequalities.

No matter what the outcome, it is quite clear that the recent developments in central-local relations raise new empirical questions: how have these changes been brought about and with what consequences?

Behind these questions lie the more fundamental problems of how this transformation of the socio-administrative structure in Denmark can be explained in relation to the development of state and class structure.

In this chapter we shall confine our attention to the first range of questions and only comment very briefly on the second in our concluding remarks.

First, however, a few words on some central developmental functions in the post-war period.

PUBLIC INTERVENTIONS AND EVERYDAY LIFE

The welfare state was primarily built up through the 1960s by Social Democratic governments in a partial alliance with fractions of centrist political parties and with support (or under pressure) from the reformist labour movement and parts of the capitalist classes.

Alongside the vast expansion of the public sector and the increasing role of the state in the provision of the means of consumption, a fundamental transformation of the social structure has taken place. The role of the family and of the local community network has crumbled away. Whether these changes came before or after the public provision of the means of consumption, the changes themselves are irreversible.

In the 1960s public authorities intervened and assured the fulfilment of the reproductive needs, when the family or the community network failed to provide the necessary help or support. But at the same time the original social structures eroded. Therefore, as the austerity programmes in the 1980s replace further developments of the welfare state, there is no longer an immediate alternative to state provision of the social services. Consequently, the retrenchments can only be realised at the risk of social chaos and thus at the (potential) risk of social unrest.

In this sense, the state is trapped in a contradiction between the financial need to cut back expenditure and the still expanding need for state provision of social consumption: this contradiction is further strengthened by public employees' resistance to the cut-backs.

In 1982 the Social Democratic government, unable to find a way out of this contradiction, gave up and left office in favour of a Conservative four-party coalition. Obviously, the contradiction was not dissolved by this change in office, but the more energetic Conservative government has made its way out of the trap through a combination of retrenchments in the social services and ideological efforts to revitalise the family as the reproductive unit.

The resulting social chaos has been well documented, especially regarding the situation of single-parent families and young people. Despite this fact there have been few signs of organised resistance against political and economic strategies of the Conservative government. The only exceptions seem to be the alleged radicalisation of public employees and (recent) scattered conflicts in the health service.

One of the main reasons for this relative lack of active resistance might be the successful dispersion of the consequences. Or - to be more specific - decentralisation of the cut-backs are achieved through the on-going transformation of the municipal financial system. This is a process to which we shall return below.

THE MUNICIPAL REFORMS OF THE 1970s

The central/local government structure was entirely reorganised in the early 1970s. The number of municipalities was reduced from about 1200 to 275, and the division of tasks between the central, regional and local authorities was restructured.

Although many tasks were carried out by the municipalities even before the reforms, the **NEW** tasks were typically fulfilled by the central state. And the municipal tasks were carried out under close central state supervision. Even the smaller details of municipal social consumption functions were governed by tight state regulations.

This picture changed fundamentally with the reforms of the 1970s. One of the prime motives behind the reforms was to relieve the state of resource demanding detailed supervision. The reforms, therefore, included a marked enhancement of the role and importance of local councils, and the creation of more powerful locally-elected political bodies. The amalgamation of municipalities gave rise to larger units with more resources. These municipalities were able to handle all the tasks that were transferred from the institutions of the decentralised state. The close supervision of details was replaced by a new kind of public management strategy. The central idea of this strategy was the state's concentration on the formulation of guiding principles and the general rules to be applied in county and municipal policy-making.

Local councils gained a considerable degree of autonomy. As long as local dispositions were compatible with the general guidelines, it was left in principle to councils to decide the priority of tasks in crucial matters such as tax levels, housing and planning policies.

Local autonomy was, however, restricted by a set of centrally fixed minimum norms and standards, a restriction that was explicitly aimed at avoiding "undue" inequalities between the levels of service in the individual municipalities.

Another important ingredient in the municipal reforms was the complete overhaul of the local finance system. Before the reforms, a considerable proportion of municipal functions were financed through matching grants. The foundation of this system was established during the 1930s, when social stability was threatened by the developing inequalities between municipalities. Matching grants were thus introduced as a means of stabilising the social system.

An important element of the reforms of the 1970s was the drastic change in the matching grant system. The main objective was to regain central control over public expenditure. Matching grants had the unfortunate characteristic that they enabled municipalities to raise local service level without raising local taxes. The remedy to this situation was the reunion of the financial and political responsibility in the municipalities. The reforms thus abolished or reduced the majority of matching grant systems, these being were replaced by a new system of general grants.

Although this new system implied changes in the municipal finance system, the whole process was completed in full appreciation of the goal of equality behind the matching grant system.

In fact the new system was explicitly aimed at establishing a uniform relationship between the municipal service level and the local tax level. This objective was operationalised in two different schemes:

a tax base equalisation scheme according to which municipalities with over-average tax bases had to transfer some of their surplus to municipalities with less than average tax-basis;

an equalisation scheme of objective needs. The fundamental idea was that a share of the municipal budget was exempted from the control of the council, because it was connected to rights given through national laws. The municipalities were to receive compensation according to their individual share of the national sum of these resource-demanding tasks. The main part of matching grants resources was transferred to this scheme.

The two schemes represented a compromise between total local autonomy and total equality. They represented a specific combination of the effort to maximise local autonomy and the effort to prevent the (extreme) results of increasing autonomy in a capitalist society.

In the past ten years this balance has been a central issue in the development of central-local relations. And at the formal or ideological level this is still the case. However, something new and quite different seems to be developing underneath the smooth ideological surface.

DECENTRALISATION IN PHYSICAL PLANNING

During the past 15 years the system of physical planning has been subject to important reforms. Along with with the local government reforms of the 70s, the National and Regional Planning Act (1973) and the Municipal Planning Act (1975) located substantial decision-making power at the regional and the local level.

The whole planning system was built up as a hierarchy whereby the central state was to produce general guidelines outlining the main political intentions behind regional and urban development. On this basis, the counties were provided with the capacity to conceive the regional plans, which were to constitute the framework for the municipal and local planning.

This model of management was first drawn up within physical planning, but it later became generalised as one of the most frequently applied models designed to regulate local authorities' policies.

The general objectives of comprehensive physical planning stated by the laws are as follows: to provide a more efficient allocation of resources, to create better means of fighting pollution, to establish better coordination of public dispositions, and to assure an equal regional development.

Looking back on ten years' experience, it seems highly dubious whether any of these objectives have been realised. On the contrary, there are many indications that this hierarchy of decision-making levels and its concomitant management model has all but broken down.

Of course, there is a complex set of reasons for this.   One main reason is that the intended system of regulation has remained an abstract principle. The system comprises several instruments of intervention in the hands of the minister and the central authorities such as directives, sanctioning of plans, authority to veto local or regional decisions, and authority to call in plans for revision.   But these instruments have hardly ever been used to set through any kind of coherent urban or regional policy. National planning has ended up in an ideological discourse legitimating current urban and regional development and carefully avoiding actual political, social and economic problems.

Due to lack of guidance from the national level, regional planning has developed characteristics of ambiguity and incoherence.

The formal system leaves the task of regional planning to the county councils who are supposed to cooperate closely with the municipalities. However, this task is not an easy one. The municipalities are placed in a situation of financial, fiscal and social stress that provokes a rather tense competition for further demographic and industrial growth.

The counties are not provided with sufficient means to settle these conflicts because of a weak formal and actual power position.   The existing finance system and the established division of functions emphasise the role of the municipalities in such a way that the regional authorities have fewer resources and less decision-making power than the municipalities. Furthermore, the counties are deprived of an efficient means of coercion as regards the implementation of plans.   This weak position is a result of the efforts of the national Association of Municipalities. When the Act was passed by the Parliament (Folketinget) in 1973, the Association succeeded in removing the counties' authority to sanction municipal plans from the Bill. As a result, regional planning has obtained very meagre results in coordinating the different public dispositions.

Finally, the assumptions of growth in regional planning are based on an optimism that lacks foundation in the economic and social crises of the eighties.

As a consequence of practically non-existent national planning and weak and incoherent regional planning, municipal planning appears as the most vigorous type of physical planning. The breakdown of regulation created an administrative power vacuum in which municipal planning bodies could operate without serious restraints. In the areas of zoning, housing policy, infrastructure and environment protection, local authorities have thus achieved a position of considerable autonomy.

The combined outcome of this situation is a form of regional planning that is patchwork-like in its structure. The revitalisation of local planning was an outspoken intention of the planning system reform of the seventies, but it is evident that the scope and contents of this decentralisation largely exceed the original intentions.

The considerable municipal influence not only produced regional planning shaped by a conglomerate of local demands, but it was also revealed by the fact that in many cases the regional plan was simply disregarded by the municipalities' actual decisions.

Many cases of "deviation" from regional planning can be mentioned: office centres have been builton the Copenhagen outskirts in flagrant contradiction to plans. Demands for industrial location in rural areas reserved for recreational purposes have caused arbitrary changes of plans, reflecting inter-municipal competition. Lately, an alliance between a local authority and the Danish branch of IBM has succeeded in locating a new administrative centre in one of the most attractive recreational areas north of Copenhagen. Even though the decision making process involved all levels of the planning system hierarchy from the county to the minister, the local alliance was powerful enough to have its way.

Another example of decentralisation of decision-making with unfortunate consequences can be found in the environmental protection field. As part of the seventies' local government reforms a wide range of matters with crucial environmental importance was transferred to local authority: sewerage, water supply, waste disposal, and control of polluting industries.

Had the government issued these guidelines, and hereby maintained the principle of total balance, then the municipalities would have been able to compensate for their loss of revenue by reducing the level of services on an equal basis.

But the government did not issue such guidelines. It was, therefore, left to struggles on the local political scene to determine the sector or the social group that was to be subject to local cutbacks. Despite the lip-service the government paid to the established principle of total balance, the government did actually reduce the grant pool without reducing the obligatory municipal tasks.

In an historical perspective, the state has thus succeeded in pushing functions out to municipal responsibility without paying for them. In other words, the principle of balance was demolished and councils were left with the unpleasant alternative of either reducing service levels or increasing local taxes.

Another conspicuous element of the 1980s' local authority financial reforms was the complete change of the role of the central state in the municipal equalisation scheme. Until 1982 the central state was directly engaged in the levelling out of municipal inequalities that took place through the two equalisation schemes.

According to the equalisation scheme of objective needs the contributions to municipal economies were almost exclusively paid by the state. And the state covered a part of the contributions to municipalities with a poor tax basis. The wealthy municipalities paid less than the poor municipalities received, so the state had to make up the difference. Due to these arrangements the state was unable to change the total amount of grant without at the same time changing the level of equalisation.

A special committee on the municipal financial system established by the former Social Democratic government recommended a reform of the whole system. It recommended first, that the state's contributions should be separated from the question of equalisation: second, the bringing together of all the different state contributions into a new grant pool, and the distribution of this grant pool in accordance with the municipal tax base after inter-municipal equalisation had taken place. When the Conservative coalition came to power in 1982, these recommendations were brought into existence with the passage of a new Act on the general grant system.

71

Although there have been massive investments in sewage systems throughout the last 15 years, there are many indications of pollution in the freshwater and coastal sea areas. Neglectful administration and defective control on the part of local authorities seem to be at the root of these problems.

DEVELOPMENT OF THE LOCAL FINANCE AND GRANT SYSTEM

The main part of local government expenditure in Denmark is financed through municipal income tax. However, grants from the central state play a significant role, although there are indications of their declining importance.

A central principle of the reform of local finances in the 1970s was to keep the existing balance between the central state and local government economy. This meant that the transfer of functions from central to local authorities did not result in increased local taxation. In other words, local governments were fully compensated for their rising expenditures due to the new distribution of tasks.

The policy of the seventies concerning local finance and grant system is thus characterised by two principles:

the principle of total balance: to keep a total financial balance between central state and the local government system through the use of compensating transfers;

the principle of municipal equality: to secure some degree of financial equality between municipalities and thereby assure an equal level of social services.

The policies of the 1980s have abandoned these principles to a large extent. Not only have the austerity programmes reduced the general grant pool, they have also introduced a new set of principles for the distribution of grants.

In her introduction to the Conservative coalition government's retrenchments in 1982 and 1983, the Minister of the Interior promised to issue guidelines for the allocation of the reduced resources. Due to the construction of the general grant pool, every single penny in it was in principle labelled. What she promised was, in other words, to specify the municipal functions to which the retrenchments corresponded to.

For the central state the gains were twofold. The Act enabled the state to change (reduce) the general grant pool without influencing the level of equalisation. The state has, so to speak, transformed itself from an engaged participant to a benefactor. Detachment from the question of equalisation was the pronounced purpose of the reform, but there is an additional political gain which can hardly be overestimated. Any further changes in the level of inter-municipal equalisation have been turned into a strictly municipal matter. Conflicts no longer involve the central state, but solely the municipalities themselves. The recent conflicts between the National Association of Municipalities and the Greater Copenhagen municipalities (who suffered most from the new Act) appear to mark the beginning of a long series of conflicts which might induce the collapse of the National Association and definitely weaken the position of the municipalities vis-a-vis the central state.

In summary it is evident that the retrenchments are more than just a quantitative reduction. They comprise a definite break with established principles for the distribution of functions between the state and the municipalities.

Clearly, the change also has consequences for the social structure. First of all, the abandonment of the principle of total balance indicates a potential dislocation of tax burdens from the central level to the local level. This would not make any difference if state and local taxes were paid on the same basis. But they are not. While the state taxes are paid according to a progressive scale, the local taxes are paid according to a proportional scale. Thus the new system openly favours high income groups.

Second, this tendency is reinforced by the transformation of the basis on which grants are distributed. In accordance with inherent inequalities in the Danish tax system this transformation results in a relative advantage for high income municipalities with a high proportion of owner-occupied dwellings, whereas the opposite is the case for low-income municipalities with a high proportion of rented dwellings.

All in all, the local finance and state grant reforms of the 1980s have implied a new distribution of burdens and resources between central state and local authorities, between different municipalities, and between the citizens of the individual municipalities. The retrenchment policies adopted by the new Conservative government are in all respects policies of redistribution towards the better off.

TOWARDS A NEW INEQUALITY

Viewed as a totality, the combined consequences of the decentralisation of functions and decision making, and the reform of local finances, indicate that the administrative system and its dominant procedures are in a process of profound transformation, involving a process that will cause new inequalities and create new patterns of segregation in the urban system in Denmark. It seems beyond any doubt that the inherent tendency in the reforms of recent years is to gain a greater state of flexibility through the abandonment of social equality. The state confines its attention to the total level of public expenditure without considering the subsequent development of inequalities in and between municipalities.

With the new finance system and the breakdown of the central government framework of regulation, it seems plausible to expect that existing economic, political and social inequalities between the municipalities will be emphasised in the future. The wealthy local authorities will make use of their high degree of freedom of manoeuvre to fortify their power position relative to the central state and other local authorities. By employing their traditional means of housing, planning, taxation and social policies, they will continuously try to secure an extended reproduction of their social basis.

On the other hand (because of their lack of sufficient resources) the poorer municipalities will be deprived of the same freedom of action. To a still greater extent, they will be confronted with the problems of rising social consumption needs, due to unemployment and social problems, and a declining tax base caused by the exodus of the middle classes.

CONCLUSION

What we have presented here is the result of a first ordering of a chaotic empirical reality. It is the preliminary answer to the question of what is actually happening in the 1980s as regards central-local relations in Denmark.

It is a first step that has to be followed by answers to more fundamental questions. For example: what are the connections between the restructuring of the central-local relations and contemporary developments in the Danish social structure? Which social forces have been able to drive the decentralisation so far beyond the original rationale?

A hint at the groups or classes behind the new policies might be found in the fact that the inherent redistributions have all been in the same direction. Whether we consider the social groups or the municipalities, resources have been moved from the poor to the wealthy in all cases. Together with the fact that the retrenchments have been accompanied by central state policies aimed at an accelerated accumulation process, this change might be evidence of a massive dislocation in the political hegemony in favour of the capitalist classes.

Thus, we would probably not be totally out of touch with the present social reality if we concluded that the capitalist class or fractions of it had succeeded in revitalising the economy through central and local state-mediated cuts in the social wage.

The point is, however, that unless this conclusion is otherwise qualified, it is a purely functionalist statement that closes off the question without providing any explanatory answers.

Although the present situation with its balance of power invites functionalist conclusions, it is quite clear that the functionalist fallacy conceals more than it reveals in this case. In other words, we still need to shed more light on the processes in the grey box between social bases/forces and the state's adoption of new policies.

What about theories of state intervention and theories of the local state? There are several which focus on exactly this complex of problems. Does the application of one or several of them provide sought-for answers?

We do not think so. Without going into a detailed discussion, we will just point out that these theories or models have not been really liberated from the characteristics of their parentage. They have incorporated and often also generalised specific French and/or British societal characteristics. The explanation of social action does in fact demand an acknowledgment of the specific societal context in which the action takes place. But it is evident that the applicability of British or French models or theories is very limited in a Danish context for the same reasons.

In more general terms it is an open question as to how far we can actually theorise social action or class struggle. Does the struggle of classes entail a basis for a general model or theory that can provide general statements about the outcome of specific situations?   Or is the outcome so unique that answers can only be found which are relevant to a specific place and at a specific time? We support the latter view.

At the present phase, what is needed is therefore not the transference of British or French models and theories, nor is it primarily the building of another - maybe Danish - theory or model of state intervention or theory of the local state. What is needed is rather a more open-minded research without pre-formed results.   To avoid a consequent critique that blames us for re-adopting the inductivist fallacy, we are of course aware that considerable knowledge about the local level has already been accumulated, and that this, together with more general sociological knowledge, will necessarily play a vital role in any research project. What we wish to emphasise is the necessity to avoid any theory or model that unconsciously "answers" questions that cannot be answered outside a specific social context such as, for example, the question of relations between policies, formulated interests and social forces, or that about which policies are formulated and implemented at which administrative level; and through which mode of interest mediation are they formulated? We hope to have demonstrated that at least Danish society has developed a much too complex and differentiated combination of policies and resource-allocation to allow any a priori generalisations on these issues to be made.

The only way forward is to launch research from a pad of minimum theoretical preconstruction and to hold open the questions to which we do not or cannot have any pre-given answers.

Although this might appear too cautious, it does not deviate too much from what we believe is the dominant tendency in contemporary urban sociology. As far as we can see, there has been a growing emphasis on empirical research both in France and Britain. Although there are also other reasons for this change, the tendency primarily seems to be founded on a recognition of the loose grip which previous theories and models have had on social reality.   As a result, it has apparently been recognised that we need both more updated empirical knowledge and further reformulation of theory beyond those made earlier. In this way, in the end we might be able to construct theories and models with a tighter grip on the social reality of Denmark in the 1980s.

4 Urban politics, the local state and consumption: problems in recent social and political theory

ROB FLYNN [1]
Department of Sociology and Anthropology, University of Salford

"The dissolution of the orthodox consensus has been succeeded by the Babel of theoretical voices that currently clamour for attention."

(Giddens 1979, 238)

"The time is over, if it ever existed, when a single theory or holy book could provide the right answers."

(Castells 1980, 129)

INTRODUCTION

This chapter critically examines some of the most important and influential arguments developed in recent British urban social science. In the last decade there has been a remarkable growth of sociological and political theory about urban questions, and particularly about state intervention and its consequences. The development of new concepts to analyse urban politics and the 'local state' has stimulated, indeed required, a significant re-orientation in research. It is therefore prudent to reflect systematically on problems and progress so far, especially when substantial claims are made for the utility of new theoretical frameworks. Despite, or perhaps because of, the idealised interdependency between theoretical ideas and empirical work, we must continuously assess the relationship between conceptualism and evidence: this is essential and routine scientific procedure. However, the overall evaluation of theories (whether between or within old or new paradigms) is much more difficult and problematic.

Evaluation necessarily presupposes some standards of adjudication, some measurements of strength and weakness, of merit and defect. In addition, if we are to compare, we must be sure that the things to be compared are actually comparable. Assessments which seek to go beyond an inventory or stocktaking also imply some normative statement of preferences, since we are obliged to indicate why something is regarded as 'better' or valued as more 'useful' than another. Moreover, all these considerations rest on a more fundamental assumption, which is that estimates of importance, value or worth essentially depend on a prior concept of purpose.

These general issues pose special difficulties in the appraisal of social scientific concepts and theories. It is surely now a well established position in the philosophy of science and methodology of the social sciences that there are no logical grounds for believing in the possibility of one ultimately 'correct' epistemology. Nevertheless, theories are conventionally evaluated in terms of their internal logical consistency and their empirical cogency. Even this approach contains problems, however, because there are different types of theory; because the status of, and differences between concepts, ideal-types, models and theories is often unclear; and because their relationship to evidence is problematic.

Of course the nature of explanation within the social sciences has always been the source of controversy. The most fundamental disputes are about whether we are seeking causal laws, whether these must provide universal or probabilistic predictive generalisations, and how patterns or regularities in social behaviour can be connected with human meaning, consciousness and action. What makes an adequate, let alone good theory, is far from clear. Ryan, for example, insisted that social scientific theory must be deductive and causal, should seek to make nomothetic generalisations with counterfactual conditional statements, or at least provide "an intelligible account of causal sequences - or if this is too strong, a coherent story about natural processes" (Ryan, 1970; 79). Whereas Giddens has argued that the stress on deductive explanations and universal laws is dogmatic and restrictive.

"Explanation, most broadly conceived, can be more appropriately treated as the clearing up of puzzles or queries; seen from this point of view, explanation is the making intelligible of observations or events that cannot readily be interpreted within the context of an existing theory or frame of meaning." (Giddens, 1979, 258)

While this view is reasonable, it still does not help us decide what is a satisfactory or valid explanation, nor how to judge between theories.[2]

Evidently, from a meta-theoretical viewpoint, difficulties abound in our effort to formulate principles and standards for evaluation and comparability, and these are compounded by disciplinary fragmentation; theoretical pluralism, and paradigm-shifts. So how then do we decide between alternative competing theoretical accounts? This is an unresolved (because probably unresolvable) question (Lukes 1981). However, I would argue that we must at a minimum adopt the following conventions based on certain normative assumptions: that social science theories ought to make general propositions of a causal kind; that such theories must consist of provisional explanations whose adequacy is measured in terms of logical coherence, operational validity, empirical cogency and breadth of scope; and, perhaps more controversially, utility for intervention. Alternative theories should therefore be assessed on these basic principles. However, even using such (admittedly vague) principles, the task of evaluation cannot proceed until we are sure about the objectives or purposes of particular theories and conceptual frameworks, their boundaries or terms of reference. In one sense theories are like tools, and while some tools are versatile, they usually have a specific purpose: we cannot in general say that a hammer is 'better than' a saw. Thus we must also consider whether different theories or approaches have common referents and objects of inquiry. It makes no sense to say that one theory is superior to another if they set out to explain different phenomena, so for purposes of comparison we have to assume that there is some empirical congruence despite apparent conceptual and explanatory differences. Of course theories have validity only at certain levels of abstraction and generality, but it can be argued that it is possible to devise a 'nested' hierarchy of more-or-less self-contained but complementary and commensurable theories for varying levels of abstraction.[3]

These remarks are necessary and very relevant in the context of this chapter which discusses the value of recent urban social and political theories in research on the local state. In this field we are face with a bewildering plethora of concepts, models, ideal-types and attempts at theory construction. Whether the variety and fundamental disagreements over basic concepts, terminology and attributions of causality are special to analysis in particular, is difficult to say.[4] What we do know is that this field has attracted the attention of writers from different social science disciplines and has recently been a competitive arena for 'neo-Marxist' versus 'bourgeois' theory.[5] Necessarily then, we should expect diversity and perhaps some confusion, as writers call upon different stocks of intellectual knowledge, work with different frames of references (spatial, comparative, historical etc.) and appeal to evidence at different levels of abstraction.

Given this diversity, of methodological and theoretical pluralism, it is not possible to provide a comprehensive overview or systematic synthesis of recent urban social theory; nor is it possible, for the reasons given above, to adjudicate between competing theories. What I shall do is discuss the main features of certain selected ideas in recent British urban politics and sociology, outline some of the problems involved in applying and using these ideas, in order to clear some ground for a fuller debate. Observations made about the plausibility and utility of concepts and theories are inescapably personal and context-dependent, but their justification, and ultimately the validation of all theory, is a matter of broader collective judgement within a scientific community.

PROBLEMS IN DEFINING THE FIELD OF INQUIRY

There are, obviously, important disagreements about the conceptualisation and identification of both the 'urban' and 'urban politics', and much argument about the specificity of 'locality' or 'locale' and the relevance of spatial/territorial differentiation in attempts to delimit local economies, local labour markets, local social structures and of course community power and the local state (see Dunleavy 1982b; Giddens 1979; Pahl, Flynn and Buck 1983; Urry 1981, 1983a, 1983b). If we confine our attention for present purposes to what is currently regarded as important or interesting about the local state and urban politics (i.e. why should we study it?), then we can sketch out some ideas about the purpose, and perhaps the value, of various explanations. While this is certainly a matter for further argument, it seems to me that reduced to first principles, we study local urban politics and the local state for these basic (but not exhaustive) reasons:

(a)   because certain activities, processes and
structures observed in localities have a <u>sui generis</u>
character, and have distinctive and separate effects
on the pattern of life-chances, power relations and
social consciousness compared to macro-societal
influences.

(b) because the institutional form and political
structure (conceived in terms of relations, not merely
organisations) of the local state is distinctive from
other forms or levels of the state, and this has an
independent effect on (a)

(c) because the inter-relationship between (a) and (b)
has a cumulative impact which changes, or at least
modifies, the nature of central/national public
policies and politics, and <u>the operation and impact
of the wider economy and polity on the economy</u>.

Clearly we must make a theoretical assumption that urban
politics and the local state have a contingent but
nevertheless specific autonomy. If we do not subscribe to
this view, the only other reason for studying the 'urban' and
locality is that it provides a convenient and useful arena for
examining the working out of societal processes: in other
words a pragmatic justification. Such a view is based on the
assumption that the political economy of cities and regions
reveals in <u>microcosm</u> the outcomes of dominant independent
variables whose consequences are nonetheless sufficiently
diverse as to merit investigation. Whatever general position
is taken will affect the delineation of aspects of reality
regarded as important, what kinds of evidence are important,
and which kinds of research methods are appropriate. The
central issue here is the discovery and estimation of local
political autonomy. The methodological and theoretical task
is one of deciding if and when one set of concepts and
variables can be logically subsumed by or reduced to, another,
so that particular empirical observations and causal
narratives can be deduced from more abstract and general
propositions - thus for example (b) above might be subsumed by
(a).

In urban social theory, the core argument is about the
identification of special attributes or properties of 'urban'
economic/political/social processes, the factors or variables
which influence them, and the degrees of independence or
causal weight attached to them. In my view the most important
and interesting aspect of this argument revolves around recent
attempts to disentangle theories of collective assumption and

theories of state intervention at the local level, which have provided new answers (or at least different proposals) to such conventional political science/political sociology questions as:

1. What is the nature of policies managed by local or sub-national government and what are the functions and outcomes of these policies for local populations?

2. What differences are there between state policies and services in their administration, and in their social and political effects?

3. What is the nature of the resource allocation process, and what are the sources of influence on policymakers?

However, these new approaches are not without their own dilemmas and difficulties. Thus, while it is now common to castigate orthodox theories for being abstract, behaviourist, deterministic, empiricist, functionalist, ideological, reductionist, teleological etc. etc..., it is not so easy to avoid most or all (or any?) of these defects. It is generally agreed that what is most distinctive and worthwhile about recent urban political social theory is its insistence on explanations which refer to structural features of the economy and polity. Nevertheless mere critique of, and disdain for other approaches which focus in depth on the actions of groups and institutions does nothing to solve the vital problem of bridging macro- and micro-levels of analysis, which is common to all theory.

I now wish to discuss some of these issues by referring to debates stimulated principally by Saunders and Dunleavy, about the boundaries, content and significance of urban politics and the local state.

THE IDEAL-TYPE OF THE DUAL STATE AND URBAN POLITICS

In seeking to unravel the intricacies of local politics, and the complex roles of local government in urban policy, Saunders has advanced a persuasive and sophisticated conceptual framework. This combined an account of the functions of state intervention with a typology of power relations which is now deservedly well-known and influential (Saunders 1979, 1981). In criticising the functionalism, tautological and teleological aspects of some recent marxian work, Saunders both emphasised the need for empirical-counterfactual theories and argued for the possibility of using elements from different theories to explain different aspects of urban policy and politics, especially to explain the apparent 'relative autonomy' of the local state. He suggested an ideal-type division between capitalist investment and consumption functions, between forms of politics and levels of the state, and claimed that accordingly, local government was the medium for consumption-based policies, and the arena for localised, competitive political struggles.

In elaborations of these ideas (Saunders 1982a, 1982b, 1982c; Cawson & Saunders 1983) Saunders claimed that the peculiar nature of social consumption, local state autonomy and the non-class character of local politics, constituted a distinctive set of processes and structures requiring a specific coherent theory with urban sociology. At numerous points he stressed that his proposals comprised an 'analytical schema', an 'heuristic device', or a rudimentary hypothetical framework, which was founded upon an ideal-type - the intention was to develop further hypotheses and guide research. Despite these caveats, however, Saunders clearly insisted that no single theory of the state was adequate, but on the contrary theoretical dualism was necessary in order to deal with the bifurcation of state policies, governmental structures, and forms of political mediation. While he accepted that in general, urban politics and policies were undoubtedly related to capital accumulation, corporate influence and central state intervention, Saunders nevertheless argued that they could be extricated analytically, and that they constituted a unique domain, empirically and theoretically (cf. Saunders 1981, 266-267, 274-5: Cawson & Saunders 1983, 24-25).

Thus according to Saunders:

> "The political groupings which arise around housing issues, education cuts, welfare agencies, and so on, are not class-based but are constituted on the basis of 'consumption sectors' (council tenants, parents, the elderly etc) which bear a 'necessary non-correspondence' (analytically though not of course empirically) to class categories." (Saunders 1982b, 186)

and "...the functional specificity of local government in Britain - the fact that is primarily concerned with the provision of social consumption - means that local political struggles are generally not constituted as class struggles. More specifically...local government...has its own specificity in terms of its function, its mode of discharging this function, and

the ideology which surrounds this function, and the
necessary implication of this specificity is that it
does not constitute an arena of class struggle."
(Saunders 1982a, 57)

Predictably, these propositions have attracted severe
criticism from marxian writers who regard the separation of
consumption from production/investment as misconceived and
misleading, and who consider the dual state/political model as
mistakenly functionalist and a historical (see Cooke 1982; Cox
1984; Duncan & Goodwin 1982a; Hooper 1982). Now Saunders
(1981, 259-260) and Cawson & Saunders (1983, 20) were careful
to indicate that consumption and investment are inter-related,
and that the capitalist sphere of production provides a "set
of constraints which shapes some of the contours of policy",
but they reject the idea that consumption processes are
necessarily reducible to production relations. Further,
although Saunders has accepted Duncan and Goodwin's criticism
that his model of the dual state is static (and possibly
functionalist) and accepted that we need an approach which is
historical and relational, he still insists that it is
theoretically valid and pragmatically essential to isolate
'local consumption processes' for analysis. Thus:

"...the local political process cannot easily be seen
simply as one aspect of the overall political class
struggle. Within...constraints...it seems that
non-capitalist interests can win at the local
level..."

"...the political forces which are mobilised around
the 'local state' cannot be analysed in class terms at
all, for the social bases on which they draw are
defined not by relations of production but by
differential patterns of consumption."

"...Because they involve different functions, modes
and ideologies, local political processes must be
analysed by means of different theoretical
perspectives from national policies." (Saunders 1982a,
63-64

Thus attempts to explain the local state and urban politics
in class terms are clearly rejected by Saunders, in favour of
a theory of competitive politics or 'imperfect pluralism'.
Moreover, he recommends abandonment of the local state concept
(1982a; 57, 64) since it is a misnomer for 'local political
processes' or 'local political struggles' oriented around
material interests derived from social consumption.

Here however we encounter difficulty in making sense of the ideal-type construction: if we cannot use the concept of the local state (because it connotes production-based determinants and class conflict), then what precisely are the defining characteristics of the object of inquiry, and what are its institutional referents? For Saunders, the object of inquiry is local consumption-based competitive political struggles, around the principles of citizenship and social need. This is defined theoretically as a set of processes rather than institutionally. But we can still argue that this begs the questions as to what, when and where are 'local' struggles, and in what sense consumption policies have to have a 'local' dimension. Saunders (1982a) argues that the questions of the specificity of local political processes is ultimately an empirical one, but of course the selection of evidence is guided by the ideal-type.

We are frequently reminded by Saunders, Cawson (1982; 72-73) and Cawson & Saunders (1983) that the ideal-type proposed is neither a model (analogue) nor a theory (causal explanation) but rather an analytical framework to help simplify complex and diverse reality. Because knowledge can only ever be incomplete, the Weberian method of ideal-types provides a means for constructing concepts which distinguish relevant phenomena, and for avoiding the problem of infinite regress implied in attempts to study totalities. We are told that the dualistic ideal-type is a necessary preliminary to generating hypotheses and thence theories, and will enable comparative and historical analysis (Saunders 1982a; 58). Ideal-types, however, are neither true or false, since they cannot be empirically 'disproven'; their utility lies in crystallising the 'essential' features of concrete reality in an abstract concept which then assists research.

So how useful is such an ideal-type in practice? One major difficulty arises out of its ambiguity and vagueness. What is it a device for, what eventually is the thing to be explained? The principal concern seems to be the relative autonomy of the local state, but the ideal-type is a composite construct of several concepts at different levels of abstraction. One resulting problem is that it is hard to explicate the ideal-type in order to make claims about real relations and to know the causal directions implied. Are local political processes consequences of the interrelation between particular economic functions, interest mediation and ideology, or vice versa? Further, Saunders's ideal-type necessarily compels exaggeration (in rejecting class-based theories of local politics and urban policies he has denied that consumption issues are a concomitant or prior struggles in the sphere of production) but the extent of exaggeration is difficult to measure. His basic dichotomy between social consumption and investment implies that social consumption policies are 'primarily' functional for non-capitalist sections of the population, and that it is contingent whether such policies are favourable for capital accumulation. But the ideal-type does not indicate what kinds of criteria or evidence would be relevant to establish such 'contingency'. We are told that the more we find evidence of attributes associated with central/corporate/class politics at the local level (and vice versa) the more we should invoke the alternative theoretical explanation (pluralist versus instrumentalist). But surely such evidence would cast serious doubt on the entire validity of the ideal-type of bifurcation and the dual state? In reply to such a question, it can be argued that an ideal-type cannot provide answers but only clues as to what and where to look, and thus even though evidence might challenge the theories, the bifurcation of functions remained valid as an ideal-type. However, it is still reasonable to ask how much evidence, and of what kind, relating to which policy fields, would be necessary to cast doubt on the plausibility of the ideal-type, remembering that as a mental construct or logical purification it is immune to empirical test? [6]

The abandonment of the concept 'local state', and its substitution by 'local political processes' poses further problems empirically. If local/urban politics are not merely miniature replicas of national/class politics, then what (and where) are they? First, there is the longstanding issue about defining 'local' and restricting analysis to particular spatial or territorial scales. Saunders rejected a spatial focus for urban sociology, but we still require criteria to isolate local processes, local state agencies, and identify local political groupings. Second, there are the unavoidable problems of indicating precisely what constitutes social consumption provisions (which flow from the conceptual/theoretical ambiguities noted above) and which institutional levels to include. Are we concerned with all elements of the 'social wage' and all organisations concerned with the welfare state? Consumption expenditures include social security and pension payments and other income transfers, which are administered at all levels of government using criteria of citizenship and social need — but does, for example, controversy over a fraud squad investigation of welfare benefit claimants in a particular city constitute a local political struggle? Public education, housing and health services may be delivered locally, policy implementation may be subject to local discretion, and may give rise to locally-based consumer movements, but primary resource allocation decisions are centralised and the policy agenda is frequently politicised in class terms at the national level. The point here is not just whether it is plausible to describe certain state policies as serving predominantly consumption rather than investment functions [7] but how to derive a realistic sampling frame of relevant policies, actors and organisations for empirical investigation, and how to deal with what Saunders himself noted was a flaw in urban manageralist approaches - the receding locus of power and infinite regress in decision-making (Saunders 1979; 135)

In my view, his ideal-type does not, so far, provide sufficiently detailed or explicit guidance in devising such a sampling frame, and moreover, the 'institutional insulation' of functions at particular levels tells us little about how to investigate the crucial question of their inter-relation.[8] However, these weaknesses are an inevitable consequence of the ideal-type procedure, since in methodological terms ideal-types are inherently impossible to operationalise (since they make no claims about real relations) and so, as in this case, their usefulness is difficult to assess.

Related substantive criticisms have been developed from a marxian standpoint by Goodwin (1982), Duncan & Goodwin (1982a; 1982b) and Cooke (1982). As already noted, Duncan & Goodwin criticise the dualistic 'theory' of the state for being functionalist and a-historical, and they reject institutional definitions of the local state in favour of a class-based model which relates local politics and autonomy to stages in the development of capital and the social relations of production (using a modified state derivationist theory). They suggest that our understanding of the tensions between centralised state control and local democracy within capitalism will be improved if we examine the significance of variations in class consciousness (due to the uneven development of class relations) and in particular the potential threat of localised political control by the organised working class. Goodwin (1982), noting that 'local social relations' are not mere reflections of national social relations, claims that 'social forces' operating locally cannot be wholly reduced to local factors. Thus:

"The important task in understanding local variations in state actions is to find out what the interlinkages are between (inter) national social processes and local social processes. The form and content of state policies in the locality will be the result of a number of different and contingent factors [sic;viz?] which cannot be read off in advance from a list of predetermined functions." (Goodwin 1982; 9)

Using some illustrative material about the historical development of public housing provision in one city, Goodwin further claimed that "... because of the importance of local social relations, no two areas will respond in the same manner to the wider social forces" (op.cit. p.12)

Here again, although this might seem a reasonable approach to the analysis of local variations, we get no guidance on what the contingent factors are, or might be, nor how to identify these sets of 'local social relations. In addition, the local state has no concrete referent (an institutional concept of local government and formal politics is implicit) and there is an a priori assertion of the uniqueness of particular localities. This does not take us much further than Saunders's ideal-type and indeed the observation that different economic/socio-political environments (systems?) in different geographical areas produce different kinds of 'urban politics' is hardly novel, and appears tautological.[9]

Cooke (1982) acknowledges the problems of operationalising abstract categories for empirical research, and concedes that from a marxian standpoint there are "genuine difficulties in connecting local, and even some regional, struggles to the available macro theory since antagonistic groupings are seldom clearly contesting as classes formed around social relations of production" (op.cit. p.187). However, he rejects Saunders's axiom that local state issues cannot be class-based, and argues instead that a modified version of Hirsch's 'class-relational' perspective helps us to explain the variability and flexibility of capital/state relations which produces relational and local 'autonomy'. Here it is important to note that Cooke's thesis is exactly the obverse of Saunders:

> "The determinants which link a local anti-motorway
> or office development campaign to struggles between
> capital and labour within the state and civil
> society at various levels will often be difficult
> to establish and will sometimes be absent or
> impossible to situate. Nevertheless they ought not
> to be assumed away by definition." (op.cit. p.199)

Thus according to Cooke, urban conflicts may take the form of pluralistic disputes which cannot be analysed as inherently production-based, but they can be related to the dynamic nature of capital accumulation and crises within it, which permits and indeed requires temporary compromises and accommodations between capital and labour, reflected in state form and policy.[10] However this argument, which rests on assumptions that state agencies and policies reflect the 'double determination' of capital and labour (so that sometimes production-relations will be determinant and sometimes they will not) is at worst tautological, and at best inadequately operationalised. While determinants ought not to be assumed away by definition, they do still have to be shown to exist, or their absence be accounted for, in ways which enable empirical validation.

We can conclude then that Saunders's formulation of the problem of local state autonomy (and recent marxian criticism of it) poses difficulties in linking the abstract with the concrete, and in specifying the conditions and degrees of causality implied by the analysis. This is perhaps inevitable because of the heuristic nature of Saunders's ideal-type, but the problem of building middle-range theory remains a general difficulty and an essential future task. What is encouraging, however, is that each approach is firmly committed to detailed empirical application of the respective frameworks, and explicitly seeks to explain the <u>disparate</u> nature of local politics and the <u>contradictory</u> character of state intervention. In particular, both approaches emphasise the necessity of examining 'local social relations' and 'local political processes' (back to community studies?). It now seems that it is through the detailed study of local labour markets, class structures, economic restructuring and state policies, that we ar most likely to refine such concepts and calibrate explanatory variables (see Urry 1981, 1983a). Hopefully, such studies will also incorporate analysis of the internal structure of the state and the policy-making processes,[11] which are often only superficially discussed and/or regarded as epiphenomenal - Saunders and Duncan & Goodwin for example are evidently more interested in 'politics' rather than 'policymaking'. Thus I would argue that even adopting the ideal-type we still require deeper understanding of resource allocation, modes of provision, service delivery and bureaucratic discretion in the administration of collective consumption or state welfare policies.[12] We also need to know if, and how, different modes in different services (education, health, housing etc.) impinge on the awareness and capacity of citizens to mobilise as consumers in particular ways, and whether the 'politics of consumption' takes the same form in different areas or cities.

CONSUMPTION SECTORS AND URBAN POLITICS

Our awareness of the politics of consumption, and the centrality of state intervention in collective consumption, is largely due to Castells and his colleagues. Of course

Castells's writings have been the object of enormous critical attention, but for present purposes I shall concentrate on the concept of collective consumption as amended by Dunleavy and Saunders to form key elements in their arguments. Briefly, Saunders criticised Castells's theory of the state and theory of labour-power, and rejected the idea that collective consumption is equated with spatial units of organisation (Saunders 1981, chap.6). Nevertheless he retained the concept of collective consumption because it was valuable in providing a framework for understanding state intervention in social/non-market provisions and he suggested that Dunleavy's reformulation also offered empirical and theoretical potential.

Dunleavy's use of the collective consumption concept stemmed from his dissatisfaction with traditional approaches to local government and urban policy. He proposed a 'content-definition' of urban politics in terms of decision-making about collective consumption processes (Dunleavy, 1980: 50-55) incorporating public services such as education, health care, housing transport, social welfare and land use planning. He stressed that his approach was not confined to state institutions, was not restricted to 'cities' or any particular spatial scale, nor to the local level of government. The criteria for defining collective consumption processes were that the policies or activities should be a service not a commodity, should be collectively organised and managed, use non-market criteria for access, and were subsidised out of general taxation.

Using this model, Dunleavy attempted to show the salience of sectoral consumption conflicts in several kinds of urban policy in Britain. Sectoral consumption cleavages were said to affect political alignment independently of production-class divisions - the social locations created by dependence/independence on public services or private commodity provision affected people's perceptions of policy issues, their attitudes towards party ideologies and their voting behaviour (Dunleavy 1980: 71-79, 163). Detailed evidence and theoretical justifications for these claims were given in Dunleavy (1979), where partisan de-alignment in voting patterns was explained partly by the contradictory and 'cross-cutting' influence of consumption sectoral locations.

According to Dunleavy:

"...consumption positions cannot be assimilated into or explained in terms of occupational class. Instead the relative independence of some consumption locations needs to be recognised." (op.cit. p.417) and

> "The concept of sector is a means of characterising
> and grouping together non-class or 'immediate' social
> interests distributed in systematic ways by economic,
> political and ideological structures.   Basically
> sectors are lines of vertical division in a society,
> such that certain common interests are shared between
> social classes in the same sector, while within a
> social class sectoral differences reflect a measure of
> conflict of interests."

It was emphasised that although consumption locations are
only partly independent of class locations, they nevertheless
have an effect on political attitudes and voting preferences.
Indeed Dunleavy argues that the apparent decline of working
class political strength (or at least fragmentation) can be
ascribed, in part, to the cumulative effect of consumption
sectoral divisions.   State intervention, moreover, may have
stabilised social formations by creating distinctive sets of
material interests cross-cutting those of economic class:
"...sectoral explanations of politics suggest that the
restricted levels of overt class conflict in advanced
industrial states reflect the partial displacement of class by
sectoral interests as bases for political mobilisation or
alignment."[13]   (Dunleavy 1982a; 189)

This appears to offer a convincing demonstration of the
distinctive nature of collective consumption, and Dunleavy has
buttressed arguments about the specificity of urban politics,
and the necessity to incorporate other forms of explanation,
in addition to those of class, when accounting for the
formation and impact of state policy.   However, it seems that
his concern to place 'local politics' within a macro-context -
Dunleavy (1980) emphasised the circumscribed nature of
so-called local politics and the significance of non-local
influences on changes in urban policy - compels him to develop
a 'radical but non-marxist structuralism' (Dunleavy 1982; 192)
which is still only partially developed.

As part of this continuing project, Dunleavy has recently
advanced a new framework for understanding 'socialised
consumption' (Dunleavy (1983).   Rejecting an undifferentiated
concept of collective consumption, he has advocated a complex
typology of modes of consumption to analyse variations in
forms and modes of consumption; historical changes within and
between modes; and the varying parameters of economic,
political and ideological functions.   Socialised consumption
is distinguished as a separate type of commodified

consumption, which is contrasted with autonomous consumption. Within socialised consumption, there are three distinct sub-categories - quasi-individualised, quasi-collective, and collective-consumption, illustrated by, respectively, home-ownership tax-relief subsidies; voluntary welfare services; and public education, housing, social services and transport.   Unfortunately space prevents a detailed description of this typology, but it offers a comprehensive scheme to account for changing forms of welfare state interventions and their relations to the market, shifts between modes of socialised consumption, and the 'functional pressures' which encourage or constrain policies.

Dunleavy particularly concentrates attention on the political implications of two aspects of socialised consumption - 'compulsory consumption' and 'coerced exchanges'.   In the former, state intervention in the market imposes a legal mandate for specific regulations and services, creates new forms of welfare need and thereby creates heteronomous control over public sector professions.   In the latter, complex changes in private/public sector provision increasingly reduce effective demand for services and/or constrain choices to one mode of consumption.   Compulsory consumption tends to increase the power of public sector professions and pressure to expand the welfare state. Coerced exchanges tend to produce consumption sectoral cleavages which further fragment the electorate.

What is evident (and explicitly acknowledged by Dunleavy) is that this typology is specifically concerned with macro questions, and ultimately with elucidating 'meta-causes' of long-term trends in socialised consumption.   Considerations about the 'local state' or 'local politics' per se thus have little or no relevance since they have to be reconceptualised in non-institutional terms: the precise role and involvement of specific state agencies and the nature of political mobilisation are contingent upon a prior theorisation of modes of consumption.   In many ways this approach conforms to that advocated by Saunders, but it is not yet clear how, if at all, Dunleavy's typology relates to the dualistic ideal-type. This undoubtedly requires the development of even more complex and sophisticated models to illuminate differences between types of consumption sectoral cleavages, and, as Dunleavy recognises, the analytical framework needs to be explicated through detailed studies at an institutional level.   Two obvious questions for empirical research are whether the political attitudes, values and behaviour of citizens, politicians and professionals are distinctive in relation to their location in quasi-collective, quasi individual and collective-consumption; and what are the additive or aggregate effects for citizens and groups occupying several consumption locations.

Clearly then consumption sectoral theory is still emergent and tentative. But such an approach, if it is to avoid rather mechanistic and post hoc impositions of the consumption sectoral idea, needs now to show how consumption locations affect action and how 'ideological structuration' works as a process. It is not yet clear how objective cleavages link up with subjective perceptions and political action. This raises the complex issues of ideology and interests, and the problem of identifying those factors which impinge on people's objective locations, subjective perceptions and their capacity and willingness to mobilise over particular issues. Another problem is the question of whether there are variations in local milieux which mediate the influence of consumption sectoral cleavages within sectors and between 'policy systems'. Further study of such matters may enable us to examine whether certain configurations of consumption locations are necessarily associated with specific kinds and styles of provision, and perhaps the likely incidence (and even probable outcome) of various types of citizen revolt or consumer protest.

From a very different standpoint, Preteceille (1981) has underlined the importance of such an analysis. It is not merely the existence of public services, or levels of public expenditure which is significant, but also the nature, organisation and ideological aspects of consumption. Further, public expenditure cuts or restructuring the welfare state must be seen as part of a continuous political process the outcome of which is segmentation of consumers by institution, access, area and type of management.[14] This then means that:

"To understand the objective conditions from which social movements arise, we should analyse the allocation and use of public funds - the quantitative aspects of the services - but also their management and the political problems involved.
(Preteceille, op.cit. p.14)

Thus while consumption sectoral analysis seems a promising avenue to explore, its principal use so far appears to be in explaining partisan de-alignment by compounding or intervening non-class variables. The role of local government,

territorial variations in urban politics, and the
institutional matrix of policy surrounding consumption
locations, have yet to be elaborated.

CONCLUSIONS

Obviously it is always easy to criticise, and very difficult
to create positive arguments and develop new theory. This
paper does not presume to make authoritative judgements, but
rather attempts to make a constructive appraisal of some ideas
which are widely regarded as important. Undoubtedly the 'new'
urban politics and sociology have shown, in fascinating and
stimulating ways, that it is imperative to examine local state
policies in the context of general structures and processes of
economic development, social stratification and power.
However, this objective is one shared implicitly, or at least
partly, by other conventional approaches. The main
difference, and the major source of difficulty and confusion,
lies in efforts to articulate complex chains and levels of
causation, in the linkages made between concepts, and
connections between concepts and empirical evidence. I do not
wholly accept Walton's complaint that we are not told how or
why the new urban sociology theoretically supersedes the old,
nor "how it explains better the empirical questions of
previous work and the anomalies that haunt conventional
paradigms, which is the whole point..." (Walton, 1983; 297).
Nevertheless, we should expect much greater precision in
specifying the units of analysis employed, the boundaries of
relevance, and especially the difference between explanans and
explanandum in theory and research.

This returns us to fundamental questions about the uses and
purposes of concepts and theories. Conceptual frameworks and
theories ought to indicate their objectives and must
explicitly clarify, in as rigorous a way as possible, what
cases or categories of phenomena they apply to. Otherwise,
critiques which point to failures in including or excluding
relevant variables will be misconceived, and cumulative
synthesis is impractical. This is even more relevant in
cross-national comparative research. Our selection of
theories and our preferences for concepts depends, as we noted
earlier, on their plausibility, logicality and
comprehensiveness for certain purposes. There will inevitably
be divergent views as to their usefulness, since disagreements
about purposes derive initially from normative assumptions
about what (and why) the 'problem' is to be explained. Thus
we cannot unequivocally assess the value of different
theories, and even if they share identical objectives there
are always likely to be disputes about evidence and

inference.[15]   Conversely, elaborating and 'disaggregating' theories should enable us to determine degrees of commonality and discrepancy, and to provide some estimate of utility.

This leads us finally to a practical question about whether contemporary urban social theory is helpful in understanding future trends.   Many of the ideas in recent theory were developed in an era of rapid economic growth and expanding state intervention.   While some writers have adapted their approach to changed circumstances, and have begun to explore different lines of inquiry, it remains to be seen whether existing concepts (let alone chains of reasoning) will be outmoded.   We have substantial literatures developing in relation to public expenditure reductions and the political economy of fiscal crisis, and some work on crises in service delivery and the social and political consequences of obsolescent infrastructure in cities.   But we do not know whether the so-called collapse of the formal (industrial) economy and the emergence of mass unemployment will mean that the 'urban politics' of the future will be qualitatively different from that of the present, and whether this will demand the creation of new concepts and theories.   Szelenyi has made powerful criticisms of recent radial structuralism, and urged us to rethink our approaches to cope with the rise of the informal economy and new questions thrown up by the dismantling of capitalist welfare states (Szelenyi, 1981). Pahl has even more explicitly recommended a re-orientation of urban sociology towards the consequences of the decline of the formal economy and the responses of households coping with varied opportunity structures (Pahl, 1983).   Others are better qualified to discuss these speculations, and to comment on the capacity of current theory to explain these new trends.   But at present we have enough interesting puzzles, and sufficient difficulty in solving them, to ensure that future debate in urban social theory will continue to be problematic, but challenging and worthwhile.

NOTES

[1]   This is a revised version of a paper presented to the Anglo-Danish Seminar on Local State Research, University of Copenhagen, Denmark, September 1983.   I am particularly grateful to Chris Pickvance and Peter Saunders for their comments; of course I am solely responsible for the views expressed here.

[2] Giddens explicitly refuses to deal with the question, raised in the last pages of the book, There is also the problem of infinite regress - puzzle surely derive from previous theory, but how do we decide which are the most important puzzles?

[3] Both Pickvance and Saunders stress this point (personal communications).

[4] Banfield (1975) observed that there were great obstacles for urban political science: disagreement about the concept 'urban'; a rag-bag assortment of theories; disagreement about appropriate empirical research; and the absence of cumulative and replicatory studies; hence there were 'many tracks but very few paths'.

[5] See for example: (ed) Harloe (1977; 1981) and (eds) Harloe and Lebas (1981); Pickvance (1984 forthcoming).

[6] How to determine whether the accentuation or exaggeration of reality (which comprises an ideal-type) is a distortion, is undoubtedly a fundamental epistemological problem inherent in Weber's procedure. I am grateful to Chris Bryant and Paul Keating for their comments on this point.

[7] See Flynn (1983) for a discussion of this in relation to land-use planning.

[8] Cawson (1982) provides a highly generalised account of state welfare policies, but acknowledges the tentative and preliminary nature of his corporatist framework - see especially chaps. 5 and 7 and pp.130-134.

[9] Arguably Duncan & Goodwin (1982b), despite their claim to the contrary, do not explicitly demonstrate causal connections, and refer to circumstantial evidence.

[10] Cooke (1983) provides a more elaborated version of his argument, using a Gramscian framework combined with a 'capital-theoretic' approach to the local state. Space prevents a full consideration here.

[11] Space prevents a discussion of the recent English literature on central/local government relations; however, it still remains to be shown how state organisational structures and relations articulate with the structure of class and power.

[12] Dunleavy (1980) deals with this very generally; and Dunleavy (1981) represents one rare and valuable effort to relate intra-state interests (especially professional) to external forces in policy formation at various levels.

[13] Franklin and Page (1983) are very sceptical of the validity of evidence about consumption cleavages. There are substantial methodological problems in measuring consumption effects, but further empirical evidence for this theory has been provided by Duke & Edgell (1984). They show that mainly private consumption locations (housing and transport) are associated with greater fragmentation within the working class; whereas mainly public consumption (education and health) are associated with greater fragmentation in the middle class. However, social class polarisation was still evident in opinions about public expenditure cuts - all 'workers' were more disapproving than all 'controllers'.

[14] Harloe (1981) and Lojkine (1981) have also argued closer attention to such fragmentation, and the significance of local autonomy in urban politics, but both stress the enormous difficulties of supplying explanatory links between theories of capitalist production and consumption relations.

REFERENCES

Banfield E. (1975) Foreword to Young, K. (ed) Essays on the Study of Urban Politics London, Macmillan
Castells M. (1980) 'Cities and regions beyond the crisis' International Journal of Urban & Regional Research vol.4 no.1.
Cawson A. (1982) Corporatism and Welfare London, Heinemann
Cawson A. and Saunders, P. (1983)'Corporatism, competitive politics and class struggle' in (ed) R. King Capital and Politics London, Routledge & Kegan Paul.
Cooke P. (1982) 'Class interests, regional restructuring and state formation in Wales' International Journal of Urban and Regional Research vol.6 no.2
Cooke P. (1983) Theories of Planning & Spatial Development London, Hutchinson
Cox K.R. (1984) 'Space and the urban question' Political Geography Quarterly, vol.3 no.1
Duke V. & Edgell S. (1984) 'Public expenditure cuts in Britain and consumption sectoral cleavages' International Journal of Urban and Regional Research
Duncan S.S. and Goodwin M. 'The local state' Political Geography Quarterly (1982a) vol.1, no.1

Duncan S.S. and Goodwin M. (1982b) 'The local state and restructuring social relations' International Journal of Urban and Regional Research vol.6 no.2

Dunleavy P. (1979) 'The urban basis of political alignment' British Journal of Political Science vol.9

Dunleavy, P.(1980) Urban Political Analysis London, Macmillan

Dunleavy, P. (1981) The Politics of Mass Housing in Britain London, Oxford University Press

Dunleavy P. (1982a) Rejoinder to Hooper Political Geography Quarterly vol.1 no.2

Dunleavy, P. (1982b) The Scope of Urban Studies in Social Science (Unit 3/4 D202) Milton Keynes, Open University Press

Dunleavy P. (1983) 'Socialised consumption and economic development'. Paper presented to the Anglo-Danish seminar on Local State Research, Copenhagen, September.

Flynn R. (1983) 'Co-optation and strategic planning in the local state' in R. King (ed) Capital and Politics

Franklin M.N. and Page E.C. (1983) 'The consumption cleavage heresy in British voting studies' Strathclyde Papers on Government and Politics

Giddens A (1979) Central Problems in Social Theory London, Macmillan

Goodwin M. (1982) 'The local state and the local provision of welfare'. Paper presented to the Political Studies Association Conference, University of Kent

Harloe M.(ed) (1977) Captive Cities London, Wiley

Harloe M.(ed) (1981) New Perspectives in Urban Change & Conflict London, Heinemann

Harloe M. and Lebas E. (eds.) (1981) City, Class and Capital, London, Edward Arnold.

Hooper A. (1982) 'Neo-Weberian political Sociology' (Review Essay) Political Geography Quarterly Vol.1 no.1

Lojkine J. (1981) 'Urban policy and local power' in M.Harloe and E. Lebas (eds) City, Class and Capital

Lukes S. (1981)'Fact and theory in the social sciences' in (eds) Potter D. et al Society and the Social Sciences Open University and Routledge & Kegan Paul, London

Pahl R.E. (1983) 'Concepts in context: pursuing the 'urban' of urban sociology' in (eds) D. Fraser and A.Sutcliffe, The Pursuit of Urban History, London, Edward Arnold

Pahl R.E., Flynn R. and Buck N. (1983) Structures and Processes of Urban Life London, Longmans

Pickvance C.G. (1982) The State and Collective Consumption (Unit 24, D202) Milton Keynes, Open University Press

Pickvance C.G. (1984) 'The structuralist critique in urban studies' in Smith M.P. (ed) Capital, Class and Urban Structure Sage Urban Affairs Annual Review no.26

Preteceille E.(1981) 'Collective consumption, the state and the crisis of capitalist society' in (eds) Harloe M. and Lebas E. City, Class and Capital

Ryan A. (1970) The Philosophy of the Social Sciences London, Macmillan

Saunders P. (1979) Urban Politics - a sociological interpretation London, Macmillan

Saunders P. (1981) Social Theory and the Urban Question London, Hutchinson

Saunders P. (1982a) 'Why study central-local relations? Local Government Studies vol.8 no.2

Saunders P. (1982b) Rejoinder to Hooper and Duncan & Goodwin Political Geography Quarterly vol.1 no.2

Saunders P. (1982c) The State as Investor (unit 25, D202) Milton Keynes, Open University Press

Szelenyi I. (1981) 'Structural changes of, and alternatives to, capital development...' International Journal of Urban & Regional Research vol.5 no.1

Urry J. (1981) 'Localities, regions and social class' International Journal of Urban & Regional Research vol 5, no.4

Urry J. (1983a) 'De-industrialisation, classes and politics' in (ed) R. King Capital and Politics

Urry J. (1983b) 'Some notes on realism and the analysis of space' International Journal of Urban and Regional Research vol.7 no.1

Walton, J. (1983) Review of Lebas E. Urban and Regional Sociology, International Journal of Urban and & Regional Research Vol.7, no.2

5 Danish local government: recent trends in economy and administration

CARL-JOHAN SKOVSGAARD AND JØRGAN SØNDERGAARD
Institutes of Political Science and Economics, University of Aarhus

INTRODUCTION

The single most important factor affecting local government during recent years is obviously the profound economic recession that began in the mid seventies. On the one hand comprehensive unemployment, and unemployment among young people in particular, has created new demands for local government activities and expenditures. On the other hand, the tax base of local government finance is shrinking. Thus any increase of an activity is now associated with either tax increases or decreases of other types of activities. As in many other countries, local governments in Denmark have been put in a position of fiscal strain.

Fiscal strain may well be more severe in Denmark than elsewhere for several reasons. First, since local government's expenditures amount to some 12% of GNP, they cannot avoid the economic recession simply by being small. Second, a large fraction of their revenue is raised by a local income tax and therefore the tax base is very sensitive to changes in the overall economic conditions of the country. Third, a wide range of reforms concerning the size, tasks and finance of local governments took place during the seventies. Therefore many local governments have been hit by the economic recession at a particularly inconvenient point in time.

In this paper we attempt to give a brief review of the Danish system of local government (section 2) and the reforms of the seventies (section 3) as a general background for the main discussion of recent trends in section 4. During this discussion we shall assess recent developments in local government expenditures as well as changes in central-local relations. In addition we shall focus attention on the internal changes in local administration and political decision making. Does fiscal strain aggravate conflicts between sectors, and which political and administrative strategies are applied in order to cope with the problems of fiscal stress? Indeed, these difficulties are likely to last for some time?

THE DANISH SYSTEM OF LOCAL GOVERNMENT

The administrative division in Denmark at present consists of three levels: the State or central government, the counties (of which there are 14), and the municipalities or local governments (of which there are 275). The only exceptions to this pattern are two municipalities (Copenhagen and Frederiksberg) which have been assigned municipal and county status simultaneously. The division of labour between counties and municipalities is quite extensive, but in certain cases, such as physical planning, the county holds a certain amount of authority over the municipalities.

Although there are many similarities between counties and municipalities with respect to political conditions, financial system, administrative structure and so forth, we concentrate on the municipalities throughout the paper. We would expect, however, that the main trends are pretty much the same for the counties as for the municipalities.

Each municipality is governed by a local council, the members of which are elected at direct elections held every fourth year. In most cases local governments are dominated by the nation wide political parties, but in some cases particular local lists play an important role.

A major part of public service provision is delegated to local government such as primary education, kindergartens, old age provision, public libraries, sports, roads, public transportation, sanitation, and town planning. Furthermore, local government is responsible for the administration of a large part of the income transfers in the Danish welfare system, including old age pensions and general assistance. Normally these expenses are fully or partly refunded by the central government.

The main source of finance for local government expenditures is a local income tax, which is levied on the same tax base as the state income tax, but at a locally chosen proportional tax rate in each municipality. Additionally, the local council is allowed to levy taxes on land and also to raise revenue by user charges on some of their services. Finally, unconditional grants (block grants) from the state are an important source of finance; additionally there is an equalising scheme in operation whereby funds are redistributed from rich communities to poor communities. In a very few cases the share of revenue from corporate taxation to local governments is also of some importance.

Danish local government is government by committee in the sense that preparation of the recommendations put to the council and implementation of the decisions are the work of committees (Harder, 1973). The only exceptions to this general rule are the largest municipalities, such as Copenhagen, Aarhus, Aalborg and Odense, which have aldermanic systems as well as locally-elected councillors. Local councils are not free to organise their committees as they please. Every local authority is required to appoint a finance committee with wide powers, whilst standing committees for the most important expenditure areas are also obligatory.

The management of the administration is the responsibility of the mayor. The normal arrangement is for the authority to be divided into five departments: finance, social affairs, education, technical department and rating. The head of the finance department is often given a special position, carrying the title of central director (town clerk), and the finance department has a special status due to the fact that the central director is also secretary of the finance committee. Thus this department prepares matters for finance committee meetings and - most importantly - prepares the annual budget on behalf of the finance committee.

CHANGING THE ROLE OF LOCAL GOVERNMENT

The Danish constitution guarantees local government some independence, which is to be regulated by law. Especially in the post-war period, when the public sector expanded rapidly, a large number of laws were passed by Parliament which regulated local government activities. These developments expanded the scope of local government, with the result that the existing structure, with a large number of small local authorities, became obsolete.

At the beginning of the 1960s proposals were introduced which aimed at remedying this situation by reducing the number of local authorities dramatically. A number of reforms were prepared around 1970 and carried through during the following years. These reforms are linked, but four issues may be distinguished: a) the division of areas, b) the allocation of functions between central, regional and local government, c) local political and administrative structure, and d) local finance and resources.

Division of areas

In 1945 Denmark was divided into 24 regional governments and almost 1,400 local authorities, consisting of 88 cities, and 1,304 suburban and rural authorities. On average, these categories had populations of between 165,000 and a little less than 3,000 inhabitants. However, these figures concealed very great variations within each category, from almost three-quarters of a million in the city of Copenhagen to a few hundred inhabitants in the smaller rural areas which, nevertheless, were in principle obliged to carry out the same tasks.

The law that laid the ground for the reform of this structure stated three essential principles:

a) efficiency should be achieved by creating demographic and economic entities appropriate for administrative purposes;

b) one city should be encompassed by one local government;

c) local loyalties should be respected by amalgamating local authorities in toto without crossing municipality boundaries.

On the basis of these principles the Minister of the Interior, with delegated authority from Parliament, then carried out the reform process in the two years 1967-69. Owing to voluntary amalgamations, the number of local authorities had dropped to 1,000 in 1967, but the reform further reduced the number to 277, since reduced to 275. The distinction between cities and other governments was also abolished.

Allocation of Functions

Although proposals to increase the number of local functions were one of the major factors that helped to overcome resistance to the amalgamation of local authorities in 1970, the distribution of functions among central, regional and local government was not outlined before 1970. Only one principle was stated: that responsibilities of each of the three tiers of government should be confined to their defined area.

The following brief overview of the present division of local government functions following the 70s reforms is based on a distinction between compulsory and non-compulsory functions (Bruun, 1979). In terms of compulsory functions, several social welfare responsibilities were devolved from central to regional and local government, and new ones have been given to local authorities. These include assistance to unmarried mothers, rehabilitation for the disabled, day- and night-care institutions for children, and recently the administration of unemployment assistance paid by central government. In the case of these institutions, the principle that a specific task should be the sole responsibility of one level of government has not been respected. Regional and local government operate many similar institutions.

All primary education (7-16-year-olds) was transferred to local government; the grammar schools (16-19-year-olds) from local to regional government. The central government still administers some grammar schools. Adult education, which is rapidly increasing, is administered and paid for by the local authorities. Before 1970 the health sector was divided between the three tiers of government. Apart from a few specialist hospitals, run by the central government, all hospitals are now administered by the regional governments, which also pay practising doctors. Local authorities take care of a few tasks, such as national health, dental treatment of children, and home nursing.

The construction and maintenance of roads are divided between central, regional and local authorities according to the size and importance of the roads. Since 1970 some former regional roads have been transferred to the central government. Local authorities administer and pay for all the roads that are used primarily for local transportation. Local administration of environmental controls was taken from state bodies and given to local government where physical planning, disposal of waste, and sewerage and water supply are of growing importance. Conservation was transferred from state bodies to regional government. Finally, when unemployment rose through the 1970s, local government was given tasks aiming at combating unemployment, especially concerning young people and long-time unemployed.

All the above compulsory functions are determined by laws which often also dictate minimum standards for the services. Local authorities, however, have other, non-compulsory responsibilities, especially in recreation, public transportation, public enterprises, and local economic development.

Local political and administrative structure

The general rules governing the organisation of county and local authorities and relations between these and central government are codified in The Local Government Act (Harder,1973). It is worth noting that the Act merely deals with the political level of local government, while administration is not touched upon, following a long tradition allowing councils to adapt their administration as circumstances may require. The Local Government Act delegates certain provisions to standing orders which are approved by the Minister of the Interior upon acceptance by the individual council. Only on exceptional grounds is permission granted to go outside the framework of the model standing order. Also the rules for the procedure of individual councils are very much influenced by a model of procedural rules circulated by the Ministry.

In general the council is the body responsible for local government. The finance committee's powers are explicitly stated in the Act and cover all matters involving finance, the appointment and dismissal of staff and staff salaries. Its position was strengthened in 1982 through an amendment to the Act stating that the finance committee should always serve as planning committee. The mayor is always chairman of the finance committee, and the political composition of the committee always reflects the composition of the council, which is not necessarily the case with the other committees. The standing orders state the standing committees' areas of responsibility, but the council has the final right to decide. The only exception concerns the Public Assistance Act, which lays responsibility for local decisions under this Act on the social committee. The council may, however, delegate authority to a committee as it chooses, and, within the annual budget, committees can make use of funds unless the council decides otherwise. It follows that the council is the body co-ordinating the - sometimes conflicting - interests of the various committees.

Local government legislation is chiefly concerned with the political organisation of authorities and contains little about local officers and departments. According to law the mayor is head of the administration and thus responsible for its organisation and staff. Since the functions of local authorities are much the same all over the country, the organisational structure follows the same pattern in most municipalities: five departments, each with its department head. Frequently departments make decisions within certain authorised limits. Delegation of authority within the administrative hierarchy will often depend on the nature of the problem and established practice, as we shall see shortly.

Local finances and grant systems

Danish local authorities have always had the right of taxation in accordance with the laws of Parliament. Apart from local taxation, grants from the central government have been their primary source of income.

Reform of the system was initiated in 1969 and several changes have taken place in the 1970s. The main element of the reform is the introduction of general grants and the abolition of reimbursing grants in most areas. Today, reimbursing grants cover only the social welfare programmes, with central government typically covering 50 per cent of total service expenditure, except for pensions which are totally financed by central government.

Two types of general grants have been introduced. First, the tax base equalisation scheme compensates those authorities who have a tax base smaller than the average. Compensation is based on an average tax rate, and the compensation ratio for municipalities below average is 50 per cent. The scheme is financed partly by municipalities with a tax base above average, partly by central government.

However, variations in expenditures are not solely due to differences in tax base. Also, expenditure requirements vary. For these reasons, unconditional (block) grants were introduced in 1973. The distribution of these grants is based on criteria which are supposed to reflect "needs" or expenditure requirements. The formula covering municipalities thus takes into consideration size and age structure of population, housing conditions, kilometres of road and space.

The distribution formula has been much debated. (Mouritzen and Skovsgaard, 1981). The City of Copenhagen, which allegedly has special expenditure requirements, in 1977 performed a determinant analysis of county and municipal expenditures. The analysis suggested that a considerable bias in the distribution of unconditional grants exists, and as a result there was a minor change in the formula which reallocates money from the western part of Denmark to the Copenhagen Metropolitan area.

Finally, a Grants of Assistance scheme was established in 1969 in order to meet the special problems of certain types of municipalities, such as those on the smaller islands. These grants are distributed autonomously by the Minister of the Interior on application. Enacted in 1977, the new budget system comprises current and capital expenditure. As a major new feature pluriannual budgets have been introduced covering a period of 4 years (Mouritzen, 1979).

From the point of view of central government, the functional structure of the budget makes it possible to combine central, regional and local budgets into one public budget. Furthermore, information on type of expenditure is a prerequisite of any effort to evaluate the conjunctural aspects of local and regional government policies. As a result, the new budgeting system has strengthened central government control to a considerable degree.

RECENT TRENDS IN ECONOMY AND ADMINISTRATION

General background

The economic recession in the Western World has been particularly deep in Denmark with more than 10% of the labour force being unemployed by 1984. This change from rapid economic growth in the sixties and the early seventies to a situation with no or very little growth in GNP is probably by far the most influential single factor behind the changes in local governments during recent years. On the one hand the recession has implied that the growth in revenue from local income tax has more or less ceased, so that any real expansion of local public services now requires a corresponding increase in the tax rate. On the other hand heavy unemployment creates new demands for local public expenditures, such as public assistance to those without unemployment insurance and temporary employment arrangements for particular groups of unemployed such as the young and the long-term unemployed. Thus many local governments are in a situation of fiscal strain because revenue is needed for the expansion of existing welfare programs and the establishment of new programmes for the unemployed, while at the same time the tax base is more or less constant in real terms. It is therefore necessary either to raise tax rates or to cut down spending on existing programmes.

In fact, the actual development since 1977 has involved an increase in the average local income tax rate from 15.7 to 18.5 per cent in 1983. However, there is a considerable variation both in levels and rates of increase across municipalities. Thus, almost one fifth of all municipalities have tax rates below 17 per cent, whilst one seventh have tax rates above 20 per cent.

Table 1. Percentage Increase in Tax Rate and Real Expenditures

Period	77/78	78/79	79/80	80/81	81/82	82/83
Type of expenditure						
Current expenditure	9.9	3.8	6.3	4.1	6.6	0.8
Income transfers	4.6	3.3	2.0	-0.9	1.3	-0.2
Capital expenditure	11.9	0.0	-19.9	-9.9	-17.2	-31.7
Total expenditure	8.6	2.6	2.0	1.1	3.0	-1.4
Average tax rate	1.3	7.6	3.0	0.0	0.0	6.3

Note: Includes all municipalities except Copenhagen and Frederiksberg.

Sources: Statistiske efterretninger and material from the Local Government Association.

Table 1 reports the relative change from year to year in real expenditures as well as in the average tax rate. Several things should be noted from these figures. First, the growth rate of local expenditures has gone down and for 1983 a reduction in expenditure in real terms is expected. Second, because 1978 and 1982 were election years there is a marked difference in tax rate changes and expenditure growth for these two years. The "menu" of the election year is paid for by a considerable tax increase one year later. Third, a widespread tendency to cut back on capital rather than current expenditure is revealed in the table. This is hardly surprising since no particular group among those currently employed by the municipality suffers directly from cancellation of future construction plans. Fourth, the expected decrease in transfers in real terms during 1983 is due to the intervention in all the transfer programmes of the Conservative government which took office during the summer of 1982. One of their proposals that passed in Parliament was to reduce child allowances, sick benefits, welfare benefits, and unemployment benefits and to limit the growth of public pensions.

Table 2 shows that there has been a reallocation of resources between functions in favour of employment arrangements, public assistance and, more surprisingly, in favour of kindergartens.

Table 2. Current expenditures on selected functions

Year	1978	1978	1980	1982	1983
Purpose	Mill. d.kr.		Index		
Roads, Environ- mental	3960	100	140	170	185
Public assistance	2085	100	143	183	224
Kinder- gartens	3558	100	157	220	244
Old age provision	4714	100	140	180	203
Primary education	8823	100	127	156	166
Employment	1215	100	101	219	287

Note: Includes all municipalities except Copenhagen and Frederiksberg.

Sources: As in table 1.

On average, Denmark has seen a considerable decline in the number of young children recently, and an increase in the number of people in all other age groups, which makes the rise in expenditures on kindergartens even more pronounced. By contrast, the increases in expenditures on old age provision and primary education are of equal magnitude when the changes in age composition of the population are taken into account.

Central-local fiscal relations

As mentioned earlier, the relative share of total public expenditures in Denmark which is controlled by local authorities increased during the sixties and the seventies. This trend continued until around 1980 when the local government's share (excl. public pensions) reached almost 1/3 of total public expenditures. There is no doubt that this was one of the important motives for the central government to propose and enact a budgeting reform in 1978.

This budgeting reform is an important prerequisite of the most radical alternation of central-local economic relations during the last decade. In 1979 a circular letter from the Minister of the Interior asked local councils to limit the growth rate of their expenditures to 3 per cent for 1980 in real terms. Before the circular letter was issued, negotiations took place between the Minister of the Interior and the Local Government Association. The spending limit was formally an agreement between the two sides, but it is clear that the central government would have put other measures into use if the negotiations had failed to reach an agreement.

The procedure followed in 1979 has been repeated during subsequent years with growth rates aimed at 2 per cent for 1981, 1 per cent for 1982 and zero for 1983. The limit on expenditure growth has also been accompanied by other circular letters aimed at weakening the requirements as to the level and quality of particular local services. Of course, the motivation for the latter is to reduce the squeeze on some local councils brought about by the expenditure limitation agreement. On top of all this the Conservative government has enacted a reduction of the general grants in 1983 and 1984.

There have been other changes in central-local fiscal relations, for example a new set of criteria for fixing the general grants and an associated change in the equalizing scheme. These changes have been designed to achieve a better relationship between expenditure needs and general grants, whilst at the same time strengthening the degree of redistribution, particularly since many poor authorities now receive smaller general grants under the new criteria. These changes are important for some municipalities, but their general impact is to produce only a minor reallocation of financial resources between the municipalities.

An important question is whether this attempt by the central government to obtain control of local budgets has the intended effects. As Table 1 above demonstrates, the growth rate of local government expenditures has indisputably been reduced. The only exception to a steady decline is 1982 (which was an election year), but it should be emphasised that the reduction in general grants for 1983 was enacted at a time when municipal tax rates were already fixed.

Even if we accept the figures of Table 1 there remains the question as to the importance of the central government policy as the cause of this reduction in growth rates. Two pieces of information raise some doubt on this point. First, an investigation of all 792 circular letters, instructions etc. from the central government to the municipalities in the year 1980 showed that about 12% were likely to reduce local expenditures, while about 21% were likely to increase local expenditures (Administrationsdepartementet, 1982). This is not to suggest that the central government has necessarily been inconsistent, but merely that local authorities are fed with expenditure demanding proposals and requirements from central government, the flow of which has been slightly reduced during recent years. Second, interviews with members of 40 selected councils and some of their executives, showed that about one half considered that central government initiatives had no or little influence on the changes in their municipal expenditures. It seems likely that only a few council members expected the growth rates associated with the seventies to continue alongside currently increasing levels of unemployment and slow growth of taxable income. Therefore, to some extent at least, most people had expected at best a slowing down in expenditure growth. Furthermore, some executives and council members may also wish to give the impression that they are good managers and thus are likely to understate the impact of the measures taken by the central government.

Local authorities under fiscal strain

Fiscal strain refers to a situation where expenditure demands are considered to be growing faster than available financial resources. Fiscal strain has been widely recognised to be a general condition of local government in many western countries in recent years (Newton, 1980). The basic reason for this has been the deepening economic recession. In the beginning of the seventies it was possible for local authorities in Denmark to increase their expenditures in real terms by 2-4% each year at a constant level of taxation. At present the feasible expenditure increase at unchanged tax rates is approximately zero on average and negative for a considerable number of municipalities.

There are likely to be several reasons why such a fall in the growth rate of economic resources causes fiscal strain within local governments. First, the change was not expected and it takes time to adapt expenditures to new conditions. In fact capital expenditure is the only one which can be reduced in the short run, primarily because it is a long lasting tradition that public employees are not dismissed unless very extraordinary circumstances emerge. Therefore current expenditure can only be reduced gradually over a long period of time. This issue is also important because there is no decline in the demand for local services which corresponds to the fall in resource growth.

Second, there has been an increase in demand for several services such as employment assistance for particular groups, old age provision (due to changes in demography) and environmental arrangements (due to legislation in the past). Thus many municipalities are in a position where expenditure increases are desirable or unavoidable in some areas, while in the short run no cutbacks are possible in other areas except on capital programmes.

Third, many municipalities may have been in a disequilibrium position before the recession appeared. The full adaptation of public services to the dramatic change in labour force participation of women and the associated changes in the roles and patterns of the family has not yet taken place. Therefore a local authority may be facing a delayed demand pressure on those services which are substitutes for traditional housework by women, even in services such as kindergartens and primary education where the demographic effect is negative.

Fourth, there may well be quite substantial differences in the service performance of local councils. Many of these have never had any real choices about services, either because of the rapid increase in resources in the past or because the local politicians have largely sought consensus. Thus it takes time to adopt a decision-making process involving difficult choices and conflicts among council members.

So capital expenditure have been cut back and it is no surprise that there has also been an unambiguous tendency towards deficit budgeting among local governments during recent years, but for most municipalities these ways of escaping the squeeze have now been precluded, since the last decade of growth in current expenditure is expected to cease from 1983 onwards. In some areas the result will be a rather abrupt change in current trends. This question is illustrated by Table 3, which shows the great variation in growth rates among the municipalities. Inflation was about 50 per cent over the period, averaging 10-11 per cent per year, so a few authorities have decreased their expenditures in real terms on primary education and old age provision, but none of them has decided to reduce current expenditure. Furthermore, there is a fairly close association between the expenditure changes on education and kindergartens and the total growth rate, while no significant correlation exists for old age provision. A closer examination of explanatory factors behind these growth rates shows that income growth and demography were the only significant determinants for old age provision, while the level of service in 1978 was an additional important determinant of provision for primary education and kindergartens. This finding supports the idea of a delayed demand pressure operating on present budgets.

Table 3. Distribution of municipalities according to growth rate 1978–82 of expenditures on various items.

Growth rate	Number of municipalities	Growth rate	Number of municipalities
Total working expenses		Primary education	
50–75%	12	30–50%	15
75–90%	15	50–60%	14
90–125%	12	60–85%	10
Kindergartens		Old age provision	
55–115%	12	40–70%	12
115–160%	15	70–95%	15
160–510%	12	95–220%	12

Note: N = 39 municipalities (a random sample)

Conflicts in local administration under fiscal strain

The issue of conflicts between service sectors is likely to be of particular importance in a fiscal stress situation because resource scarcity simply makes resource allocation much more difficult. It is relatively easy to allocate resources that are growing steadily. If you don't get a "piece of the pie" this year, you might expect to get something next year. But if the budget share for a service is reduced, when fiscal strain has set in there is a severe risk that that share will never be regained. Under such conditions the decision-making process becomes more demanding: decision makers have to know more about their services, and the consequences of decisions. The adjustments required make innovative administrative and political thinking necessary, a point to which we return.

But the potentials for conflicts are also increased. Changes in allocations within services and particularly between services, which must take place when fiscal strain is combined with demographic changes or other changes of needs, are likely to be met with resistance from the services which are about to lose their share of the budget.

Two factors seem important for an understanding of the likely outcome of such a situation. One is the relative strength of the different services: another is how conflict resolution takes place.

During interviews of senior officials in 39 local authorities the central directors (town clerks) were asked to answer several questions pertaining to such factors.

Central directors were asked to indicate which of the three most important services would best be able to retain appropriations in case of general budget cuts.

The figures in Table 4 leave no doubt that there are wide variations as to the relative strength of the three sectors and it should be noted that these figures fit very well the expenditure trends presented in Table 2.

Table 4. Central directors' evaluation of sector strength (%)

N = 39	Social affairs	Education	Roads etc.
Strongest sector	53.8	20.5	7.7
Weakest Sector	5.6	19.4	69.4

Note: "Roads etc." is used as a common designation of roads, environmental measures, water supply and so on.

It might be asked why social services are considered so much stronger than the others. The interview data point to the following factors as being the most important ones: social services have by far the best possibility for arguing that central government requirements make expenditures necessary.

They have the best-developed plans for future service provisions, and they have a higher degree of political support in the council.

These factors touch upon the rules of the game for solving conflicts between services in local government, but only to a certain extent however. In order to gain further knowledge about the conflict-solving mechanisms, the heads of the social service and education departments respectively were asked whether they felt their task was to ensure as much money as possible for their own service, irrespective of other services' wishes or whether it was to ensure a fair share of the budget for their own service. (Wildavsky, 1964).

The answers given to this question by the two heads of departments indicate that the head of department with a "fair share of the budget attitude" is doing better in terms of attracting resources to his department. In other words, a service advocate who puts all his strengths into advocating more resources to his own service is not necessarily a strong service advocate. Of course, the causal relation can go both ways, but cautiously interpreted, these responses indicate that conflict resolution in local government is characterised by negotiation and mutual adjustment rather than simple majority decisions.

Political and administrative innovations in local government under fiscal strain.

In a situation where local authorities move from a situation of general resource scarcity into fiscal stress the need for innovative thinking increases in order to make the necessary adjustments.

Cut-backs are only short-term solutions if not accompanied by adjustments. For instance typical short-term solutions such as delaying maintenance and capital expenditure cannot be maintained over a prolonged period without creating a need for higher expenditures in the long run.

Innovations may be either new policy solutions, which may be called strategies, and administrative restructuring or changes in the processes, which we call bureaucratic innovations.

Strategies

The strategies available may be categorised into two main types: those designed to increase revenue and those which reduce expenditure. They may be either aiming at short-term or long-term effects. The most important strategies may be summarised as follows:

Figure 1. Strategies for handling fiscal strain in local government

	Short-term	Draw on liquid assets
		Increase debts
Increase revenues		Increase taxes
	Long-term	Increase user fees and charges
	Short-term	Delay maintenance
		Delay capital expenses
		General reductions
Decrease expenditure		Programme specific service reductions
	Long-term	Stop for appointing additional personnel
		Dismissal of street-level personnel
		Dismissal of administrative personnel Purchase agreements

Which strategies have been implemented by local authorities at various stages of fiscal strain? Based on our data, four fiscal strain stages can be identified. Stage 1 appears in 1978-79, when some municipalities experienced some fiscal difficulties. Stage 2 refers to 1980-81, when some municipalities were under increasing pressure and a few municipalities under severe fiscal stress. Stage 3 refers to 1982-83, when the majority of municipalities had severe fiscal difficulties.

On the basis of material from 31 of the 39 sampled municipalities, we can identify some main trends in strategy choices by local authorities at different stages of fiscal strain.

Little innovation occurred in increase-revenue strategies during 1978-79, when some municipalities are experiencing the beginning of fiscal strain. During Stage 2, the municipalities preferred short-term strategies: drawing on liquid assets was a favoured strategy. During the same period, municipalities under severe pressure more often chose long-term strategies, primarily that of increasing taxes. During stage 3 with fiscal difficulties for many municipalities, the trend is clearly towards long-term strategies such as increases in taxes, and raising user fees and charges.

As far as expenditure-reducing strategies are concerned, we find a repetition of the pattern of increase-revenue strategies at Stage 1, with no innovations reported in the 1978-79 interval. During Stage 2, a few authorities delayed capital expenditure and stopped appointing additional personnel. Some municipalities with severe difficulties both delayed capital programmes and maintenance work, with a few adopting more long-term strategies. However, during the 1982-83 period of severe difficulties, Stage 3, a wide range of long-term strategies was introduced, specific programme reductions being the most frequently used strategy. Reducing administrative staff was found in only one municipality.

Our analysis thus suggests some general trends. In low-stress situations when the pressure is relatively light, revenue-increasing strategies are preferred together with delays in capital programmes and a halt in staff recruitment. As the pressure increases, a wider range of strategies is introduced, whilst in the severe strain situation the whole range of strategies is adopted, with expenditure-reducing strategies clearly preferred.

Furthermore, in the situation characterised by relatively low strain, short-term strategies are preferred to long-term. As the situation tightens, long-term strategies take over. Certain types of strategies may thus be attributed to certain degrees of fiscal stress.

Bureaucratic innovations

The bureaucratic innovations adopted may be categorised into two main types: innovations in administrative processes and innovations in the organisational structure. The most important innovations may be summarised as follows:

Figure 2. Bureaucratic innovations for handling fiscal strain in local government.

Performance

    Performance measures

Per unit norms for resource allocation.

Percent increases on specificbudget items

Process measures   Surveys

Distribution of budget on "bound" and "free" expenditures

Per client or unit increases

Multiyear budgeting

Prognoses

Budgeting

Coordination of budgets and plans

Sector-specified budget ceilings

Priority-setting debate or –game

Organisational measures

Administrative sector heads participation in finance committee meetings

Representation

Economic department personnel participation in sector committees' budget meetings

The implementation of some of the items mentioned in figure 2 is summarised in Table 9.

Table 9. The implementation of selected bureaucratic innovations 1982-83. (Per cent)*

	High strain municipalities	Other municipalities
Performance measures	52.6	41.7
Resources per unit norms	84.6	58.3
Survey of increases	89.5	75.0
Survey of "bound" and "free" expenditures	68.4	41.7
Survey of expenditure per client	68.4	75.0
Priority debate or game	78.4	83.3
Sector head representation	73.7	75.0
Economic department representation.	47.4	75.0
N =	19	12

* Per cent of municipalities using the tool in question.

Since only data on 1982-83 are available, comparisons are made between local authorities in a severe fiscal situation and the rest of the sample. These comparisons should show to what extent bureaucratic innovations occur in municipalities under severe fiscal strain as compared to municipalities in a less strained situation.

The figures in Table 9 show that the first four tools are used by a considerably higher proportion of the high stress authorities than by the other municipalities. The lower half of the table shows precisely the opposite trend, which is interesting, given the different nature of the tools. Those concerning ways of handling budget meetings and hearings differ from the other tools because their adoption requires the involvement of local politicians, whereas the others may be adopted by the finance department alone.

Our findings indicate that the finance departments in high stress municipalities are doing much to adopt bureaucratic tools to implement fiscal strain strategies, but that the local politicians are not as willing to fight fiscal strain as is the case in the other municipalities, a finding supported by other research, suggesting that the local political will is an important factor in easing fiscal stress. (Skovsgaard, 1983).

CONCLUSION

In Denmark there is a saying that "it is difficult to prophesy: in particular of the future". However, there seems to be a widespread agreement that even if economic growth improves there is every reason to expect such problems as unemployment and balance of payments difficulties to continue throughout the eighties. This situation makes Danish local politics (as elsewhere) substantially different from the seventies where most Danes expected a recovery to appear 'just around the corner'. This change in widely-held expectations is not the least important reason why local government expenditures continued to increase fairly rapidly until the beginning of the eighties. This situation reinforces the difficulties of political decision-making and public resource allocation during recent years. However, we would expect not only fiscal stress, but also the very difficult resource allocation situation for local authorities to continue throughout the eighties.

And the difficulties caused by the severe economic recession have been aggravated in Denmark by demographic trends, including a rapid decrease in the number of children, which will create excess capacity in schools and kindergartens, whilst the number of old people is growing, thus calling for increased services for the elderly. These trends will continue in Denmark at least until the mid-nineties.

It is easy to understand, therefore, why it is extremely difficult for some local authorities to avoid tax and expenditure increases in the future. We also expect a continuation and strengthening of central government's control over local government. The ruling conservative coalition government has paid particular attention in its fiscal policy to the limitation of public expenditure growth, and local government expenditure has been under tight control. There have also been examples of direct central government pressure on individual municipalities, itself an innovation in Danish politics. Yet, the increased importance of central control of local budgets is unlikely to be much affected if a different coalition government should take office.

Under conditions of continuing fiscal strain and tight central control of the economy, a search for new solutions and innovations seems pertinent. Ideally, the objective is to find ways of solving problems and providing services which are both cheaper and better. The possibility of implementing new solutions in this ideal sense thus depends upon the extent of inefficiency in present administrative practices and possible changes in citizens' demands for local government services (Kommunernes Landsforening, 1984).

The adoption of both political strategies and bureaucratic innovations has already begun. Municipal budget directors expect that the use of service specific budget ceilings will be the most important tool, and other important ones include the more extensive use of forecasts and of performance measures, linked to the increased coordination of budget plans in connection with multiyear budgeting.

But bureaucratic innovations aimed at increasing the efficiency of the decision-making processes will not be sufficient to cope with continued fiscal strain. Especially in the service areas which are labour intensive and more seriously affected by the demographic changes, there will be a need for accompanying policy changes. In such areas new political strategies will have to be introduced in the years to come. Alternative strategies will have to be considered, aiming at explicit political choices, and the demands on political decision-making will increase.

One might expect such new strategies to cause a reduction in service provision of the traditional form from local government institutions, and instead increasing the privatisation of such services. A few examples of such changes have appeared recently, often based on political arguments making a virtue of necessity. However, the search for new service solutions during fiscal stress is likely to point towards cheaper and to some extent poorer services than those that exist today.

REFERENCES

Administrationsdepartementet (1982), Statslige forskrifter for kommunernes virksomhed. Delredegørelse om regelforenkling.
Bruun, Finn (1979), Danske kommunalreformer siden 1945, Aarhus Universitet: Institut for statskundskab.
Harder, Erik (1973), Local government in Denmark, Copenhagen
Kommunernoes Landsforening (1984), Kommunal perspektivredego-/relse, Kommunetryk.
Mouritzen, Poul Erik (1979), Current Trends and Issues in Central Government Steering of Local Government, The Danish Case. Paper prepared for the workshop on "The Emerging Federalism", University of Washington, Seattle.

Mouritzen, Poul Erik and Carl-Johan Skovsgaard (1981), Regression Analysis and Principles of Equalisation, p. 107–134 in Measuring Local Government Expenditure Needs, OECD Urban Management Studies, Paris.

Newton, K. (1981), Balancing the Books, London, Saga.

Skovsgaard, Carl-Johan (1983), Budget-making and Fiscal Austerity. A Case Study of Danish Local government. Report No. 12, Institute of Political Science, University of Aarhus.

Wildawsky, Aaron, (1964), The Politics of the Budgetary Process, Boston, Little Brown.

6 Fiscal pressure and central-local relations in Britain

EDWARD PAGE
Department of Politics, Hull University

INTRODUCTION

In retrospect, the development of the study of central-local financial relations in Britain has undergone a remarkable number of transformations in the past decade. It was only really beginning with Boaden's 1971 classic that the widely accepted "agent" model of central-local relations, which saw central Government as "controlling" local government decision making, including local resource allocation decisions was effectively challenged. A number of studies of local government expenditure followed on from this which reinforced the notion that local factors determine or influence local spending decisions rather than national ones. Studies of local government grants or local government policy making found little evidence of any concrete effects of grant dependence upon local expenditure decisions, so much so that by the time the Layfield Committee reported in 1976, its use of the phrase "he who pays the piper calls the tune" as well as its concentration upon finance as a factor leading to centralisation seemed curiously passée.

The questioning of the old received wisdom began to change into a positive analytical framework of central-local relations through the pathbreaking and still influential "Rhodes Framework" towards the end of the 1970s (Rhodes, 1981).. This framework, with its emphasis upon resource exchange and bargaining made the British system look very much like the American, German and French. No sooner had this formulation begun in earnest than academic concerns, spurred on by the financial stringency which set in after 1976, turned back to issues more characteristic of the agent model - the constraints upon budgetary choice and the degree of control that central government can exert on local government through the grant system. The way in which central government in Britain has transformed the environment of local government since the mid-1970s, as well as the actual policy instruments that the centre has given itself, show the underlying weaknesses of local government in its relationship with the centre. The aim of this paper is to present the development of the financial system from one perceived to be based upon the absence of instruments of control, to one in which the presence of such instruments is unambiguous. The chapter will then go on to point out how the developments reflect the underlying weaknesses of local government in the British system, although these are not necessarily the automatic consequence of unitary state structures.

FROM GIFT RELATIONSHIP TO COERCION

From the introduction of a block grant in 1958, replacing specific grants, to the mid 1970s, the grant income of local authorities grew steadily in real terms, with few short interruptions. Given the structure of the grant - around 80 per cent of it was unrelated to specific items of expenditure - and given the fact that the regular increase in the amount of grant reinforced the "assumption of growth" that permeated the whole of local government decision making, it is hardly surprising that studies of the role of grants in central-local relations failed to see grants as an instrument of central control. Similarly, the centre's ability to set some sort of limit to local authority capital expenditure had been present for the whole of the present century, yet in the 1970s there were even signs that this instrument of control was being relaxed with the move towards capital financial planning which was supposed to give local authorities broad discretion for capital spending within particular categories of expenditure rather than making capital approvals on a project-by-project basis.

Yet it soon became clear that at first the 1974-9 Labour Government and then the Conservative Government of 1979 onwards thought that its grant and capital expenditure powers were instruments of control. The financial system of central-local relations underwent four main changes: first, capital allocations, traditionally the first casualties of government cuts, were dramatically reduced; second, grant was

124

reduced; third, grant was restructured; and fourth, penalties were introduced so that the government could discriminate between authorities which, in its view, had made sufficient efforts to contain its expenditure levels from those which had not, and penalise those which had not made such efforts by taking grant away from them. Fifth, legislature gave the Minister (power?) to limit the amount by which selected overspending authorities could raise local taxes in the financial system, capping the rates (local tax). These changes are set out in more detail below

Reducing capital expenditure

Local capital spending has traditionally been regarded as one which can be influenced fairly easily by central government in pursuit of macroeconomic objectives, whether retrenchment or expansion. In the period since the mid 1970s the cuts in capital spending have been particularly dramatic – capital budgets were the first casualties of financial stringency. Local authorities indeed indicated under the Labour Government that they would be more willing to accept lower capital than current expenditure levels. In constant terms (using the GDP deflator), local capital expenditure in 1983–4 ran at only 49 per cent of its peak in the 1974 (see Table 1). The major spending head affected by this, of course, is local authority housing investment. Furthermore, in 1980 central government strengthened its control over capital expenditure in the Local Government Planning and Land Act by requiring that levels of capital expenditure as opposed to capital borrowing be approved by central government.

Reducing grant

The main block grant to local authorities is calculated on the basis of setting a level of expenditure (net of some charges) that central government is willing to finance, (relevant expenditure). The total grant provided through the main block grant is then expressed as a percentage of relevant expenditure. There are consequently a variety of different ways of producing the same effect of reducing the amount of money that local government as a whole receives in grant. First, the percentage of relevant expenditure to be financed by grant can be reduced. This stood at a record 66.5 in 1975–76 and was progressively reduced by both Labour and Conservative governments to its 1983–4 level of 53 per cent.

Second, grant can be reduced through the amount of relevant expenditure which the government is prepared to finance being reduced. In cash terms, of course, the level of relevant expenditure has increased. However, when inflation is taken into account (but not the relative price effects for local government services) the level of relevant expenditure dropped from its 1976-77 level by around 5 per cent in real (GDP deflated) terms by 1983-84.

Third, grant can be reduced in real terms by limiting the amount that the government is prepared to pay to meet the level of wage and price increases in local government services. This was a strategy first introduced in 1976 under the Labour Government which put "cash limits" on local authority grants. Prior to cash limits, local authority expenditure and grant was calculated in a notional denomination ("survey prices" otherwise known as "funny money") which was in principle to be automatically supplemented by an amount reflecting the increase in local authority prices and wages. Cash limits set an upper limit to the increase in respect of pay and price changes and, under the Labour Government, they began to be used to squeeze local authority grants through the estimated rate of price and wage increases on which these limits were based being set unrealistically low. The Conservative move towards "cash planning", under which it professes to allocate expenditure in cash terms is not radically different from this, since it also contains the principle that local government grant levels should be divorced from the actual movement of local authority costs.

Table 1. Local Government Grant, Current Expenditure and Capital Expenditure 1972-1983 (constant money terms using GDP deflator)

(1972=100)

	1972	'73	'74	'75	'76	'77	'78	'79	'80	'81	'82	'83
Central Grant	100	108	123	147	161	161	152	150	152	151	142	138
Capital Expenditure	100	141	141	126	109	96	80	75	75	67	59	58
Current Expenditure	100	103	115	116	118	120	117	120	123	124	127	130

Sources: Annual Abstract of Statistics, 120, 1984: 181-185; Economic and estimated Trends, 366, 1984: Financial Statistics 166, 1984: 48-49.

The fourth way of reducing aggregate grant is a novelty introduced under the Conservative Government - withholding grant from local government because of overspending on a centrally defined total. While this option was available to the government in a limited form (and some suggested it was legally dubious), the Local Government Finance Act of 1982 allowed deductions to be made from the block grant in the event of overspending by local government. In the last financial year, 1984-85, £455 million was held back in penalties. This represented around 4 per cent of the total block grant in that year.

Overall, insofar as one can tell, grants to local authorities have fallen by 13 per cent since their peak value in 1975-76 using the GDP deflator (see Table 1) with the sharpest fall coming in 1977-78 under the Labour Government.

Reallocating Grant

It is certainly not unusual for an incoming government in Britain to change the way in which grant is allocated to different local authorities in order to bring more money to the sorts of areas in which the government party has greater support. While the changes made to the principles of grant distribution since 1979 by the Conservative Government conform to this expectation, with money being directed away from the urban areas and towards the shire counties, the grant reforms of the Conservative Government, started in the Local Government Planning and Land Act of 1980, went well beyond this. One of the major objectives of the reform was to reverse the perceived bias in the grant system to reward high spending local authorities. This occurred through two routes. First, the resources element of the Rate Support Grant which made up for imbalances in the value of the local tax base (i.e. notional rental value of properties) meant that, ceteris paribus, areas which spent more and had higher rates would get more grant merely because the government was, as it were, acting as a ratepayer. Second, actual spending levels in recent years formed the basis for calculation of "needs" for the "needs element" of the grant. Spending levels were the dependent variable in a regression equation which calculated weightings of demographic factors to be used in distributing grant - although these were admittedly diluted by various techniques (e.g. "damping") which were designed to minimise the changes in distribution for one year to the next.

The government's new method of distributing grant (sold, incidentally, as a simplification of the old arrangements), sought to break the link between spending and entitlement to grant by the mechanism of the Grant Related Expenditure Assessment (GREA). The new block grant first calculated an entitlement to grant on the basis of the difference between the total spending of an authority and the amount of income that could be raised if each class of local authority levied a uniform rate. Local authorities, however, only received their full entitlement of grant if they did not overspend on centrally defined levels, the GREAs. These were levels of expenditure for each individual local authority which were calculated by assessing the approximate number of clients (the elderly, for example, but for most services the assessment of the number of clients is, to put it mildly, crude) for local authority services. Overspending on GREAs meant a reduction in grant entitlement via a set of penalties which increased in severity the higher the authority spent above its GREA.

Bringing in Penalties

The set of disincentives imposed by the GREA system was arbitrary enough, with local authorities according to their own self-perception "Thatcherites before Thatcher was born" such as Kensington and Chelsea losing grant along with the rest of London and the metropolitan areas. The government added more confusion when in 1981 it called for an across the board reduction in local authority budgets of 5.6 per cent in volume terms below the 1978-79 figure under threat of additional grant penalties. Thus it appeared for a time that even compliant local authorities spending at or below their GREA could be penalised for not making the 5.6 per cent reductions, although subsequently they were omitted from the 1981-82 holdback penalties. The system for penalties changed further in 1982-83 when a "minimum volume budget" for each individual local authority was calculated (its arbitrariness makes detailed discussion of how it was derived superfluous) with these being used to identify where grant should be held back in the event of local government as a whole overspending.

The whole system of penalties has become very complex and, to judge on the basis of past experience, is likely to be changed in future either in the direction of abolishing these penalties, (since rate-capping has taken away their importance, so that the right local authorities, mainly Labour city authorities, are singled out for the most severe penalties. The whole of the changes up until 1985, however, can be summed up as an attempt to build into the grant system an initial disincentive for high expenditure levels in striking the rate, with the subsequent possibility for the Secretary of State for the Environment, the minister responsible for local government, imposing more severe penalties if the disincentives do not work.

128

Capping Rates

The Conservatives had pledged in 1979 to reform the local taxation system. The context in which rating reform was discussed made it clear that the government was not proposing a reform in the spirit of the 1976 Layfield Report, which was concerned with the effects of the existing rating and grant system upon local responsibility and accountability and proposed the introduction of a local income tax to supplement income from the local rates or property tax (a curious tax based upon the notional rental value of domestic and non-domestic property and only subject to periodic revaluation, with the last revaluation in England and Wales taking place in 1973). Rather, it was discussed in the context of keeping local expenditure under control by central government. It always appeared unlikely that the government could find a way to reform the local taxation system without appearing to give greater influence over taxation issues to the type of authority with which it appeared to be permanently engaged in battle, such as the Greater London Council (currently due for abolition), and the issue of local income reform was periodically reported to be high on the government's agenda and then dropped. In December 1981 the government published a Green Paper "Alternatives to Domestic Rates" (Cmnd.8449) and in September 1982 the Parliamentary Select Committee on the Environment published a report: both of these documents explored the alternatives to the existing system. The publication in August 1982 of the Government's White Paper (setting out its intention to legislate) "Rates. Proposals for Rate Limitation and the Reform of the Rating System" (Cmnd 9008) seemed to confirm what had been apparent for some time; that the government did not envision introducing any changes in the structure of local government income, and that "rates should remain for the foreseeable future the main source of local revenue for local government". Although local tax reform has subsequently returned to the political agenda, given added impetus by the embarrassing consequences of the revaluation exercise in Scotland which produced massive rate increases for large numbers of those who were most likely to support the Conservative Party, reforms are unlikely to be introduced, if at all, before 1987 or 1988.

Through the Rates Act 1984, the government has introduced measures which have limited the discretion of local authorities to set rates. The rate limitation capacity of central government has developed furthest in Scotland, where a significantly different (in this respect at least) statutory framework and a separate ministry for Scottish affairs, the Scottish Office, makes for substantial differences in central-local relationships. Since 1919 Scottish local authorities have not had the statutory ability to levy supplementary rates in addition to the main rate. Therefore, any capacity of the central government to make reductions in grant within the financial year while at the same time blocking other possibilities for making up the shortfall of income, such as accumulating balances or short-term borrowing, is virtually identical to cutting local expenditure. The government gave itself the capacity to cut grant in this way in the Local Government (Miscellaneous Provisions) (Scotland) Act 1981, and was used to cut the budgets of seven local authorities in 1981-82 and two in 1982-83, notably the left Labour councils of Stirling District and Lothian Region on both occasions. Since then the Scottish Secretary has acquired the powers to demand that any reduction in expenditure be followed by paying back surplus rates to ratepayers.

In England and Wales the use of supplementary rates was abolished in the 1982 Local Government Finance Act, which replaced a bill rejected by Parliament because of its inclusion of a class requiring that proposals for levying supplementary rates be subjected to a local referendum. The 1982 Act did allow for somewhat less direct control over spending than appeared to be the case in Scotland because the requirement that the penalties imposed by the basic principles according to which grant would be held back within the financial year were set out in advance of the rate being struck (one of the concessions gained during the committee stage of the legislation in Parliament) allowed local authorities some scope for budgeting for grant penalties.

The government's recent changes in the rating system involve a far more direct limitation of local rating and spending. The government is now to limit rates according to a selective rate limitation scheme and, if it wishes, a more general rate limitation scheme.

The government introduced the selective scheme in the financial year 1985-86. It is based upon the government identifying a set of authorities which overrated and overspent in the previous year (i.e. 1984-85). This group of authorities have, if they do not agree to make reductions, been given a maximum spending and rating ceiling for 1985-86 which is set by statutory regulation. The general limitation scheme does not involve the naming of a specific group of authorities but general levels of rate increases would be set for all local authorities similarly to the way in which GREAs and holdback targets are presently set.

The overall effect of the financial squeeze on local government is difficult to quantify precisely because of changes in the calculation of spending and price bases. Table 1 gives some broad indication of the movement of local grant and expenditure taking 1972 as a base and using the GDP deflator. Grant has clearly declined in real terms, by 17 per cent compared with its peak in 1976, and capital spending has declined by 51 per cent from its 1974 peak. Local authority expenditure has, according to the figures in Table 1, continued to grow, with real cuts in local expenditure relative to movements in GDP prices occurring only in 1978.

However, this finding shows the limitations of the use of the GDP deflator to measure volume changes in local expenditure since local authority wage and cost increases have grown faster than this general measure of price changes in the economy in the past decade. On the basis of the government's own figures, 73 per cent of the rise in local expenditure in real (i.e. GDP deflated) terms is explained by wage cost increases rising faster than changes in the GDP deflator. This would make an index figure for 1982 of 122 instead of 127 for current expenditure if volume terms were employed, and a figure for 1983 of 118. In view of this, the safest conclusion is that in volume terms there have been massive reductions in capital spending, a heavy reduction in the volume value of central grants to local government which has been met by local authorities more or less holding constant their volume spending since the onset of stringency in the mid 1970s.

WEAKNESSES OF LOCAL GOVERNMENT IN BRITAIN

The Conservative approach to local finance has involved, like the best-turned-out weddings, something old, something new, something borrowed and something blue. The reduction in levels of relevant expenditure, capital expenditure, percentage grants and the use of cash limits were old devices used under the previous Labour government. The client group method of calculating block grant as well as the tapering mechanisms were, it has been suggested, lying around in the Department of the Environment under the Labour government, and can be classed as something borrowed. The holdback penalties and the system of rate capping are something new. The party affiliations of the people responsible for much of the assault on local government spending add the colour.

The analogy of the wedding is not, however, one that can be pursued very far since there is no equivalent to the divorce courts. Relationships between central and local government are strained in a way that the literature on central-local relations in the 1970s, with its stress on interdependence and bargaining, had no real grounds to imagine. Central government has passed other items of legislation which run flatly counter to the expressed interests of many local authorities, including the mandatory sale of council houses, redefinition of capital expenditure, limitations on the discretion to set council house rent levels; and the abolition of the metropolitan counties and the Greater London Council. The government's schemes for "controlling" local expenditure themselves appear to have a substantial symbolic element - local government, especially Labour authorities which openly espouse their rational policies, should not be able to take on central government and win. Consequently the changes to the financial system in the past few years appear to be framed according to the principle that the system will go on being changed until central victory is total and unmistakable. In addition, the Conservative government has pursued, at least in a number of important sectors, a strategy of policy formulation which has been termed "anti-corporatist", by which is usually meant that the large interest groups formally influential in the policy process are now being omitted from it. This strategy has especially affected the national associations of local government who, in 1981, launched a publicity campaign of limited achievement under the "Keep it Local" banner: such campaigns are, according to all good textbooks, the characteristic sign of a pressure group lacking in influence within the executive.

The actions of the Conservative government show quite clearly that local authorities in Britain are weak relative to a central government which can, as long as parliamentary support is forthcoming, impose unilaterally its own policy priorities against the bitter opposition of local government and its national interest groups. Moreover, the Parliamentary support for local government interest groups appears to be rather unpredictable, and under no circumstances at present could one point to a strong identification of MPs with either the interests of their own individual local authority or the local authority associations. Undoubtedly, the bargaining between central and local government that was supposed to characterise their relationship still persists in a variety of fields from environmental health legislation to the training of social workers as mental health officers. Undoubtedly, also, local authorities still retain substantial discretion to determine spending priorities within these aggregate levels.

Yet the fact remains that central government has great scope for unilateral action in the most sensitive of areas, of which finance is one example and the abolition of metropolitan counties and the Greater London Council would be another.

Such unilateral action, with only relatively minor concessions to local authority interests, would be unimaginable in federal states such as the United States and West Germany as well as in many unitary states such as France. How is it possible for central government in Britain to take such unilateral action? After all, Britain has been, at least since the days of von Gneist, regarded as the international model of "local self-government", so how is it possible for central government to impose its policy priorities against the vociferous opposition of local authorities?

It has been possible because the traditional model of self-government in Britain has been one which limits effective local government opposition to central government actions. Goldsmith and Page (1985)have identified three major dimensions to the central-local government relationship. First, there is the dimension of the range of functions that local government is expected to perform. Local self-government appeared to be strong in Britain partly because local authorities were entrusted with a wide range of functions, unusual for a unitary state, such as education, police, social services, housing and, before the reorganisation of the NHS after the war, health services. Second, there is the dimension of the discretion that local authorities have in carrying out these functions. Local government was not directly subject to the tutelage of central government authorities: local government legislation is frequently broad and permissive in nature, and the role of inspection by central officials appeared to be weak even at the beginning of the twentieth century with inspectors adopting the role of advisers than enforcers of laws and standards. Thus on the second dimension, local government in Britain appeared to be the embodiment of an extensive system of local self-government. However, it is on the third dimension, access to central decision making processes, that local government in Britain is weak, and its weakness on this one dimension is crucial in understanding the ability of central government to take unilateral action against local government since the mid-1970s.

It has been frequently noted that local government in Britain is "separated" from national government. Bulpitt (1983) has argued that there is in Britain a "dual polity" with "high politics" (policy areas such as defence and foreign affairs) being the preserve of national politicians who were

133

quite happy to leave issues of "low politics" (with its images of the parish pump) to local politicians who were broadly compliant with national politicians' wishes and who did not use their hands on control over local administration to oppose central government policies. Greenwood's (1981) argument citing a cultural disdain for local government within British political elites reinforces this argument. Further, one could identify the weak links between MPs and their local councils as further evidence of the separation of national from local politics. However one characterises this precisely, it is clear that the interpenetration between national and local politics, found within federal states and some unitary states such as France and Italy, is absent in Britain.

Relationships between central and local government are, in the absence of direct links between local and national actors in a system in which national and local policy processes are closely interrelated, predominantly conducted by national associations of local authorities and their officials and central government. In this relationship, the distinctive privileges of local government in terms of its access to central decision making are lost - its legitimacy as an elected body with the statutory right to make decisions about a wide range of state services provide it with a claim to privileged access, yet, through the absence of direct contacts with the centre and the mediation of national associations, local authority interest groups increasingly took on the characteristics of other functional interest groups, but without the cohesion of the more powerful service-based professional interest groups.

Certainly the national local authority associations appeared to be bargaining with central government on issues of local finance, at least up until the onset of financial stringency in the mid 1970s. Yet this bargaining capacity was more related to the financial climate of the period than to any strong bargaining resources possessed by British local authorities and their associations. As Heclo argues, in the period from the 1950s onwards, the expansion of the welfare state was relatively "painless", with "triple affluence", to use Rose and Peters' (1982) characterisation, meaning that priorities for social welfare as well as other state services rarely became issues on which politicians had to struggle and build coalitions and consequently "few groups had difficulty in showing that their needs were unmet". In this climate it is hardly surprising that central government should appear to be bargaining and making concessions to local authorities via their associations, not only in the aggregate amount of grant that they gave local authorities but also in the form of grant which appeared to renounce all influence over most spending priorities.

The reality of central-local bargaining on issues of finance during the period to the mid 1970s, however, presented an illusion of near-equality in terms of bargaining between central and local government on questions of finance, with central government having let lapse its ability to influence local finance through the grant system. Hence one can understand the emphasis upon bargaining and the downgrading of grants as an instrument of central influence in the 1970s literature interpreting British central-local relations. However, with the onset of financial stringency and the desire of central government (whether the macroeconomic assumptions are correct or not) to contain local spending growth, it became clear that central grant was the only means that central government had within the existing array of policy instruments to control expenditure; moreover, it had to be changed to act more effectively as such. Further, it became clear that the claims of local authorities, via their associations, to influence central policies towards local government were merely the same as those of other groups and could be ignored as such, especially given the general "anti-corporatist" predispositions of the Conservative government. If the major resource of local authorities in bargaining with the centre was the ability to embarrass the government, then the 1979 Conservative government showed quite quickly that it was probably the most unembarrassable government since the war.

CONCLUSIONS

Individual members of local authorities, members of national associations of local government as well as academics have heralded many of the previous actions of central government since the mid 1970s as being one of the final nails in the coffin of local government. If fully implemented, the rate limitation powers remove, local finance and spending decisions from local politics, by which I mean struggles for power within individual local authorities. Instead, such decisions will be taken in the course of national policy processes in a manner similar to the taking of decisions about the national allocation of government grants, in which the national associations of local government are, under conditions of financial stringency, unlikely to have any substantial influence.

The government has become too committed to controlling local expenditure, and the symbolic importance of central government gaining power over the local authorities has become too great for it to countenance serious defeats. The future looks bleak for local politics since local government has few inherent resources on which it can draw to protect itself from further central intervention in local financial decisions. Rather, the only possible hopes for some relief from central government continuing to increase the potency of its instruments for securing reductions in local expenditure lie in a change of government in Westminster and/or an end to financial stringency. The Labour leadership has insisted that change at Westminster is the only real means of restoring local spending as well as local decision-making power, and has failed to support more radical Labour councils in either testing the law or simply breaking it. The Labour leadership's insistence on change at the centre as the only realistic and legitimate strategy underlines precisely how deep-rooted the basic weakness of local government in Britain is.

REFERENCES

Boaden, N. (1971) Urban Policy Making, London, Cambridge University Press

Bulpitt, J. (1983) Territory and Power in the U.K., Manchester, Manchester University Press

Greenwood, R. "Pressures from Whitehall in Rose, R. and Page, E. (eds.) (1982) Fiscal Stress in Cities, London, C.U.P.

H.M.S.O. (1981), Cmnd.8449: Alternatives to Domestic Rates

H.M.S.O. (1982) Rates: Proposals for Rate Limitation and the Reform of the Rating System

Heclo, H. (1974) Modern Social Politics in Britain and Sweden, London, Yale University Press

Page, E. and Goldsmith, M. (1983): "Centralisation and Decentralisation: a Framework for comparative analysis". Paper presented for E.C.P.R. Research Session, Trento, Italy.

Rhodes, R. A. W. (1981) Control and Power in Central-Local Government Relations, Farnborough Gower

Rose, R. and Peters, G. (1982) Can Governments Go Bankrupt? London, Macmillan

7 Deconcentration or decentralisation? Local government and the possibilities for local control of local economies

RAY HUDSON
University of Durham
and
VIGGO PLUM
Roskilde University Centre

INTRODUCTION

In this chapter we examine some aspects of local government re-organisation; the division of state power between central and local government, and the redefinition of the boundaries between local and central governments' spheres of competence and responsibilities as one element in a more general restructuring of capitalist states in western Europe. In particular we will upon the extent to which local government re-organisation has merely involved a deconcentration of state powers from the centre as opposed to a decentralisation of power to the local level, especially in relation to local government control over or responsibility for economic affairs and a more effective exercise of locally based control over local economies.

Central to our discussion are the concepts of "deconcentration" and "decentralisation" and as the distinction between these is a crucial one, it is important to specify it at the outset. By political "decentralisation" we refer to a situation where effective control over events in their area is given to residents of that area via their control through democratically elected political representatives of the machinery of local government. Thus goals and objectives can be decided at the local level rather than merely being handed down from the centre, as can standards of public services and facilities, while the capacity exists to raise money at the local level and/or spend money distributed from a central tax pool by central government in pursuit of such aims unfettered by central government constraints. Given this definition of decentralisation, it is more accurate to denote much local government creation, organisation and reorganisation as an attempt to produce more efficient management by the State via devolving some functions to local government, changing the territorial level from national to local in the pursuit of more efficient, effective administration and exercise of State power. For decisively, the room for manoeuvre at local government level remains tightly constrained by central government, in terms of finance, as well as the specification of objectives, norms and performance targets. For example, in the U.K. between 1974 and 1981, 70-80% of total local government expenditure was absorbed simply by those expenditures that local government necessarily undertook on behalf of central government. This is not to deny that political responsibility - or blame - may be at the same time transferred from central to local level, with the intention of legitimating central government policies and reinforcing central control via discrediting local government and thus more generally underwriting dominant power relations. The effects are not necessarily always those intended, however, as the centrally-imposed constraints on local government can lead to attacks on central government for attempting to dismantle local democracy (as events in Liverpool in 1984, triggered by central Government's attempts rigidly to control local government expenditure via its "rate-capping" legislation have demonstrated).

There is a further point that is important in this connection, however. For while the original creation and subsequent transformation of local government essentially involves a deconcentration of state power from the centre, giving more tasks to local (or regional) government levels subject to strong centrally-imposed constraints, it may also, albeit unintentionally, create some scope for a limited degree of political decentralisation, at the margin as it were. Such decentralisation can occur precisely because day-to-day state administration and provision of services take place at the local level through institutions which are organised in respect to areas at this level, then their provision is thus more susceptible to locally-based pressure groups both inside and outside of formal party political structures: further locally-based bureaucrats also have more scope to divert from strictly Weberian concepts of bureaucratic rationality in their actions. While the scope that exists for departing from centrally set criteria and goals may be small in quantitative terms, the fact that it exists may be qualitatively very important politically in demonstrating that there _is_ the possibility to challenge the power of the centre - maybe even of the state itself - at the local level. Nevertheless, leaving this important qualification aside for the moment, it remains the case that local government activity essentially involves a deconcentration of State power in the quest for more efficient methods of management and control.

This leads to another issue that is central to our concerns in this paper: the relation between such forms of political deconcentration and what is often referred to as the decentralisation, though more accurately deconcentration, of production as part of a changing spatial division of labour, typically in the form of routinised functions to branch plants located in areas outside of major urban-industrial metropolitan regions. We prefer the term "deconcentration" here precisely because, like their counterparts in the local government levels of the State apparatus, such branch plant managers have little freedom of manoeuvre as choice of product, production technique, quality specifications etc. are given to them from central offices. In part this relation arises because of competition between local (and regional) political authorities and organisations for industrial employment and investment in parallel with, or as part of, a locally-based policy response to replace, central government regional industrial policies to encourage the deconcentration of production. But the effects of such State policies (both those of central and local government) cannot sensibly be understood outside the context of the changing spatial divisions of labour within industry, capitals' attempts to match the requirements of different stages in the total production process to the characteristics of specific locations in the interests of profit maximisation, and the relation between this spatial deconcentration and fragmentation of production with the increased centralisation of control in an increasingly small number of locations and transnational corporations.

For it is precisely in the context of critiques of the "external dependency" that such branch-plant economies bring that the alternative of autonomous, decentralised development, based on indigenous small and medium-sized local capitals, has been advanced, from right to left across the political spectrum (though admittedly for different reasons). The parallels, both in terms of analysis and subsequent political prescriptions (capitalist development with definite territorial allegiances) with the Latin-American underdevelopment/dependency theorists is striking. In a sense, though, such small firm development does bring a greater degree of "decentralised" control over local economic affairs, especially when their products are destined for local or even national markets. For as long as the market is at least a national one, then the <u>potential</u> exists for a degree of political control to regulate market conditions, though whether this potential is realised is a contingent matter. But it is important to recognise the heterogeneity of the category "small and medium-sized firm", and to recognise that increasingly such firms are drawn into wider circuits of capital. Thus while in a formal sense there may be a greater degree of decentralised control over the local economy within capitalist social relations of production, the real effect of the growth of these forms of capital organisation capital is to create new dependency relations and fresh forms of integration into the international economy, points to which we return and amplify in the final two sections of the chapter.

For the moment, the point we wish to stress is that there is no <u>necessary</u> connection between political deconcentration and the deconcentration of production or the autonomous growth of local capital in the form of small manufacturing firms. An important implication follows from this, however: local government reorganisation, or the re-allocation of tasks from central to local government, does not guarantee growth in the "local" economy. Conversely, though, if there <u>is</u> a real decentralisation to the local level, will there be sufficient political power lodged in small sub-national territorial units to control investment and disinvestment decisions in economies increasingly dominated directly and indirectly by major transnationals which have demonstrated the capacity to resist or manipulate State power exercised at the national level? Thus we are left with the seeming paradox that, whatever the route followed, there are imminent dangers of undermining "local" economies in ways that cannot be controlled by power exercised through a (capitalist) State in a capitalist society.

What we would emphasise, though, is the inter-relationships between local politics and the changing international division of labour: local politics affects capitals' decisions as to where to invest and disinvest while those same decisions affect local politics and indeed have wider effects through the civil society. To give a contemporary example from North East England, the decision (April 1984) of the Japanese Nissan car company to establish an assembly plant at Washington New Town reflects the effects of a combination of national government financial incentives, the efforts of the New Town Development Corporation and Local Authorities, and considerable reserves of relatively passive and "green" (at least in relation to car production") labour, while the decision to locate the plant there will have effects on trades union practices and the local political debate on the advantages and disadvantages of "selling" the area to transnational capital. But the "local" effects will not simply be felt in Washington but also in other areas where jobs in car production will be threatened or actually lost as a result of the Nissan investment (for example, in Coventry or Liverpool), and Nissan avoid the political problems of further car imports to the U.K. by assembling cars there. Thus the relations extend not just between local politics and transnationalised production, but also, as a necessary corollary, with international trade patterns and national trade policies.

One further point by way of introduction: in directing attention here primarily to the issue of the links between political decentralisation, deconcentration and local control over local economies, we do not intend to deprecate the importance of local government involvement in issues such as land use planning, collective consumption and living conditions (environmental improvement, housing, education, health care etc.); not least, action in such areas has often been seen as a necessary precondition for the attraction of manufacturing investment and jobs. But it is important to recognise that local governments' room for manoeuvre in these matters is generally tightly constrained by financial controls as well as by central government directives as to norms and standards, so that even where there is some capacity to raise money at the local level the uses to which this can be put are limited. Nevertheless, the fact that provision of basic services (education, health etc.) is to a degree organised at local government levels can be very important in so far as this can lead to their becoming foci for political struggles, with resultant constraints upon the State in so far as there are historically-determined minimum levels of service provision that must be maintained in the interests of legitimation. For it is precisely the fact that many more people come into contact with local government bureaucracies and institutions delivering these services in the course of their daily lives than are involved in a struggle with capital at the actual point of production that creates the scope, potentially at least, for a more generalised process of learning to organise and fight politically in defence of living conditions and the right to live, learn and work in a particular locality.

The remainder of this paper, then, falls into five sections. First, the background to the growing recent deconcentration of political power and decentralisation of responsibility for economic well-being to local and regional levels is examined. In the next two sections, we consider in rather more detail some examples of this, allied to local government reorganisation in Denmark and the U.K. As we show, there are considerable similarities but also significant differences between the two cases, although we use the two cases to illustrate different, more general, points rather than simply repeating the same points in each of them. In the next section, we comment upon the limits to decentralisation and local economic initiatives in the context of the contemporary and evolving international division of labour and transnationalisation of production. Finally, we summarise some of the conclusions arising from our analysis.

Why switch political responsibility for economic well-being to local and regional levels?

Within much of Western Europe, there is a long tradition of local government and administration, though with little real decentralisation of power. There is also considerable variety in the balance of locally-raised taxes in relation to funds redistributed by central government for funding these activities. In the U.K., for example, the property tax of the "rates" provides 59% of all revenue raised locally by local government, while since 1975/6 over 50% of local government expenditures has been financed by central government via the Rate Support Grant (RSG). Thus in the U.K. local government expenditure, on average, remains very dependent upon central government decisions, not only with respect to RSG (which has been progressively cut since 1979), but also because of current central government limits on the levels of rates that some local authorities can levy (the so-called "Rate-capping" legislation).

More generally, a recurrent feature in the recent and contemporary political situation over much of Western Europe has been and is a restructuring of the State so as to deconcentrate some limited powers and shift considerably more political responsibilities for some aspects of the economy and employment to regional and/or local political and administrative levels. Such tendencies are visible (inter alia) in Belgium, Denmark, France, Italy, Portugal, Spain and the U.K. Why should this be so?

To begin to answer this question, three rather distinct but nonetheless related issues must be brought together, focusing upon their fusion in the actual course of political and economic developments in these states. The first relates to demands, often long-established, for a greater degree of local autonomy and a increased degree of control over the local economy to be decentralised away from central government to local or regional administrative or political organisations. Put another way, these demands are an expression of a deeply-rooted desire for a more decentralised political power structure, one more open to democratic local control. Such desires are by no means recent, however; to understand how and why they became partially realised (in the sense of a further deconcentration of power) at particular points in time requires relating them to the other two issues.

These themselves are closely interrelated: the failure of central governments' national economic and regional industrial policies and the reorganisation of local government, sometimes explicitly linked to initiatives to develop more effective forms of regional planning, in an attempt to create some of the pre-conditions thought to be necessary for the "success" of the former sets of policies. For the deconcentration of parts of the overall process of industrial production to peripheral regions, as an intended result of the implementation of a centrally-directed regional policy designed simultaneously to reduce regional inequalities and accelerate national economic growth rates, presupposed the creation of appropriate general conditions of production in such regions. In turn, their creation partly depended upon the effectiveness of the actions of local government. To guarantee this, the structures and procedures of local government required modernising.

In practice, however, the combined effects of the policies of often-restructured local governments and central governments' regional industrial policies diverged sharply from their intended outcomes. In the 1960s and early 1970s, they were associated with the emergence of new spatial divisions of labour within the territories of national states and with the penetration of transnational capital into peripheral regions, with the growing integration of peripheral regional economies into national but increasingly international patterns of production. Thus in this period the effects of these policies in helping create branch-plant economies, vulnerable to externally-taken decisions and external control, became a cause for concern in peripheral regions. As the 1970s progressed, such concerns were rapidly and increasingly overtaken by those linked to the generalised industrial decline of much of the West European economy. This accelerated and generalised industrial decline, associated with the failure of central governments' national economic and industrial policies (although in some cases, notably the U.K., aggregate industrial decline has not been at all inconsistent with the intentions of central government's policies), has been accompanied by the deepening and intensification of existing regional problems and the emergence of new regional, urban and inner-urban problems. Thus the generalisation of spatial policy problems has been set against a background of national industrial decline and an increasing unwillingness and/or inability on the part of central governments to formulate and implement policies to cope with, or at least contain, these changes. Under these circumstances, it has been politically convenient for central governments to allow the growing transfer of responsibility for local and regional economic conditions to more locally-based authorities. Not least, it allows part of the blame for local and regional economic problems to be shifted onto that locally-based part of the overall political structure at the same time as central governments cut the resources available to local authorities as part of broader strategies to control public expenditure.

In summary, then, this decentralisation of responsibility has taken place as part of a restructuring of capitalist states involving deconcentration of tasks and functions from central to local levels in response to a profound crisis in the capitalist economies of Western Europe as the effects of quite fundamental changes in the international division of labour began to work through into them. To a substantial degree, it reflected central Government's recognition that they were no longer able, or no longer wished, to exercise effective control over economic and employment conditions.

LOCAL GOVERNMENT RE-ORGANISATION, FORMS OF TRANSFER OF ECONOMIC RESPONSIBILITY TO LOCAL AND REGIONAL LEVELS, AND LOCAL CONTROL OVER LOCAL ECONOMIES: SOME EXAMPLES FROM DENMARK AND THE U.K.

The Scottish and Welsh Development Agencies.

These were introduced in December 1975 and represent, in the U.K. case, an almost unique form of deconcentration of power to regional level authorities, certainly one with no parallel in terms of England. The reasons for their creation and subsequent mode of operation are instructive of the problems that can accompany such a deconcentration to regional levels.

Their origin must be seen, at least in part, as a response to the politics of nationalism and fears as to the possible break-up of the U.K. State. This provided, as it were, the proximate cause of their establishment which in turn permitted the further transformation of the U.K. State's regional policy from one concerned with employment provision in peripheral regions to one that, increasingly from the mid-1960s, had became concerned with the restructuring of the national manufacturing base in an attempt to preserve, enhance or restore international competitiveness.

This trend becomes very clear if one examines the budgets and powers granted to the two Agencies, and, particularly in the case of the SDA, the ways in which they have exercised them. Broadly speaking, their powers fall in two main areas: environmental improvement (which is not particularly relevant to our concerns here) and industrial regeneration. In part, the powers in this latter area simply involve co-ordinating some existing activities (such as industrial estate and factory provision, industrial promotion abroad, and some aspects of encouraging small businesses). More important, however, the DAs were given powers to invest - either by taking share capital in existing companies, entering partnerships with such companies, or establishing new companies (though these were subsequently cut back by the Thatcher government after the 1979 election).

In particular, the SDA actively pursued this investment role after 1975, allocating 40% of its initial £300 million budget to it. The Agency was also very explicit about the criteria that were to govern its investment allocation. It saw its "proper concern" as long-term profitability and explicitly argued that it should not have a short-term "rescue" function to protect employment. Furthermore, the SDA saw one of its key roles as producing a technological transformation, pursuing this goal in two ways. One was to seek out and develop, via its own investment activities, industries using "forward technologies", while recognizing the risky nature of investing in them. In brief, it was to act as a "venture capitalist", one of the last entrepreneurs. The other was to evolve a specific sectoral strategy to promote Scotland as a location for (USA and Japanese) transnational capital involved in micro-electronics production, identifying specific companies with strong growth prospects and seeking to persuade them to locate part of their operations in Scotland. This strategy has not been without some success in relation to the SDA's objectives (and has in fact had a greater impact than its own investment activities, having survived the 1979 election result largely intact).

More generally, though, both DAs have had only a very partial success in terms of their more broadly specified goals of economic regeneration and modernisation, although this need not concern us here, beyond pointing out that their policies have only had a very marginal effect in terms of reducing unemployment from what it otherwise would have been in Scotland and Wales. What does concern us here, however, especially in the case of the SDA, is that as the actions and policies of the two Agencies abundantly reveal, deconcentration of a degree of economic power did not mean a greater degree of regional control and closure of the Scottish and Welsh economies. Rather the contrary; for as part of a restructuring of the UK State itself, they represented part of an attempt to cope with and manage the UK's changing role and status within the evolving international division of labour and in fact thereby facilitated the opening up of the Scottish and Welsh economies to new forms of penetration by transnational capital, new forms of external dependency and control.

Local government reorganisation and economic initiatives by local authorities in the UK:

The recent growing involvement of local government in the UK with economic and employment issues, though its main concerns are still in the sphere of the reproduction of labour-power and land use planning and infrastructure provision, has to be seen in the context of earlier changes in the structure of local government and the discrepancy between the intended and actual outcomes of central government's national economic and regional industrial policies. These changes also have to be seen in the context of the public sector absorbing a growing share of GNP and with local government's share of total public expenditure rising to around 25%, although with increasing central government attempts to reduce this from the mid-1970s, especially after 1979, via cutting the block grants (via the RSG) and limiting rate rises. Two significant legislative changes both reflected and set the context for central government's attitudes and views as to the role of local government in the overall State regulation of economy and society.

The first was the 1968 Town and Country Planning Act, which replaced the original 1947 Act and subsequent amendments, and by which local authorities, as the statutory planning organisations, were required to produce new forms of land use plans (structure and district plans). These were intended to generate new and supposedly technically more efficient, in the context of the requirements of accumulation in a modern capitalist industrial economy, land use planning procedures. The second was the (belated) 1974 reorganisation of local government itself following a prolonged public debate leading to the 1972 Local Government Act; the subsequent modification of its proposals, and the creation of metropolitan counties (seven in number, including Greater London) and larger basic county (39 in England and 8 in Wales together with 10 Scottish regions) and district units, along with a reorganisation of non-elected boards involved in the provision of health, water and sewerage services at regional level and some reallocation of functions between these various levels. The legislative basis for local government had been confirmed in Acts of Parliament in 1888 and 1894 but, as the twentieth century progressed, and especially after the 1947 Town and Country Planning Act gave planning functions to local authorities, the pattern of units inherited from the nineteenth century became increasingly problematic. The essential logic of these changes, then, was to ensure a more uniform provision of services throughout the national territory while cutting the unit costs of service provision via centralisation onto bigger local units as the public sector share of GNP continued to rise. However, these 1974 changes have themselves come to be seen as problematic so that currently there are proposals to abolish the metropolitan counties.

The combined effects of these changes and central governments' regional industrial policies were increasingly to open local and/or peripheral regional economies to external influence by making them more attractive to big national and transnational capital. Net investment was increasingly replaced by net disinvestment in the 1970s, however, reflecting the UK's changed position in the international division of labour. This trend was especially marked after 1979 when the switch from a Labour to a Conservative central government brought the abandonment of any pretence at formulating national government policies designed to decelerate or reverse deindustrialisation. Rather both became encouraged (particularly via the removal of controls on capital export), so as to promote a restructuring of industry in the UK in search of the elusive goal of international competitiveness.

In these circumstances, concern and political responsibility for economic development and employment issues were partly foisted onto local authorities as central government retreated from an active engagement with them. But it was partly also a defensive measure of their own choosing, in response to local pressure over unemployment levels. Local authorities tried to fill a policy void in economic and political circumstances that was not of their own choosing (not least because of central Government cuts in finance for local government). This activity has given a certain legitimacy to the role of local politicians and to the administrative structure of local government. What emphatically has not resulted from this transfer of political responsibility (without any commensurate real transfer of political powers) is a greater degree of local control and autonomy; in some ways quite the reverse.

For the result has been that local authorities (even down to the level of district councils) have attempted to enter into competition with one another for jobs. Despite the fact that they lack both the resources and expertise necessary for this type of activity, local authorities have also entered into a competition with one another to be granted Enterprise Zone and/or Free-port status by central government in order to improve their competitive position in the desperate scramble for investment and jobs (a competition that bears a heavy ideological price in relation to legitimating the Thatcher government's broader position as regards economic policy). But whether successful in this or not, local authorities have generally recognised their limited capacity to sell their areas to capital on what is more and more a world market for labour and production sites - more and more, their problem is how to cope with the impacts of deindustrialisation as capital withdraws from their areas and further new inward-investment is not forthcoming. Consequently, their efforts have turned more and more to encouraging indigenous small firm formation and growth <u>within</u> their own areas.

It might be thought that such a policy would yield increased "local control" over local economies but there are several reservations about the validity of this proposition. First, such policies typically yield little in the way of new employment, especially relative to other job losses and unemployment levels. Second, such developments as do occur characteristically take the form of small capitalist firms, which in turn poses certain problems. One is that even if control of production is more rooted in local areas, markets lie outside of these. A second is more fundamental in so far as the acceptance of trying to solve "local economic problems" in this way grants an ideological primacy to the logic of capital, to the equating of economic development with the model of the competitive entrepreneur, and in so far as these entrepreneurs are to emerge from the labour rendered redundant to the needs of other capitals, such a policy can have a sharply divisive and fragmenting effect within the working class. It accepts the legitimacy of seeking a solution to the problems thrown up by the uneven character of capitalist development in terms of capital's own logic, rather than posing the question of socialist alternatives to these.

The Danish case: deconcentration or decentralisation?

In the last two decades, paralleling changes in the UK, a considerable deconcentration of Danish manufacturing has taken place. Jobs in manufacturing have been reallocated from the capital (Copenhagen) and the bigger traditional manufacturing

148

centres, like Arhus in East Jutland and Odense on the island of Fyn, to the more remote peripheral regions in North-, West and South Jutland. There has also been a reallocation from these traditional manufacturing centres and from medium size provincial towns to small towns with between 5-10,000 inhabitants. In contrast to the UK, however, where manufacturing capital increasingly abandoned central and peripheral regions alike, the restructuring of industrial location has been even stronger in Denmark in the last decade than in the 1960s. These tendencies have been strengthened at a time when the restructuring could no longer be related back to the lack of labour measures in the traditional industrial towns, since the crisis has raised the level of unemployment all over the country. The national unemployment rate is now (1983) 11%.

In 1970 a drastic restructuring of the Danish local government structure started. Decentralisation was the key word. Deconcentration was the practice. Many government functions were transferred from central government to the new, larger municipalities and counties, a process of restructuring of local government system paralleled in many West European countries. The Danish restructuring was especially influenced by that started in 1962 in Sweden. Part of the explanation for the reorganisation is the growth in economic output and the associated growth in the State activities – the expansion of the Welfare State. On another level, the explanation is partly to be found in terms of a response to administrative and political problems, in that promoting deconcentration while calling it decentralisation was seen as the best way of giving people the _feeling_ that they have some impact on the political system.

Even though the tasks of local government ar mainly concentrated in the field of reproduction of the labour force and infrastructure provision, it seems that, from an empirical point of view, the two deconcentration processes could have been very closely linked, or that the changing location of manufacturing has reflected deconcentration on the political level. We do not believe that the political deconcentration means that Danish local government has any possibilities for decisively influencing the restructuring of manufacturing industry or to increase its influence over local economic matters. Before we devote ourselves to this debate, we want to describe the deconcentration to the local government level.

Deconcentration in the Danish political system

The roots of Danish local self-government can be traced back to last century, while the electoral system at local level, with equal rights for men and women, goes back to 1909. The people elect the municipality council every four years and it elects the mayor. Before 1970 Denmark was divided into 24 counties and nearly 1100 rural municipalities. Beside these, there 88 city governments of provincial towns and boroughs of the Copenhagen region. The municipalities were able to decide on rates of property tax and of direct personal income tax to the municipality. The counties only had direct taxation powers on property. Until 1970 central government increasingly used local governments to take on public sector responsibilities and then refunded some of the money (50-90%) used for these purposes. Standards for many functions were decided in detail and controlled by central government. Only the city municipalities and the counties had a professional staff, and they also had a higher degree of self-government. In rural municipalities, the local administration was executed by council members and a single civil servant responsible for taxation.

In 1970, as a first step in the local government reforms, the territorial basis was changed. Two principles lay behind the reform. The first was to enhance administrative efficiency by increasing the range of functions taken on by local self-government and by creating units large enough in demographic and economic terms to allow decisions to be taken locally relating to provision of public services involved in reproducing the labour force and to carry out some planning and development of infrastructure. The second principle was that each city should be surrounded by a single local government area. Thus 275 municipalities and 14 counties were created. In principle there are at least 10,000 inhabitants in a municipality, though a few have less and some big municipalities have up to 250,000. The Capital region is still divided into many municipalities, with Copenhagen municipality having more than half a million inhabitants. The counties have on average 350,000 inhabitants, but range from 50-60,000. The electoral system is still the same, but many people feel that contact with council members is less than before and especially that the distance to the town hall is now rather large. Previously people knew council members personally from daily life but now they know them only from the newspapers.

The next stage of reform was to give more power and responsibility to the local and regional levels, followed by a change in the method of financing local government expenditure. Income tax at the municipal level was raised, and the counties were given powers to raise direct personal income tax. But the main change was that the central government stopped nearly all refunds for local government expenditure (except pensions) and instead paid general block grants (rather like the Rate Support Grant in the UK) to the municipalities and counties. The size of these grants depends on the number of inhabitants, the geographical size of the municipality or county and on the proportions of children and old people in the municipality and county. The overall effect of these changes can be seen from Table 2.

TABLE 1: Revenue for local governments, 1981 (Municipalities and counties) [1]

Personal income taxes	50 billion kr	57%
Tax on property	5 billion kr	6%
Refunds from central state	10 billion kr	12%
General grants from	22 billion kr	25%
	87 billion kr	100%

The importance of the role of local government expenditure is further revealed by the fact that, apart from transfer-payments (which are to a large extent determined by special legislation), counties and municipalities today account for 68% of total government current and 55% of capital expenditure (see Table 2).

Of course local government activities are to a large degree regulated by Acts of Parliament and by central government. But in health, education and social services, local governments have considerable influence over the level and standards of public service. In some fields certain minimum standards have been established via guidelines from the central state, but in practice the local state has chosen to set higher ones.

The municipalities are responsible for primary and secondary schools, social welfare services for children and the elderly (including child day care institutions and institutions for the elderly), local roads, sports facilities, local planning, environmental protection and social assistance to problem families, etc. The counties are responsible for hospitals, high schools, county roads, regional planning, and some

TABLE 2: Current and Capital Expenditure by Central and Local Government, 1982.

Expenditure for consumption

Central state	42 billion D.kr	32%
Counties	27 billion D.kr	20%
Municipalities	63 billion D.kr	48%
		‾‾‾‾
		100%

Expenditure for investment

Central state	9 billion D.kr	45%
Counties	3 billion D.kr	15%
Municipalities	8 billion D.kr	40%
		‾‾‾‾
		100%

Source: Statistical Yearbook 1983.

welfare services. There is a special council for the
metropolitan region around Copenhagen, of which the 50
municipalities and the 3 counties in the region are members.
The metropolitan council is responsible for collective
transport, infrastructure planning, hospitals and regional
planning.

To control local governments' activities, a sectoral
planning system was developed, with Annual Reports on
medium-term programmes being made to the relevant ministries.
A budget and accounting system has also been developed, which
makes it easier for central government to ask local
governments to stop increasing their budgets and to demand
some cuts in services, especially after the start of the
crisis. Central government cuts the general block grants and
demands that local government taxes do not increase further,
in much the same way as has happened in the UK since 1979.
Denmark's local government restructuring is thus more a
deconcentration rather than a decentralisation of power. And
by giving less in general block grants to the local
governments, central government has a very efficient weapon
with which to control the level of local expenditure, at a
time when the crisis makes it virtually impossible to let
direct taxes increase at local government level. Further,
today there is a big differences in how much a family pays in
tax, depending on where they live. In rich municipalities
with few social problems, personal income tax is only 12%; in
poorer municipalities with a lot of social problems and

spending on development, the tax rate is 23%. On top of that there is the county tax at 6-9%. For a family with two wage-earners the difference in taxation between one municipality and another can amount to the price of having a car - 20,000D.kr. This process of differentiation, especially in the Copenhagen Region, has been increased by the politics of decentralisation.

The Danish manufacturing deconcentration - a success story!

In 1960 33% of the population and 50% of the manufacturing jobs (in firms with 6 persons or more) were located in the Capital Region, with a further 15% in the 3 big provincial towns of Arhus, Odense and Alborg. In 1982 only 30% of manufacturing jobs were placed in the Capital Region and the 3 big provincial towns had only 11%. At the same time, the peripheral regions in Jutland (North-, South- and West-) have increased their share of the manufacturing jobs from 15% to 32%.

Compared with the number of people living in them, these peripheral regions are today more dependent on manufacturing than is the Capital Region. In the sixties the medium size provincial towns gained from the restructuring of local government. The centralisation of economic activities was followed by a concentration of manufacturing firms in them. The rural areas lost some small firms and the Capital Region lost firms which moved out to find labour reserves and a cheaper labour force. In the 1970s even the smaller towns gained from restructuring, with many new firms setting up there. These firms have not moved out or re-located, but have started up production from scratch, and are partly oriented to the international market and partly as subcontractors.

In the late 1970s there has been growth in manufacturing jobs in municipalities with less than 20,000 inhabitants. The biggest growth has been in a few towns with less than 5,000 inhabitants. Table 3 shows that the decline in manufacturing jobs in the country was 12% between 1972 and 1982. In 1980 18% of those employed were in manufacturing. The figure also shows that the decline has been most marked in the Capital Region - 30%. Odense, and the island of Fyn is a traditional manufacturing area and here manufacturing jobs fell by 18%. The peripheral regions in Jutland all increased their number of manufacturing jobs. The traditional rural regions all have more jobs in manufacturing than in agriculture. Copenhagen municipality is now facing English-type inner-city problems, with the loss of half of the manufacturing jobs in 8 years and an above-average unemployment rate.

TABLE 3. Index of manufacturing employment (in establishments with minimum 6 employees) in Danish Counties 1982. 1972 = 100.

1982

	1982
Total all counties	87.3
Copenhagen and Frederiksberg municipalities	52.9
Copenhagen county	81.4
Fredensborg county	89.0
Roskilde county	83.4
THE CAPITAL REGION	69.5
Westzealand county	82.6
Storstrøms county	89.2
Bornholm county	97.2
Fyns county	82.0
South Jutlands county	103.4
Ribe county	117.2
Vejle county	94.8
Ringkøbing county	115.3
Arhus county	91.6
Viborg county	138.8
North Jutland county	104.9

Note: shows counties with a development better than the average for all counties.

Source: Industrial Statistics 1972 and 1982.

The changing location pattern of Danish manufacturing industry thus accelerated after the crisis started. The political need for it is less than before, but the economic imperatives seem to be stronger. Whether this will continue to be so within Denmark remains to be seen - the English experience suggests it may well not be.

Local governments and local economic control?

The Regional Development Agency in Denmark provides some cheap loans for investment and some economic aid to firms establishing themselves in West-, North- and South Jutland and in some of the islands south of Sjaelland. It is a central government agency and its expenditures are said to have created around 2000 new jobs a year in the 1970s. This figure contrasts with the UK case, where it is generally recognised that in the 1970s regional policy expenditures ceased to have an effect on employment levels in peripheral regions, in contrast to the 1960s when it is claimed some 20,000 jobs were created per year through such policies. Nevertheless, it has been argued that in the Danish, as in the UK case, many of the firms would have established themselves in the peripheral regions even without the support from the Regional Development Agency.

The Regional Agency can also help some municipalities to establish industrial estates with low interest loans. A few have established such estates, where private firms can rent a building rather cheaply. Some smaller firms have used these possibilities, but the main restructuring of industrial location has not involved such industrial estates. Another way in which municipalities compete in attracting industrial firms is to create the required infrastructure. They can also try to keep a firm by ignoring pollution or by letting private households pay a large part of the necessary investment in environmental protection. The municipality can also (or could before the crisis) build up day-care institutions to attract firms using a lot of female workers. The municipalities have a few weapons to compete with one another in attracting private investments but no economic or political control over the resulting economic activities. The central government has a very liberal industrial policy, if it has any policy at all. The regional Master Plan, made by the counties and accepted by the central government, specifies where manufacturing firms are allowed to locate, but no one can control or demand that firms to establish themselves in this or that region. In a small way the taxes are used to promote competition between different municipalities in attracting industries. But now with unemployment in all regions, this could easily result in a waste of public money. One symptom is that prepared industrial sites are already over-provided in most municipalities.

Fundamentally, there is no control over where firms invest, so that they can take their profits out of the region and invest the money elsewhere in Denmark or in a country offering better chances of profitable production. Several firms have closed or moved out of Denmark, leaving the resultant social problems to the municipalities. The acceptance of free international capital movements and the new international division of labour means that these economic tendencies are setting the scene for local politics and at best are only leaving room for a decentralisation in relation to the level of public service for reproduction of the labour force. Even so local governments are dependent on the degree to which capital finds that a location in this or that municipality fits in with the need of the private accumulation process. Local governments depend on taxes, which in turn depend on how many people are employed and on the level of wages they can get. Furthermore, the very large degree of vertical integration of the international production process means that imports and exports for a single firm are often very big, so that the multiplier effect within a particular region is rather limited.

In connection with the long period of high growth rates, deconcentration in Denmark has helped to raise the standards of public services. The central government's decision to build up a better school system all over the country - even in the rural municipalities - has raised the educational standards of school leavers, providing a better qualified workforce nationally. Infrastructure has also been developed. This homogenisation of Denmark could have helped many new industries to locate in the traditional peripheral regions; or, to put it another way, the traditional industrial regions with a skilled workforce, a highly developed infrastructure and possibilities for a horizontal division of the production process inside a region, have lost a little while the peripheral regions have gained a little relatively in the competition for manufacturing jobs. But such a result could have followed with a central government policy of building up service facilities in the peripheral regions. It might be that political deconcentration presented as decentralisation is a cheaper way to do it, but the main reason could equally be to remove some of the political pressure from central government and better legitimate the political system by giving a broader scope of power and responsibility to local level units.

The crisis shows more clearly how the new international division of labour is setting the scene for local politics. Or to put it in another way, the tendencies in Denmark and the free enterprise zones and free ports in the UK show us that we will have to work with implications of the internationalisation of local politics.

THE LIMITS TO DECENTRALISATION AND LOCAL ECONOMIC CONTROL ION THE CONTEXT OF THE INTERNATIONAL DIVISION OF LABOUR

In the previous three sections we have commented briefly on the limits associated with deconcentration as a solution to local economic problems within the framework of capitalist development, not least in terms of the way in which such "solutions" reinforce the legitimacy of this framework itself. The point we wish to emphasise here is that the contemporary international division of labour will result in any attempt at purely local level solutions to local economic problems within

156

a capitalist framework being extremely problematic: more and
more, transnational capitals are becoming active agents in
local politics.

If the logic of ceding responsibility, if not power, in the
economic sphere to the local level was the failure of national
governments via their macroeconomic, fiscal, industrial and
regional policies, to control the impacts of the changing
international division of labour within their domestic
economies, then it is surely nonsensical to expect local
government to be able to do so. For capitalist firms of all
sizes, large and small are drawn more and more into an
international economic order that is largely controlled,
directly or indirectly, by a relatively small number of
transnational corporations. If national governments lack the
political power to control the activities of such firms, then
it is patently ridiculous to expect local government
authorities to be able to do so. What the latter might do,
however, is to seek ways of encouraging forms of economic
activity that put some space between themselves and the forces
of international competition and the world market – though the
degree to which they will be able to do so will be heavily
constrained by the economic policies pursued by national
governments.

Conclusions: what are the lessons to be learned?

We here summarise some of the implications of the preceding
discussion. Local government restructuring and reorganisation
is not to be confused with increasing local control of
economic and social affairs.   In fact, it has often had
precisely the reverse effect, simultaneously opening up some
local economies to penetration from capital that is
increasingly linked to international markets and leading to a
flight of capital from other local economies: both the Danish
and UK experiences point clearly to this.

Second, the scope for local government to taking economic
initiatives at the local level is critically constrained by
national government attitudes to economic policy. This is
true at two levels. The first can be illustrated by reference
to local authority initiatives to promote small firm
development within the UK, which have been severely hampered
by central government's monetary policies, credit and interest
rate policies, as well as by central government limits on
local government expenditures for these purposes. Thus even
within the logic of a capitalist economy, this conflict in the
objective impacts, if not necessarily the intentions, of
central and local government policies is heavily weighted
against local government's aims of promoting small firm

formations and growth and has severely hampered, if not effectively prevented, them being realised. The second is obvious, but nevertheless important to state. For if the attitudes of central government involve an acceptance of the logic of capitalist development and of the market as the principle economic steering mechanism, then the scope that remains for local government initiatives that break with this rationality is, to say the least, severely limited. The experiences of local authorities in the UK, such as those in London and Sheffield, in trying to develop such locally-based economic initiatives, provides ample support for this claim.

Third, unless there are local government initiatives and policies that do not regard the competitive forces of a capitalist (world) economy as sacrosanct economic steering mechanisms, then there can be little, if any, real hope of meaningful local control of, or autonomy for, local economies. For the political space needed to allow such initiatives to develop hinges crucially, as a necessary but not sufficient condition, on national economic policy measures. This is <u>not</u> to say that <u>nothing</u> can be done at the local level in the absence of appropriate national economic policies being adopted, but it is to acknowledge that what can be done will be extremely restricted, probably of a defensive character, and reacting to the debris produced within the local area by capitals' strategies for accumulation. Moreover, it is politically important that this be widely understood if a deconcentration or even a limited decentralisation to local government is not merely to be used as a mechanism for central government to pass off the responsibility for deteriorating economic conditions.

Fourth, for there to be the possibility of meaningful control of local economies presupposes a considerable decentralisation of not only administrative competence but also of the political power to allow local communities the scope for economic self-determination. Equally, it has to be recognised that there is no guarantee that providing such scope will result in progressive social and economic policies, even in circumstances when they are being pursued by government at national level.

Fifth, considerable emphasis has in practice been placed by local governments on encouraging the development of small firms. In so far as the space within which local economic initiatives are to be pursued is one that is given to them as defined by the parameters of a capitalist society, then small firm policies should be framed in such a way as to increase the degree of closure of local economies by encouraging input-output links between both manufacturing and service firms within the local economy. This statement needs qualifying in several ways, however. If the ruling logic is that of capitalist development, then it is very probable that small firms will be able to purchase commodities and services more cheaply outside of the immediate local area. Moreover, the financial capacity of local government to intervene to try and guarantee local buying and selling (by subsidies etc.) will be hampered by lack of resources, by the limited range of economic activities actually present in local areas, and by central government regulation. Furthermore, markets for final products most probably will lie outside the boundaries of the local area. For such reasons the degree to which the local economy can be closed will be severely limited. Finally, but by no means least, there is the danger that promoting this sort of small firm development, based upon assertions as to a cross-class unity of interest between capital and labour, will lead to super-exploitation of workers, low wages, bad working conditions – and so maybe greater demands on those services provided by local government in relation to the reproduction of labour power.

Sixth, in so far as local governments have, with varying degrees of enthusiasm, taken such opportunities as are open to them to develop more positive local economic and employment initiatives from within the range of available options – a range so drastically limited as to predetermine that these initiatives would fail even in their own terms of creating some new employment – it has allowed central governments to off-load at least some of the blame for rising unemployment and growing economic problems. If unemployment rises in particular areas, so central governments can argue that this reflects the failures not of their own but of local government's economic policies. In this way the deconcentration of State power and the growing formulation of local government economic initiatives has fulfilled a crucial ideological role.

Lastly, decentralisation has fulfilled such a role in another sense. In the desperate struggle for such new employment and investment as capital is making within the territories of states such as Denmark and the UK, local governments enter into fierce competition to sell their areas to capitals. Thus the focus of attention is shifted from questions such as "why is national unemployment so high?" or "why is capital fleeing from Denmark or the UK?" to those of how best to secure a share of such investment and new employment growth as is on offer for one's own local area. Such competition between areas and people living in them is thus reinforced as an "inevitable" and "normal" aspect of everyday life in a modern capitalist society.

REFERENCES

In this paper, we have drawn on a variety of sources, the more important of which are:

Anderson J., Duncan S. and Hudson, R. (eds) (1983) Redundant Spaces in Cities and Regions?. Academic Press, London, (especially the editorial introduction and the chapters by Anderson and Cochran).

Bugge L., Jensen H.T., Plum V., Cauchi P. and Schou B., (1983) Erhvervsstrukturens udvikling i Danmark, 1901-76. GEO-RUC

Carney J., Hudson R. and Lewis J. (eds), (1980) Regions in Crisis, Croom Helm, London.

Fröbel F., Heirichs J. and Kreye O., (1980) International Division of Labour, Cambridge University Press, Cambridge.

Grønlund B. and Jensen S.B., (1982) Nordiske storbyer, Copenhagen.

Hartoft-Nielsen P. (1982) Industriens strukturelle udvikling

Hudson R. and Lewis J. (eds) (1982) Regional Planning in Europe, Pion, London (especially the editorial introduction and the chapter by Toft Jensen)

Jensen H.T., (1983) "Municipal government a an element in the politico-administrative system", Anglo-Danish Seminar, Copenhagen.

Lorentz Nielsen, (1981) Growth limit for local government expenditure, Copenhagen.

Løtz J. (1980) Kommunernes finansiering, Copenhagen.

Maskell P. (1932) Industriens regionale omlokalisering 1970-80, Copenhagen.

8 Central and local state relations in UK land supply

GILL WHITTING
School for Advanced Urban Studies, University of Bristol

INTRODUCTION

This chapter sets out to illustrate the inadequacy of referring to central/local government relations in abstract terms given the complexity of other intervening relationships, particularly those existing at the public/private interface. The chapter also attempts to combine the theoretical traditions of organisational sociology, which has tended to focus on the 'organisation' as the unit of analysis, with more structural concerns about central and local state function in the local political arena. The concepts of 'central control' and 'local autonomy' are crucial to the discussion; the chapter explores how power, interest and dependency determine degrees of control and autonomy during the life of a policy. The process of policy change is determined by alliances between actors and agencies involved in the policy sector. These changes reflect both the way in which the interests consolidate and evolve over time in response to new circumstances, and the effect of earlier misconceptions on behalf of policy makers about the interaction between dependent interests, resulting in frequent policy revision.

The policy in question is the Community Land Scheme, the Labour Party's third attempt to recoup development gain in the interests of the community. Introduced in 1976, the scheme gave additional powers to local authorities in England and to a new, separate land agency in Wales. These agencies were empowered to acquire land for private development net of development land tax otherwise paid by the vendor, thereby realising the full development value for the community at the point of resale to the private sector. The experience of local authorities in England, the operational difficulties and performance achieved, provide the data for this chapter.

The discussion that ensues relates to one of the central questions for urban political analysis: for what purpose and in whose interests does the state function in the construction of the urban locality? The theoretical approach of the paper pursues the contradictions within 'local state' terminology; is it possible to fuse political, administrative analysis with political, economic analysis and what are the implications for understanding the central/local state functions in the local political arena?

THEORETICAL BACKGROUND

The emphasis on power, interest and dependency arises from a concern to develop a radical theory of society in which organisations are accorded a central role (Burrell and Morgan, 1979). The common criticism of traditional organisational theory is its formality, the inability to perceive informal, political process and the absence of a structural or contextual analysis.[1] The contrast is made with structuralist writers who address the historical dimension of their subject, who emphasise the importance of class relationships and/or the role of the State and who account for the phenomena of social change.[2] The preoccupation in recent theoretical work is to fuse together the two distinctly different approaches (Saunders, 1979; Offe 1975; Dunleavy 1980). Theoretically, the debate has developed in sophistication to contrast Weberian and Marxian structuralist approaches. Burrell and Morgan (1979) for example, illustrate the dilemma more succinctly by suggesting that the radical Weberian and Marxian structuralist perspectives tend to draw upon relatively distinct intellectual traditions and focus upon different areas of interest. The former (Weberian) stresses political administrative structures, corporatism, power, the factional analogy; the latter (Marxian) stresses political economy, economic structures, monopoly capitalism, contradiction, the catastrophe analogy. Both approaches, it is argued, analyse social formations from different perspectives which lead to the use of different analytical constructs with emphasis on different elements of the total social formation. The authors suggest that synthesis between the two approaches is possible, and a systematically developed theory would offer many new insights into understanding organisations in society.

This chapter uses a framework which is sympathetic to the need for contextualisation at all levels of analysis; it falls short of a systematic developed theory of the type demanded by Burrell and Morgan (1979 pp.389/390), but as a framework it allows linkages to made between structure and administrative process and consequences.

In analysing the social organisation of a policy sector, Benson (1980) argues that sectors have levels of structure with the deeper levels determining within limits the range of variation on the surface levels.   Levels and components distinguished are:

	administrative arrangements (division of labour)
Level I	policy paradigms
	interorganisational dependency

| Level II | interest-power structures |
| | rules of structure formation |

A policy sector is defined as 'a cluster or complex of organisations connected to each other by resource dependencies and distinguished from other clusters or complexes by breaks in the structure of resource dependencies'. The analysis of inter-organisational policy sectors should, according to the author, be comparative in three senses:

(i) between sector comparisons within a society
(ii) comparisons between policy sectors of different societies
(iii) comparisons of the social structures of whole societies.

The analysis should also consider the historical processes through which a sector has been structured, the current social organisation of a sector and the tensions and inconsistencies within the present structure and in its relations to the larger society which portend further development.

The levels of analysis distinguished by Benson are described in the following way:

Administrative arrangements are defined as the patterns of differentiation and control over activities in a sector. Differentiation defines a set of rules according to which activities are allocated. Control refers to the extent of control and the bases of control exercised over activities. Policy paradigm refers to the commitment to a particular set

163

of policy options selected from a wider range of potential policies. It is emphasised that a policy paradigm must be inferred from practices; declarations of policy intent are useful as indications of assumptions and values but are not guides to the paradigm. Interorganisational resource dependencies consist of relationships of resource dependence between organisations which arise in part from the degree and form of the division of labour.

Administrative arrangements and policy paradigms must be understood in relation to an underlying power structure. The analysis of power structure requires as a first step the identification of 'structured interests' and rules setting boundaries upon the operation of the sector. The rules restrict the range of alternatives available with regard to policy paradigm and administrative structure. Negotiations and bargains occur within the range of available alternatives. Movement of a sector beyond these boundaries would be met with various control measures. The rules of structure formation are neither stable nor consistent; contradictions occur as one set of rules develops in the context of an existing set. The limits upon one policy sector are connected to the limits upon other sectors. The structural formation rules are generated by the requirements of the larger social formation. In the case of advanced capitalist societies these requirements stem in part from the changing demands of capital accumulation and legitimation. The variation in policy paradigms and administrative arrangements are limited by the necessity to maintain the accumulation process and to produce justification for the order of things. These limits would vary between sectors and would depend upon the location of the sector relative to the core problems of accumulation and legitimation.

A number of issues arise in relation to methodology and application of the Benson framework. For example, what is it that Benson is offering? What are the underlying assumptions? Does the framework adopt a particular theoretical stance? How much space is there for redefinition and clarification? In response, it is argued here that Benson's framework provides essentially the concept of an interorganisational policy sector which is multilevelled, a deep structure of rules and interests determining a surface level of substantive policy and administrative arrangements. The policy sector is conceived as a structure of interorganisational dependence relations. The framework is primarily responsive to a view of theory as contextualisation; theory is conceived as a comprehensive mapping of the social world which provides concepts and propositions at a macro level. It is suggested by Benson that theory in this broad sense makes practical, not merely theoretical, contributions to our understanding. The policy sector which is the focus for analysis is introduced below.

EMPIRICAL BACKGROUND

The Community Land Scheme, combining the Community Land Act 1975 and the Development Land Tax Act 1976, was introduced to achieve two main objectives. First, it was designed to enable the community to control the development of land in accordance with its need and priorities (positive planning), and second, it aimed to restore to the community the increase in value of land arising from its efforts (public profit).

Land within the scope of the Act was defined as land needed for relevant development within 10 years; land outside the scope of the Act included that with planning permission on or before the day the White Paper was published and that owned by a residential or industrial builder on or before White Paper Day. Land was identified for development in two ways, either within the planning framework or by the private sector bringing land forward for planning applications giving the agency the opportunity to consider whether public acquisition could take place.

Local authorities in England borrowed from the Land Scheme in a new Community Land Key Sector. To avoid expenditure falling on the rates, the cost of land administration and interests was treated on a capital basis and financed from borrowing. At the onset of the Scheme, the basis for central government approval of expenditure was intended to be the five-year rolling programme to be submitted annually to the Secretary of State. Block borrowing approvals for expenditure were also intended. During the life of the Scheme central government issued a number of guidance notes and circulars[3] introducing major policy and procedural revisions to the Scheme's operation, viz:

the overall resources available for the Scheme were reduced by almost half in December 1976;

rolling programmes and block loans were suspended and local authorities in England continued to apply for funds on a site by site basis;

'opportunity purchasing' in response to planning permission applications was discouraged;

criteria for land holding times and rates of return were made more explicit which served to discourage local authorities.

During 1978 there was some minor relaxation of these revisions, although the Scheme was at this stage implemented in a climate of uncertainty pending the forthcoming election. In May 1979 the Scheme was virtually curtailed [4] when the Conservative administration came to power. The CLA was finally repealed in 1980, thereby ending the English operation; the Land Authority for Wales, the separate agency implementing the CLA in Wales, was nevertheless retained, albeit with major operational revisions. [5]

ANALYSIS

Implicit in the Community Land Scheme was an attempt to restore to the community, via local government, the ownership of certain local planning decisions and the 'gain' or increase in land values arising from development activity. The importance of local needs and circumstances in determining expenditure under the CLS was a major feature of the Scheme initially: central interest and control, administered via a general block approval by central government within agreed five year rolling programmes, was secondary to the local determination of needs and expenditure by local government. The financial and administrative rules of the scheme, as enacted, provided the framework within which central and local government negotiated. But the revisions in rules and procedures throughout the life of the Scheme radically altered the relationship between central and local government. The 'theoretical' framework, introduced earlier in the chapter, will be used to illustrate the dimensions of the changing central/local relationship and the way in which the state intervened as representatives of other major 'interests' which were not immediately visible in the Land Scheme as originally enacted. The role of power, interest and dependency and the constraints on local autonomy will be observed through a discussion of structural roles, and their consequences for interest, dependencies, administrative concerns and behaviour.

Rules of structure formation

The intervention by the UK government into regional and local planning to manage the forces of change experienced by society has reflected certain social values. These values were a reflection of a concern to protect society not from change per se but from changes which might cause serious dislocation to the existing social system and status quo. The legal framework established [6] (Hall, 1973; Ratcliffe 1976, 1979) is inextricably linked to questions of land ownership, rights over development and the conflicts surrounding land use and land use planning which have been acted out in the three attempts by the Labour Party to recoup betterment from private land-owners in the interests of the community.[7]   If, as Benson (1980) suggests, structural rules stem in part from the changing demands of capital accumulation and legitimation, an analysis of capitalist land-ownership and its relationship to capital accumulation will clarify the form and content of those rules and the ensuing pattern of social relations. Massey and Catalano (1978) identify three different forms of private landownership - former landed property, industrial landownership and financial landownership, all of which produce distinct contradictions for the accumulation of capital. Their analysis suggests there is no single group based on land-ownership by capital which can be said to be a distinct and coherent faction.   The category land-ownership maintains its centrality as a structural rule but with certain ideological and political refinements.   These refinements illustrate the shift over time away from landed property landownership to industrial and financial interest and the dominance in recent years of finance capital over the system of private landownership.   The industrial shifts relate to the contradictions emerging from the process of capital accumulation and the conflicts existing within and between each pattern of landownership.

Interest power structures

Our understanding of interest and power structures is assisted by identifying those interests which are embedded in the policy sector.   Benson (1980) argues that the structured interests are those groups whose interests are built into the sector, either negatively or positively, in the sense that the operation of the sector serves or conflicts with their interests.   The Massey and Catalano analysis of landowners (1978) is one approach to the identification of structured interests and serves to illustrate power relations in the UK land market by identifying political dependencies and linkages.

The major part of manufacturing industry in Great Britain, owning the land on which the productive sections of its activity are located, comprise the bulk of industrial landownership.   The landed aristocracy, the Queen as an individual, the Church and the landed gentry comprise former landed property, owning some 40% of the total area of land in Great Britain.   This category is directly represented in the

House of Lords, on county councils and as Justices of the Peace and the group are numerically significant in the rural membership of the Tory Party. In addition, the Church has direct institutionalised links to the State. Although former landed property has a large representation in formal terms, its political power at the national level is weak, a contrast with <u>financial landownership</u> whose political significance is expanding through different channels and increasing overall. This category includes pension funds, property companies and insurance companies and is particularly significant because of its domination over the shape of the land market. The interests of this type of landowner are represented in the House of Commons, where there are a high number of business connections to both property companies and financial institutions. Politically, former landed property is overwhelmingly concerned to defend itself against increases in wealth-based rather than development-related taxes and against increases in the power and security of rural tenantry. Conversely, financial landowners' political struggles concern urban development and over investment of money capital. Massey and Catalano argue (1978, p.171) that all the groups of landowners and financial institutions in particular are not only a dominant force but also central to the dynamic of capitalism itself. Any attempts therefore to resolve the contradictions posed by the financial form of landownership would be challenging not just an isolated land-owning group but some of the interests of banking capital itself.

What is important about the identification of structured interests is not so much who they are or what they are, but the nature of contradictions which are posed and the conflicts and tensions which emerge. It is argued here, following Massey and Catalano's analysis, that the CLS itself was a response to a situation generated by the competitive and contradictory elements of landownership, particularly financial landownership. The Act was therefore concerned with pre-empting landownership by property companies and financial institutions. This is illustrated with reference to the circumstances to which the CLS was a response; the passages of the CLS through Parliament before its enactment and the implementation of the Scheme.

Responding to circumstances

In the early 70s, the economic position of a development industry powerfully placed in the economy mirrored the economic performance of the country as a whole, and, although a number of factors came together to produce the circumstances, the role of financial institutions and their increasing dominance in the sphere of landownership was perceived to be damaging to the national economy. The force of finance capital was in essence destabilising capitalism by generating political interest within the community and by attracting capital away from industrial development.

The political and ideological repercussions were voiced by community groups, inner-city residents, trades councils and trade unions who were concerned about the spatial restructuring of urban areas. Rising land prices which affected both the cost of living and access into the home-ownership market created a dilemma for the Labour government who were committed to expansion of home ownership. British industry was undergoing a severe profitability crisis at the same time as financial landowners were apparently making enormous profits. The core of the problem was diversion of investment towards the already affluent sections of the development industry and away from production activity which was fast declining. In challenging the 'unacceptable face of capitalism' the demands on the state were twofold: to aid British industry and to negotiate long-term wage restraints with trade unions. The solution proposed was public ownership of development land enacted through the Community Land Act and Development Land Tax legislation.

Passage through Parliament

In following the passage of the Community Land Bill through Parliament and analysing the debate and eventual outcomes, the relative power positions of different interests are emphasised. First, despite the White Paper's strong commitment to state organisation and ownership of land and widespread demands for land nationalisation, intervention under the CLS did not challenge either the power of private landownership, or the concept of private property; instead the CLS was confined to public ownership of <u>development</u> land and limited to land uses. The state was therefore concentrating activity on those sectors of the economy most affected by the dominance of financial landownership, that is industry and housing construction. The controversial aspects of the Bill centred round the extent of local authority compulsory purchase powers, the definition of development land, what types of land would be included in the exempt/excepted categories and taxation of development gains. Exempt and excepted categories of development land are particularly crucial for identifying structured interests. Status of land on White Paper Day was a major determinant of involvement in the Scheme and in practice protected a large number of private landowning and development interests.

It has been suggested that there were three ways in which landowners might have been affected by the Scheme (Massey and Catalano, 1979, p.176): by the acquisition of their land for relevant development; by the inability (in the future) to acquire relevant development land on a freehold basis, and by having to pay development land tax on increases in land values due to development. But the impact on different types of landownership was also inextricably linked to their specific relationship to land and the effect which the CLS would have on this relationship. Massey and Catalano concluded (1979, p.185) that former landed property would as a whole be relatively unscathed; industrial landownership would survive intact with none of its constituent groups being seriously threatened; financial institutions would be less affected by the legislation than property companies. The latter would be under more pressure since the provisions applied to them with more force and because landownership and development gains are almost their sole source of income. Because of their relatively immune position, it was suggested that financial institutions were likely to increase their control over a challenged form of landownership. In terms of the struggle between banking capital and industrial capital over land, banking capital emerged from the legislation relatively unscathed.

Implementation

The implementation of the Land Scheme by local authorities in England encountered a number of conflicts of interest – these conflicts were between central and local government in relation to general criteria for the acquisition of land, and between local authorities and competing agencies in relation to the disposal of land.

Behind central government's criteria for approving land purchase schemes was a financial imperative founded on the basis that the Land Scheme would be self financing. The hip as a source of income. It was predicted therefore that financial and industrial landowning interests would not be affected by development land taxation although some construction interests within industrial landownership where income from landownership was important might have been adversely affected.

In design, the Community Land Scheme consisted of ideologies and political interests intended to shift the dependency relationship. However, in terms of stated (and unstated) intentions, the Land Scheme could have been a very different

animal. The next section, policy paradigm, discusses some of
the alternative arrangements excluded by the policy option
enshrined in the CLS.

Policy Paradigm

As it was first envisaged, the Community Land Scheme amounted
to the gradual nationalisation of development land over a
period of years. It was aiming to address both land use and
land values by facilitating 'positive planning' in accordance
with local needs, and by restoring 'public profit' to the
community. There was however a substantial difference between
intentions for the Land Scheme in theory and eventual
implementation. This section will concentrate on options
which were 'closed off' by amendments to the Scheme in the
Parliamentary discussion period during which the Bill became
an Act, and during the 'transitional' stage of implementation
when the political imperative for effective legislation was
significantly reduced. In 1975 and 1976, excesses of the
property boom subsided together with community responses with
the effect that commitment by the Labour government to
implement the Scheme fully was lost. Three themes will be
considered: land nationalisation, positive planning and public
profit.

Land nationalisation

The policy paradigm of the Community Land Scheme did not
include nationalisation of land despite the identification of
the CLS with outright nationalisation during the ideological
and political debates of the early 1970s. The Land Scheme was
primarily concerned with public ownership of some development
land, not all; the relevance of land to the Scheme was
seriously restricted by the definition of relevant development
and exempt and excepted categories. It is important
nevertheless to appreciate that full nationalisation, as
Massey and Catalano explain (1978 pp.186-190) would not by
itself bring an end to land-related issues. With
nationalisation, the concept of property would still be based
on the exclusiveness of the rights of an individual agent, in
this case the State, and would still have an effect upon the
overall process of accumulation in a capitalist society. This
is because landownership is not fundamental to a society like
Britain where the social system is structured around
capitalist commodity production and the success of a scheme
involving full nationalisation of land would still depend on
the motivations and activities of the development industry and
the State's intervention in these activities.

Positive Planning

The paradigm of positive planning within the CLS was to be achieved by site identification and acquisition, site assembly using compulsory purchase powers if necessary, and site preparation and infrastructure works in line with the planning framework. By owning the freehold of land (except housing) local authorities had greater powers to control the form of development. The paradigm was neutralised throughout the life of the Scheme in a number of ways. Some of the influential factors were unrelated to the Land Scheme itself, like, for example, the economic climate and the depressed state of the land market which substantially affected land acquisition and disposal prospects. As far as the Scheme itself was concerned, there were a number of inhibiting factors: the reduced level of resources; the emphasis on financial return; the lack of incentives to generate financial returns; and certain operational problems such as delays on loan application decisions and lack of tolerance between financial years. These factors came together to affect the level of activity by local authorities using the Land Scheme and, in doing so, to reduce the capacity of local authorities to undertake development in the long term interests of the community or to achieve particular social and economic objectives at the local level.

Public Profit

The paradigm of public profit within the overall Scheme was to be generated in two ways. First, by land trading and rapid turnover with specific emphasis on buying land net of DLT and, after the Second Appointed Day, at current use value. Second, surpluses on the land accounts were to be shared eventually between the Exchequer and the authorities themselves. The impact of DLT gain on local authorities was of course affected by the level of activity generally and by the number of transactions where DLT was a significant factor (S. Barrett et al, 1978).

The major point to be made about the paradigms of positive planning and public profit in the context of a short time horizon is their intrinsic conflict with each other. A longer-term perspective on the basis of a rolling programme, block loan allocation, financial tolerance between years, more resources overall and, most importantly, a political commitment to the Scheme on behalf of central government would have facilitated balanced programmes of profitable and non-profitable schemes.

Illustrated here is the necessity to examine practices pursued in a policy sector in addition to declarations of policy intent. The latter indicate a set of assumptions and values inherent in a policy sector but attention to practice illustrates actual commitment to a particular option. What is interesting, where the policy paradigm is ambiguous and contradictory, is the form of control employed to enforce desired action particularly when those responsible for implementation are not necessarily those involved in the formulation of policy. The administrative arrangements within the Land Scheme provide the key to understanding the control mechanisms employed throughout implementation.

Administrative arrangements

The organisational and financial details for the Scheme were documented earlier in the background to the CLS. In practice, throughout the life of the Scheme, the administrative role prescribed for central government ensured considerable control over the scope of the Act in England. The extent of control determined the limited performance by local authorities who were having to observe the strict rules on site identification, approval of schemes, terms of borrowing, the nature of disposal.

The administrative capacity of institutions to carry out certain duties is a significant theme of this paper. The concern with local autonomy assumes an interest in local bureaucracy and the extent of independence maintained from the centre (Blau 1969). Local authorities in England were not allocated many additional resources to support the CLS operation. Local government typically pursues a multiplicity of objectives and the Land Scheme was merely an additional piece of legislation to enact within the existing bureaucratic structure and with virtually the same level of staffing. But as organisations with multiple and conflicting objectives and different accountability mechanisms, there was capacity for interpretation of the Scheme in their own interests (S. Barrett et al (1978). The analysis shows how the scope of this local autonomy was severely limited by central government controls administered through the many guidance notes and circulars.

The evidence shows that central and local government objectives for the Land Scheme in England were fundamentally in conflict with one another. There was a clear difference between central and local government objectives for the Land Scheme, which hinged around the kind of benefits sought and the timescale within which they were expected. Central government's view stemmed largely from the way the Scheme had been structured as a self-financing, land trading system, and from original restrictions placed by the Exchequer on resources to be made available to the Scheme. The emphasis was on 'balancing the books' within a short timescale, to satisfy the Exchequer that the Scheme would indeed be self-financing and on achieving rapid through-put on land transactions to generate growth potential without additional call on public funds. The criteria for success for central government were to do with a healthy balance sheet and reductions in public borrowing. Local authorities, not surprisingly, viewed the Scheme as a source of <u>powers and funds</u> in the context of their overall responsibilities. Their emphasis was therefore on plan implementation and investment to achieve long-term economic and social benefits and to coordinate and control development, rather than short-term financial gains. In addition, the economic and political power of financial and property interests affected by the Land Scheme were such that the Conservative Party had pledged to repeal the Scheme in its manifesto. This concern was excessive given the constraints on activity and performance already imposed by the Labour Government but nevertheless the Scheme was still an important political issue for the Conservatives. As would be expected from the logic of these arguments, the Land Scheme was effectively stopped after the election by an immediate withdrawal of the Scheme and then totally repealed as far as England was concerned with the passing of the Local Government, Planning and Land Act, 1980.

The arguments contained in this discussion on the strength of bureaucratic control mechanisms, internal and dynamic to the organisation, or imposed from outside, appear to be consistent with the Marxist notion of bureaucracy (Mouzelis 1975; Giddens 1971). Central government's role in the formulation and implementation of the Land Scheme can be interpreted as bureaucracy consolidating and perpetuating the class division of labour which is implicit in the capitalist mode of production. The attempt by local authorities to pursue local social and economic objectives in the interest of the community can be interpreted as bureaucracy having a certain autonomy, making conflict with the capitalist class possible. The scope of this autonomy is, as Marx explained, determined by the existing forces and relations of production, in this case the private financial and property interests of the land market and development industry.

DISCUSSIONS AND CONCLUSIONS

The use of Benson's framework (1980) facilitated the search for structural explanations of social outcomes and reinforced the desirability to integrate macro and micro levels of organisational explanations. The discussion illustrated the way levels impinge and impact on other levels and the extent to which structural interests determine policy sector, inter-organisational dependencies and bureaucratic control mechanisms. In turn, these institutional forms of control have the capacity to reinforce administrative style and limit the ability to revise and change policy and procedures.

Central control and local autonomy

The major conclusion is the interaction of central/local government tensions with conflicts inherent in land use planning between the demands of private rights over development and the production of development for social need. The analysis of the Land Scheme described the legislation as a response to a situation of crisis generated by the dominance of the financial landownership interest and the state intervening to reduce these destabilising influences. The objective of the Scheme to recoup betterment in the interests of the community ('public profit') was nevertheless reduced in scope by the power of land and property interests concerned about their own profitability. Central government effectively sold out to local authorities by maintaining and preserving certain interests and neutralising the impact of 'public profit' on the profitability of key interests in the development market.

Central/local tensions also stem from the opposing objectives of the Scheme - 'positive planning' and 'public profit' (Cmnd.5730 1974), and the concern by central government to reduce the time horizons for profitability of the Scheme. This control was imposed by strict criteria for holding times and disposal to emphasise land trading and financial return. Local authorities contradicted central government by wanting to implement the 'positive planning' elements of the Scheme and pursue longer-term economic and social gains, or at least have the opportunity to prepare balanced programmes which took account of both objectives. Local authorities were constrained to do so by the restrictive financial and administrative procedures introduced by central government to encourage an emphasis on land 'trading'.

Since the early statements about the Land Scheme proposals were made in 1974 by John Silkin [9], the political and economic imperative for state intervention had, by 1975/76, been neutralised by changes in the economy and the land and property market. It is suggested that central government operated as an interest mediator between local authorities and the land, finance and property sectors in the context of a changing economic market. The instruments of mediation took the form of controls imposed by central government through expenditure cuts and reasserting the criteria for land holding times and disposal and through the inflexible controls on approvals for land acquisition.

It is also argued, following Benson (1980), that the perception of the land market policy sector in public debate did not correspond equally to the sector measured by resource dependencies. The ambiguities inherent in the Land Scheme support this point. Central government's perception of the market and relationships within the market, including the extent to which some local authorities were significant actors, was based upon uncertain information about an environment characterised by unpredictability. Irrespective of the intentions of the policy, symbolic or otherwise, the information around which government formulated its policy was a misconception of existing dependencies between interests. It then makes sense to interpret administrative changes as attempts to correct this mismatch.

Given the constraints set by the philosophy behind the legislative framework, in particular the conditions attached to the 1947 Town and Country Planning Act and the vesting in the state of development rights only (Ratcliffe 1973, 1976), there are some points of consensus between central and local government on responsibilities and roles and there is some scope for substitutability between the agencies involved. But in times of resource constraints overall, and a deterioration in central/local relations over questions of scope for action and autonomy at the local level, there is a tendency for issues of consensus to become severely strained. Analysis of the land, property and finance sectors points to the contradictions over land use and the role of central government to maintain and preserve the rights of certain influential private interests at the expense of the interests of local government and the community.

This conclusion should also be fed into the nationalisation debate referred to earlier (Massey and Catalano 1978). The main point was that full nationalisation of land was not a guarantee that questions of land use would be resolved because fundamental decisions would still rely on the exclusive rights of an individual agent – the state – and the nature of the relationship between agent and the development industry. Land nationalisation would not prevent the state intervening in a way which protected certain private production 'rights' in the same way as central government ran the Land Scheme in the interests of certain finance and property interests at the expense of local government and the community.

NOTES

[1] A number of authors criticise traditional organisational theory for the lack of political and structural insights, for example: B. Hern and D. Porter (1980); G. Salaman, (1979); P. Dunleavy, (1980); S. Clegg and D. Dunkerley, (1980)

[2] Structuralist writers who analyse on the basis of class, state function and address the historical dimension, contrast with the above. For example: R. Miliband, (1969); R. Miliband, (1977); J. Winkler, 'Corporatism', European Journal of Sociology, Vol.17; N. Poulantzas, (1973); J. O'Connor, (1973); C. Cockburn, (1978); P. Saunders, (1979); C. Offe, (1975).

[3] Guidance Note for Local Authorities (GNLA) 12, 1976, was the most important DOE instruction introducing major policy and procedural revisions.

[4] GNLA 20, DOE, 1979 curtailed expenditure under the CLS with the intention of repealing the CLA.

[5] Local Government Planning and Land Act 1980 abolished the CLA but retained the Land Authority for Wales.

[6] For the legal framework refer to Town and Country Planning Acts 1947, 1971; Local Government Act 1972.

[7] The 1947 Town and Country Planning Act introduced the first of three attempts by successive Labour governments to solve the compensation, betterment problem. the 1967 Finance Act introduced a capital gains tax and the 1967 Land Commission Act introduced a betterment levy. (All three attempts, 1947, 1967 and 1974 were abolished by incoming Conservative Governments.)

[8] This project monitoring the implementation of the Community Land Scheme was funded by central government through the Department of the Environment (DOE).

[9] John Silkin was the Labour Minister responsible for putting together the Land Scheme and pushing it through Parliament in 1975.

REFERENCES

Barrett, S. et al (1978) 'Implementation of the Community Land Scheme', Occasional Paper 3, School for Advanced Urban Studies.
Barrett, S. and Whitting, G. (1983) 'Local Authorities and Land Supply', Occasional Paper 10, School for Advanced Urban Studies.
Benson, J. K. (1980) 'Interorganisational Networks and Policy Sectors: notes towards comparative analysis', University of Missouri, Columbia.
Blau, P. (1969) 'The Dynamics of Bureaucracy' in Etzioni ed. A Sociological Reader on Complex Organisations, Holt, Rinehart and Winston.
Burrell, G. and Morgan, G. (1979), Sociological Paradigms and Organisational Analysis, HEB, pp.365-390
Dunleavy, P. (1980), Urban Political Analysis, MacMillan
Giddens, A. (1971) Capitalism and Modern Social Theory, CUP
Hall, P. (1973), The Containment of Urban England, Allen & Unwin
Cmnd.5730, LAND HMSO 1974
Community Land Act, HMSO 1975
Local Government Planning and Land Act;, HMSO 1980
Massey, D. and Catalano A. (1978), Capital and Land, Edward Arnold.
Mouzelis, N. P. (1975) Organisation and Bureaucracy, Routledge and Kegan Paul.
Offe, C. (1975), 'The Theory of the Capitalist State and the problem of policy formation' in Lundberg, Alford, Crouch and Offe, Stress and Contradiction in Modern Capitalism, Lexington Books.
Ratcliffe, J. (1976), Land Policy, Hutchinson
Ratcliffe, J. (1979), An Introduction to Urban Land Administration, Estates Gazette.
Saunders, P. (1979), Urban Politics, Hutchinson.

9 The labour movement, local politics and spatial sociology: some recent Danish experience

JENS CHR. TONBOE
Institute of Development and Planning, University of Aalborg

INTRODUCTION

The relationship between the local labour movement (labour parties and local unions) and local politics in Denmark today seems to present a strategic starting point for the study of three problem areas, namely relations between the central and local state; between the Social Democratic Party and the unions, and relations between spatial–geographical structures and social processes.

These are normally treated in isolation, but it would seem fruitful to approach them in their everyday relationships.

CENTRAL–LOCAL STATE RELATIONS

Where have the last 10 years of restructuring the Danish public sector taken us in regard to the functional relations between the central state apparatus and local municipal institutions? Many collective service functions have grown dramatically while at the same time being decentralised, with financial responsibility being thrust upon the municipalities. At the same time the state budget has increasingly been used to regulate municipal and sector activities, especially during the cut-back period beginning in 1979–80. Evidence seems to support Saunders's dual-state theory: the division between an investment oriented state level, and a service-consumer-oriented municipal level (Saunders 1979, 1981).

On the other hand, real life seems to be more diverse and dynamic than Saunders's ideal type would indicate. Of prime interest for our purpose are class dimensions which seem to be of more importance for local politics compared with possible consumption-based alliances crossing class lines as suggested by Saunders and Dunleavy (Saunders 1982, Cawson and Saunders 1983, Dunleavy 1979). At least class relations and class conflicts seem to have been reactivated after a period of dormancy. Here our observations are closer to Cooke's, when he shows how class competition cuts through territorial/functional based relations (Cooke 1983). In fact we may have to reverse the argument and, with Valentin (1981) claim that it is national rather then local politics which are blurred by user and corporatist structures. (Valentin 1981), Alternatively we may claim that while central state policy is carried through by (bourgeois) capitalist interests for production and profit, local politics is increasingly based on wage earners' interests in reproduction and their standard of living. We arrive, so to speak, at built-in class conflict within the political-administrative system which can be particularly central and dynamic in a way we have not met before (Tonboe 1981a). Perhaps these differences from Saunders's thesis derive from differences in time or from real differences between the allocation of services in Britain and Denmark as well as differences in the social-economic structures involved in local politics. Danish municipalities have greater functional and fiscal independence with more capital responsibilities than the British, where to a larger degree local state agencies supplement and direct municipal activities.

The relationship between labour unions and the Social Democratic Party has been analysed at length and with insight at the national and international-comparative level (Przeworski 1977, 1980; Minkin 1978; von Beyme 1978; Ibsen and Jørgensen 1979; Christensen 1981; Bild 1977, 1981). However, whereas the theoretical depth and historical perspective is impressive, an essential source of dynamics in that relationship has escaped these studies: the concrete links between economic-material, organisational and political structures, as well as on matters with a direct bearing on unions and their members, such as employment, pay, standards of living, union structure and organisation, infrastructure and service, and employment policy at the local level. The most important "mediator" between the economic-production sphere and statal-political sphere i.e. what we with Gramsci and Gouldner call the Civil Society, is almost absent in those analyses (Gramsci 1971, Gouldner 1980). Nevertheless, what we observe at the national level of party activity is - one way or another - "reflections" of economic, sociological and political conditions and relations on the local and personal level. Although there has been much abstract discussion about structural contra personal causal relations, and about democratisation and bureaucratisation, we know very little about the actual process of this so-called "reflection". Urry's and Flynn's plea for studies of local labour movements, class structures and municipal policy seems well justified (Urry 1981, 1983, Flynn 1983). It is of special importance here to shed light on the increased political orientation of labour and the tendency towards more and more serious conflicts between labour unions and the Social Democratic Party.

The relationship between physical-material structure and social-political processes remains an almost unexplored area in recent urban sociological research or, more precisely, is unknown to the "map" of spatial sociology. The revolt against the "wisdom of the elders" - social physics and the human ecology of the Chicago School - led by David Harvey and Manuel Castells (Harvey 1973, Castells 1977, Harloe 1977), tabooed the subject and concentrated efforts almost exclusively on explorations of the economic, political and ideological background to spatial structures. Again Urry's and Giddens's plea for the introduction of the spatial aspect into critical analysis is a justified contribution (Giddens 1979, 1981; Urry 1981a,b), and both Urry's and Cooke's recent research in this direction is promising (Cooke 1983; Urry 1983). Considering the geographical variations in class structure and behaviour and in political power constellations, general aggregated analysis of these relations on the national level appear to be more or less meaningless. The same applies to the analysis of municipal-state relations by authors like Hirsch and Grümer (1974). Perhaps it is precisely these geographical variations that have hindered the recognition of class phenomena, especially when approached from a more abstract, generalising theoretical basis? Nonetheless, it is exactly through local variations and processes that class relations appear and are reproduced, just as it is only on this level that relations between economic-material and political-organisational processes and resulting structures obtain their real meaning.

The fact that these three apparently independent areas are, in reality, closely related and ought to be approached and analysed as such, can be seen from our studies of the local labour movement in North Jutland. From this we can point to significant mutual relations between economic, organisational and political structures and levels, and to relationships between those and personal-civil activities, which see in particular local characteristics, (variations in time and space), a meaningful response to the fundamental general relations between labour and capital, state and society, production and reproduction. We arrive at this new perspective almost automatically, as we take our departure from the local labour movement and its relations to local material-economic conditions, and to the local state - the municipality and county.

However, our research is not yet complete and cannot be said to deal fully with the problems raised above. We have only entered into a partial class analysis, with the main weight on the traditional labour class and its local political-economic power structure. The main emphasis is placed on the local as opposed to the national. At present what we offer is a comparative analysis of two out of the five municipalities researched, on the basis of part of the collected material (Møller and Tonboe 1983 a,b; Tonboe (1981a; 1983).

Though based on this analysis, what follows is a provisional attempt to develop and justify the position outlined above.

THE MUNICIPALITY AND LOCAL UNIONS

The role of the municipality, as opposed to that of the regional and national levels of government, grew quantitatively and qualitatively during the period 1970-82. This restructuring was directed administratively by the municipal reform of 1970, and economically by the budget reform of 1977. In addition there was the development of the national-local planning system dealing with the sectors of health, environment, traffic etc., and a thoroughgoing decentralisation of town planning between 1972 and 1974 (Bogason 1978). What was decentralised and further developed at the municipal level was not only the HEW functions, but also work on the infrastructure services such as roads and housing. However, at the same time as this decentralisation took place, the government tightened its control over standards for different services, as well as those for investment and expenditure.

The number of public employees reflects this development. While full-time government personnel increased from 1972 to 1983 by 20,000 to a total of 200,000, the municipal personnel in the same period increased by 210,000 to 468,000.

The share of the local and regional authorities of public expenditure grew to 47% in 1981 and to well over 50% in 1983.

Of great significance for the financing of local authorities is the taxation of income and property, which now covers almost half of total local expenditure. The rest is mainly covered by block grants (ca.20%) and by refunds of various kinds (averaging 15%). Between 1970 and 1983 local authority tax rates increased from an average of 16% to an average of 25%, actually varying between 17% and 29%. (Mouritzen 1983; Skovsgaard and Søndergaard 1983). As part of this decentralisation and the development of local autonomy, the central contribution to the municipalities was switched from special grants to unhypothecated block grants. And it is these block grants which are now being cut back.

The rate of increase in public expenditure, especially that of local authorities, has been increasingly limited by the government since 1980. By threatening legislative action, the state has in effect forced municipalities not to increase their total expenditure or their tax rates. At the same time, local authorities' expenditures on unemployment programmes and public relief have greatly increased. Typically municipalities have reacted to this crisis by reducing capital expenditure drastically. Such expenditure fell by 13% per year between 1979 and 1981, with a further reduction of 25% planned for 1983.

The activities of local authorities have been limited even more than the public sector as a whole, especially with regard to health, education and welfare services and for building and construction (Mouritzen 1983a). By contrast state support, direct and indirect, to private business has climbed by 11-12% per year (Ministry of Finance 1983). Further investments in other infrastructure programmes, (energy, communication, traffic), have increased. In spite of government regulation, and marked cutback of service standards and investment, the municipal tax rate has also continued to increase. Thus people who depend more than ever on the public sector are forced to pay more for inferior services. Unemployment has now climbed up to 12% of the work force (autumn 1983), and in a number of municipalities to more than 20%, due in part to cutbacks in local expenditures and services. The number of long-term unemployed dependent on the local municipality for retraining is greatly increasing.

Like the rest of Scandinavia, wage-earners in Denmark are highly organised. Though we can distinguish between three types of unions (for academics, functionaries and workers), they all have something special in common, namely that the fundamental basis of the union structure is still skill based. Only in part of the economy are there unions based on particular sectors or industries.

At the top of the "wage-earner class" we find 18 individual unions (academics) gather in AC (Academic Central Organisation) with 99,000 members (economists, lawyers, engineers, high-school teachers etc.). Typically these unions have only one national section, sometimes with subsections, and with clubs, representatives or shop-stewards in larger institutions or firms both in the public and private sector.

Second, there are 85 unions for functionaries and civil servants (school teachers, nurses, bank functionaries, social workers etc.) who are amalgamated in the FTF with about 334,000 members. Like AC, FTF is in principle politically "neutral", as the few unions which are markedly political can vary from the extreme left to the conservative right.

Finally, there are the traditional unions of manual workers, lower functionaries and public workers. There are 35 national unions gathered together in the LO (the Danish TUC) with 1,340,000 members. It is here that we find the politicalised union movement working closely with the Social Democratic Party, the most important "working class" party. And it is precisely this interaction between the LO unions and Social Democracy at the local level which provides the focus of the discussion which follows.

Together with the Social Democratic Party the, LO and its members provide, at least formally, one of the largest and most important political power structures in Denmark. From around 1879, this importance rested on a clear division of labour between the economic struggle (undertaken by the unions) and the political struggle (undertaken by the Social Democratic Party). Locally, as well as nationally, there is mutual representation between the organisations of the party and those of the unions, including also some of the co-operative production units which still exist. A growing and direct political alliance nationally between the national unions and LO in particular has clearly emerged during the last twenty years, during the corporative phase (1969-82). In this period of politics the state regularly intervened in collective bargaining and instituted laws regulating the labour market and conditions of labour, as well as attempting to introduce genuine tripartism on many occasions (Ibsen 1983; Ibsen and Jørgensen 1979). However, the direct political engagement of local unions at the local level has been of a more recent date and of another character.

These new activities at the local level are based on local and regional union associations (FO), which were developed in their present structure after the municipal reform of 1970, reflecting the administrative and functional structures and geographical borders laid down by that reform. However, most local unions are not based on municipal borders, but rather on local economic structures, production centres, plant location etc., and therefore often cross municipal lines. The local (municipal) association of unions, which in some places had already existed before the reform of 1970, originally had the task of co-ordinating the organised economic struggle among the unions at the local level. As the national unions and LO developed, this function was centralised. The restructuring and spread of local associations of unions after 1970 added local political work to the previous functions of the FOs. FOs are now found in almost half of the country's 275 municipalities, and no longer only in larger towns. The 14 regional FOs (FO associations) in Denmark's 14 counties are new. Besides dealing with regional politics and development policy (development agencies), they co-ordinate and serve the municipal FOs. And in turn they are served and directed by the LO to a large extent.

However, the qualitative differences between local and national political activity have still not been accounted for and documented. The gradual breakdown of the division of labour between the party and the unions on the national level, due to the increasing political orientation of the unions, can clearly be traced back to a series of fundamental structural changes.

First, the increased intervention of the public sector in the general production-reproduction process, due partly to the period in political power of the Social Democratic Party, has made political activity especially important to union members, not least from a broad welfare perspective

Second, the Social Democratic Party's class basis (members, voters) has gradually moved towards the middle of the political and occupational spectrum, not least in terms of its parliamentary representation. This is now overwhelmingly dominated by public sector employees at the expense of workers. Some of this change is due to changes in production/reproduction structures, but a good deal derives from the party's attempt to obtain maximum support in terms of votes and mandates. Naturally, personal qualifications and aspirations also play a part in this development. All in all the Social Democratic Party has developed into a typical catch-all-party, resulting in a shift of its political aims and profile (von Beyme (1978), Minkin (1978), Bild (1977)). Even though the party and the unions have much in common, the party's change in support and aims has put it on a collision course with the unions.

When the state and employers, through intervention in the crisis, hinder improvement and even worsen employment, salary and working conditions of union members, it is quite natural that the unions turn their attention and resources towards the political sphere and collective consumption of goods and services.

This situation also obtains, generally, to local political activity by the unions, but in addition there are a series of other factors to be noted.

First, to begin with, it is the local, rather than the central government, reproduction functions that most directly affect the working class today. While the central state formally acts as a generally directing force, it frequently operates, at least currently, as a counterweight which limits the municipalities' responsibilities and resources to the advantage of owners of capital, who are supported by central government policies and financial aid.

Second, the municipalities not only play a central role in the public sector but are more important employers of labour than is the centre. In the FTF more than half of the members are employed by municipalities, and a further 1/4 by central government. In most localities, the municipality is the largest employer of LO-members, and is the dominating counterpart to a series of local unions, even though collective bargaining is negotiated centrally between national unions of municipalities and counties. On average, between one third and one quarter of local LO members are employed by the municipality or are indirectly dependent, as employees of private firms, on municipal construction activities. In some unions a majority are employed by the municipalities (Municipal Workers, Cleaners and Domestic Workers) or they form a rather large proportion (Commercial and Clerical Workers, General Workers). In addition, there are municipal retraining programmes for the unemployed and an increasing municipal involvement with local occupational training and local industrial policy.

Third, in comparison with national policy-making processes, local processes are far less corporative, and far more characterised by class contradictions. The corporative tendencies at national level are due mainly to the Social Democratic Party and its politically dominant position, at

136

least until the Conservative minority government arrived in 1982. By contrast, the Social Democratic Party is clearly in the minority in most municipalities, and more or less in opposition. Only in the large urban municipalities does the S.D.P. have substantial influence and/or a majority position, and consequently a significant participation by organisations in local political processes.

Among the most significant consequences of the political-organisational involvement of unions in local politics is its contribution to the growing split between the central government and the municipalities. This leads, at least in the short run, to further contradictions between production/reproduction and capital/labour. In the long term such local involvement will probably encourage local politics to become more production orientated. Both perspectives are subjected to overall economic fluctuations and developments in production technology. Another consequence is that local political activity involving co-operation between local unions will contribute to the decentralisation of union efforts, thus possibly weakening the national unions and LO.

THE NORTH JUTLAND CASE

The general tendency for an increase in union participation in local politics can be illustrated by the following statistics from Northern Jutland.

In the period 1978-81, the Social Democratic Party had 173 seats or 32% on the 27 municipal councils and the county council. Together with the other parties and groupings on the left, they had 182 or 34%. At the 1981 local election, the party dropped to 163 seats or 30%, while the total of left-wing mandates climbed to 185 seats or 35%. There was thus a weak radicalisation both within the municipal councils and on the Left. At the same time the share of union representation on the Left climbed from 15% to 18%, due, amongst other things, to quite extensive political work from the union side. Normally the Social Democratic list was supported as a whole, but in 1981 in many places voters supported only the union candidates on the list. Generally the unions were not satisfied because union representatives were placed low on the S.D.P. list, where their chances for election were small, especially when one takes into account the fact that the Party's political battle was largely financed by the Unions. In many places the unions even wished to present their own list, something so out of the ordinary that it would automatically lead to the exclusion of those so listed from the party.

A great deal of the dissatisfaction from the union side can be explained by some other figures from the 1981 election. Before 1981, 48% of the left-wing voters were public employees who form around 30% of the work force. After the election, it was 54%. Since school teachers represent a significant part of these, the problem, which was quite clear to the unions, can be termed the unions' "school-teacher syndrome". On the one side one acknowledges that professional workers in the public sector have the time, abilities and insight which are necessary for political work: but at the same time others felt that the standpoint and interests of the workers are not always properly represented. Many workers refuse to support the Party in that situation or, in protest, cast their votes to the left or right of the S.D.P. Normally the Party obtains more local votes at parliamentary elections than at municipal.

In our research we have attempted to explain how the labour movement, and the Social Democratic Party in particular, has co-operated with the bourgeois-liberal group in the town council. In one North Jutland municipality, Hjørring has co-operated with the bourgeois-liberal group in the town council, while in another municipality, Dronninglund, where, with the same relative strength, they have been in opposition. We wished to investigate further what effects might follow from co-operation or opposition.

Though the two municipalities are of the same size geographically, Hjørring, an urban municipality, has twice as many inhabitants as the rural municipality, Dronninglund (30,000 against about 15,000).

Originally Hjørring was an old county and trade centre, but during the sixties it became industrialised. It is today North Jutland's second largest union stronghold, just after Aalborg, the regional centre. The Association of Unions (FO) in Hjørring has 10,500 members, and the largest unions are the Commercial and Clerical Workers (24%) and the General Workers (24%), with a subsidiary group of unions of similar size (Municipal Workers, Women Workers, Metal Workers and Cleaners and Domestic Workers).

Until 1974 local politics were dominated by the Conservative Party, but in that year the Social Democratic Party formalised co-operation with the Liberals, who gained the Mayor's seat. Since then it is primarily the Liberals who have gained seats, and the left-wing opposition to the S.D.P., previously with no seats, now has two.

Dronninglund still remains a typical rural municipality with a number of small towns throughout. In contrast to Hjørring, Dronninglund is still growing in industrial employment, but even so the unions remain quantitatively weak. Of the 2,700 members of the Association of Unions almost half are from the General Workers, and the leadership is dominated completely by unskilled workers and Clerical Workers. The Liberals regularly hold the Mayor's office, while the Social Democratic Party, aggressively in opposition, have increased their seats from 5 to 7 during two elections (1974 and 1978). Since 1978 there has been a "General Workers List", which has gathered the union left wing, but as they still have only one seat they cannot be taken as a serious threat to the Social Democratic Party. Within the municipalities there are a number of commuters to larger towns outside, which means that a great deal of those skilled workers employed in industry, building and construction etc. work outside, and are thus not represented in the unions in Dronninglund.

Table 1. Distribution of Employment in Municipalities 1980 %

	HJØRRING	DRONNINGLUND
Agriculture	10	21
Manufacturing	17	14
Building and Construction	7	9
Commerce and Hotel etc.	16	15
Transport	4	4
Banking, Finance	8	5
Education	7	6
Public Services	16	15
Public Administration	10	7
Other services (publ.& private)	5	3
Undeclared	–	1
TOTAL	100	100
N	16.649	7.391

Sources: Denmark's Statistics. Registered Workforce. September 1982

Third, if we try to explain why the political strategy of the Social Democratic Party in the two municipalities differs, as far as Hjørring is concerned, the answer seems as follows.

After a great electoral defeat in 1974, the Conservatives attempted to exclude both the Liberals and Social Democrats – the two largest groups – from political influence by keeping

189

the Mayoralty and committee chairmanships. They attempted to continue the bourgeois coalition without thinking about co-operation with the Left. Dissatisfaction amongst the Liberals and Social Democrats, as well as personal ambitions in both groups, forced them into a formal coalition where the two Parties shared the leading posts. At the same time they entered into agreements on a series of issues, the most important of which were the maintenance of high service levels, with taxes, especially property tax, kept to existing levels. The reason why this co-operation could take place without serious resistance within the two parties depended on the following conditions.

First and foremost is the economic structure. Most of the industrial employment in Hjørring was, and is, in the processing of agricultural products and in the production and repair of machines and buildings for agriculture. In 1974 agricultural productivity and its affiliated industries steadily improved. Furthermore, many of those employed in food industries were formerly farmers or from a rural background. As the numbers employed in agriculture dropped sharply, many sought industrial employment. Small farmers with full-time industrial employment have also become widespread.

Political co-operation between workers (Social Democrats) and farmers (Liberals) was therefore only a natural extension of the mutual economic dependence which already existed. The socialist class consciousness of the unions was weakened by farmers who were rarely active members, and by many who were first-generation workers.

Second, however, the organisational/structural relations have played and continue to play an independent role, itself strongly influenced by economic structures and, also, by spatial structures. While the Social Democratic Party in the one-town-dominated municipality is centralised in one party organisation, the unions are divided. The distribution of trades is even, and the two unions, which together almost form a majority, have neither professional nor political interests in common (Commercial and Clerical Workers and General Workers). The board of the Association of Unions has seven members representing seven different unions, and none of them will allow any other to dominate. The result is that the labour movement speaks with many tongues, none particularly strongly or clearly. Thus, structure, union conflicts, and organisational structures neutralise the political resources of the labour movement, especially when confronted with the more centralised and more decisive Social Democratic Party, itself dominated by moderate public employees with political ambitions of their own, since public employment has grown even faster than industrial employment, not least in local regional and state institutions.

As for Dronninglund, the situation is rather different. Politically, the Liberals, the farmers' party, have always been the dominating party in the bourgeois bloc. The Social Democrats have always played the role of opposition, originally based on farmhands, unskilled workers and skilled workers in building and construction. The growth in the public sector strengthened the party notably. It could make deals with the Liberals, who felt themselves secure in power, but who also supported an increase in spending on housing and other public services. The relationship between the Liberals and the Social Democrats on the political level was thus characterised more by competition than by co-operation or conflict.

As far as Dronninglund's economic structure is concerned there is no (nor has there ever been) any important relationship between farmers and workers. Agricultural products are not made in Dronninglund, and the local agricultural service industry is of minor importance. Many people work outside the municipality: they only live there. Cheap houses have been readily available in Dronninglund. Later on an abundance of public services attracted new citizens. Local industrial employment had been stagnating for a long time, and not until the end of the seventies did it begin to grow again. It was the unskilled and uncertain work connected with house building and later with public construction activity which dominated the unions and union structure, and later the increasing numbers of public sector workers.

The spatial structure of the municipality is made up of competing small towns and rural areas, where local loyalties often mean more than any party allegiance. Each local area has its own set of party organisations and its own representatives on the municipal council, they often compete with the representatives from other local areas for municipal services. Together they attempt to expand budgets and raise the tax rate, so that there will be enough for all of them to have a share of the cake. The common party leadership is subjected to pressure from the seven small local Social Democratic Party organisations, and attempts to resist by instituting a more principled socialistic line. On the other hand the unions are relatively united and have the strength to pursue a more or less left-wing labour policy. The General Workers' Union is the only union which is large enough to support a local section in the municipality, and together with

191

other unskilled and the Commercial and Clerical Workers they completely dominate the local Association of Unions. The labour movement in Dronninglund is small enough to be directed and developed by a small dynamic informal leadership, which usually achieves good results in competition with not always inspired farmers on the defensive.

Table 2: Current and Capital Expenditure per inhabitant in Hjørring and Dronninglund 1978–83. (Kr. per inhabitant)

Year	Hjørring		Dronninglund	
	Current	Capital	Current	Capital
1978	5200	1400	5000	400
1979	5700	1300	5650	350
1980	6000	1100	6500	300
1981	12000	1800	11200	1000
1982	23000	1700	21500	500
1983	25250	1600	25250	100

Naturally, this is a quite simplified presentation of a far more complex structure; more of a snapshot than a film record. So far, we have discussed the situation up to the end of the seventies: now we turn to more recent developments.

The municipal budget gives a good impression of municipal activities, especially the reactions to the economic crises of the last few years.

We see in Table 2 the municipal outlays during the real expansion period in Denmark for the two municipalities. It is worth noting that while the two budgets are quite similar for current expenditure, they differ quite markedly for capital expenditure. This seems to raise questions about local autonomy. By deflating and indexing the figures, we can obtain a more precise picture of real growth which will enable a better comparison to be made.

We can see in Tables 3–5 that Dronninglund maintained a high level of current expenditure at the cost of their capital expenditure and, as we shall see later, a higher level of taxation. Both the cut in capital expenditure and the increased tax rates fall harder on the traditional manual worker than on any other group in society. Not only do many

Table 3: Calculated, indexed real increase for current expenditure per inhabitant in Hjørring and Dronninglund. 1978-83.

	Hjørring	Dronninglund
1978	100	100
1979	100	100
1980	100	100
1981	150	140
1982	240	235
1983	180	184

Table 4: Calculated, indexed real increase for capital expenditure per inhabitant in Hjørring and Dronninglund 1978-83.

	Hjørring	Dronninglund
1978	100	100
1979	85	90
1980	75	75
1981	100	95
1982	80	80
1983	60	5

Table 5: Calculated, indexed real increase for current and capital expenditure per inhabitant in Hjørring and Dronninglund municipalities 1978-83. 1978 = 100.
Av. increase in prices = 10%

	Hjøring	Dronninglund
1978	100	100
1979	98	99
1980	110	95
1981	140	145
1982	190	190
1983	160	175

of them lose their jobs, but they are forced to pay a higher tax on their unemployment compensation, while at the same time, being poor, having no possibility of tax reductions.

In reality the differences in welfare services of social institutions, schools etc. in the two municipalities are relatively small, with Dronninglund maintaining a somewhat higher standard. Both rank somewhat higher than the national

average. The real significance of this is apparent only when
we compare service levels with financial resources available,
especially with regard to children's institutions, where there
is real local autonomy and variation. It is on these services
that the Social Democrats in Dronninglund since 1975 have
pressed more than any other party in the municipal council. In
relation to its tax base and compared to similar
municipalities, Dronninglund offers services of an
impressively high standard, while the direct opposite is true
of Hjørring.

The average income in Dronninglund and thus the average tax
base per taxpayer is lower than in Hjørring (32,000 kr.
compared to 37,000 kr. with a county average of 36,300 kr. in
1980). In order to maintain the same and in some areas even
higher service level than in Hjørring (the wish of the
political majority), Dronninglund requires a far higher tax
rate than in Hjørring (22.5% compared to 17.7% in 1983). In
1984 as well as in 1981, Dronninglund had the nation's highest
local taxes. Thus every single taxpayer in Dronninglund pays
20% more in local tax than in Hjørring. As local tax in
Denmark is not progressive, the burden falls most heavily on
the lowest income groups and on those with the lowest tax
deductions, i.e. unskilled workers, pensioners and the
unemployed, the number of which is increasing. Thus the
members of LO lose income and perhaps their jobs due to
municipal cutbacks, which mainly, when the service levels are
maintained, affect municipal construction works (investment
capital). Public employees on the service side (working
capital) keep their jobs at the very least.

Unemployment in Dronninglund is traditionally higher than in
Hjørring and higher than the regional and national average. In
1981, for example, it has 17% compared to 15% in Hjørring and
13% for Denmark as a whole. But variations between unions as
well as between corresponding unions in the two municipalities
are considerable. The Clothing and Textile Workers in
Hjørring in 1982 had, for example, 41% unemployed, while
Cleaners and Domestic Workers had 6%, and Carpenters 28%. The
corresponding figures for Dronninglund in the same period were
16%, 17% and 19%. Unemployment and the reasons behind it have
become extremely significant to the members' and the Unions'
political orientation and activities. Generally, it is the
problem of employment rather than wages that leads the union
agenda. In 1982 the Building and Construction sector,
comprising 14% of the insured workers in Hjørring, contributed
33% of total unemployment and 52% of the unemployment amongst
men. There were corresponding figures for Dronninglund. As
employment in this sector is particularly sensitive to
political decisions at the national and local level, it is

here that we find part of the explanation for the fact that it is the skilled and unskilled workers precisely from this sector who are especially politically active. Employment in the metal industry on the other had depends more on international conjunctures and long-term national cost policy, that is, a policy that will be in direct conflict in many ways with a policy which favours construction activities and/or stimulates consumption. It follows therefore that there is political disagreement within the labour movement locally. Unemployment amongst Metal Workers is more stable and generally lower than the national average, aside from which the Metal Workers are better paid. They are, therefore, less politically active, especially on the local level, and more conservative and market-oriented, especially when compared to the supporters of state intervention amongst the unskilled, locally-dependent unions (General Workers, Women Workers, Domestic Workers etc.). Though Metal Workers is only the third largest union next to General Workers and Commercial and Clerical Workers, it has great influence in the labour movement. It is well organised, has large economic resources, and more often behaves as an ally of the Conservative government rather than as a member of the Social Democratic opposition.

We can summarise the costs and benefits of co-operation and competition in Hjørring and Dronninglund, in short, as follows.

In Hjørring in the short run political co-operation gave personal political influence to a few Social Democrats, a reasonable maintenance of services and of construction and investment activities together with a low tax rate. In the short run these economic gains for the workers were limited, if one relates them to the service improvements which could have been achieved in this municipality without large cost increases. One might also add that the economic gains were more than offset by the political losses suffered by the Social Democrats and the Social Democratic labour movement. A left-wing opposition resulted, and splits occurred between the party and the unions, especially between public and private employees.

In the long run many things point to the fact that previous co-operation with the Liberals will encourage new organisational and ideological struggles and gains as a reaction. The reactions in the unions against the previous political achievements have now grown so strong and active that it is about to drag the Social Democrats away from co-operation with the Liberals towards a more marked, socialist labour policy. If this succeeds without service and

195

taxation policy becoming unbalanced, then the Social Democrats, together with the left wing, the unions, as well as part of the public service workers, could possibly form an electoral majority that has previously not been activated.

In Dronninglund there were in both service and politics gains to be noted in the short run. The number of Social Democratic voters and seats increased election after election. Co-operation between party and unions, private and public employees, manual workers and functionaries has apparently strengthened and deepened. When the crisis became really serious in 1981, it became quite clear that the public sector and services had expanded beyond what local sources could hope to provide. And when at the same time it became clear that the majority of the municipal council (including the Social Democrats) would sacrifice construction activities as well as the necessary supplies for institutions in favour of maintaining service jobs, severe conflicts became apparent. Significant groups in the unions began to distance themselves from the party, some leaving the party completely. The General Workers, the Women and the Domestics, who lost their jobs due to public sector cutbacks whilst Clerical Workers and functionaries kept theirs at the same time as taxes climbed and services declined, were clearly angered. The unity of the party and the unions cracked, and antagonism towards public employees broke out. A "left-wing" opposition to the Social Democrats based on public employees may now develop, but the split in the labour movement will prevent the formation of a left-wing majority in the municipal council for many years.

Before we jump to conclusions, two further areas will be investigated in order to illuminate the three themes sketched in the introduction: the significance of spatial dimensions, party-union relations and municipal-state relations.

The first area is an attempt to explore the significance of the fact that the Social Democratic Party and the unions are organised on a widely different basis geographically. This difference poses another and more fundamental problem from that of the varying organisational structures and resources from municipality to municipality, which we already have discussed.

Generally the party is organised according to administrative-political borders, i.e. borders of municipalities and counties, and is therefore naturally well-suited to mark itself on the parliamentary-political scene, especially concerning questions of reproduction, as membership is based on residence. On the other hand, local unions arise from the area and location of economic activity and plant structure. Historically, the organised economic struggle bases itself on the production sphere, whereas the political struggle mainly derives from and influences the reproduction sphere. As a rule, a local union embraces at least the area that would give a satisfactory membership in order that it may maintain a "battle post": office staff, economic resources etc. Today a minimum of between 500 and 1000 members is necessary. This means that a union can cover part of a municipality to many municipalities, and can on occasion cut through municipalities, dependent on where employment is available and on the density of plants. In other words, unions have widely differing spatial boundaries.

We can gain an impression of the significance of these boundaries for our two municipalities, Hjørring and Dronninglund. The union centre at Hjørring houses 23 local unions, while in Dronninglund there is only one office, the General Workers. Also, most of the unions in Hjørring, with the exception of General Workers, cover other municipalities, with which they may also be politically involved. Similarly in Dronninglund there are unions which lie outside the municipality, mainly in the regional centre, Aalborg, which can have political interests in Dronninglund. Normally a union would concentrate on its main base, that is concentrate the resources of the whole section there, but generally the more municipalities they cover, the more likely they are to hold back from local political engagement, and consequently be more interested in county politics. The Clericals in Aalborg, for example, which covers Dronninglund, also covers over 16 other municipalities. In Dronninglund, however, it means that the General Workers are alone on the local political scene, and are more or less free to push their own interests. Thus the General Workers-dominated Association of Unions has developed into an alternative or a supplement to the Social Democratic Party, which furthermore is divided into seven sub-sections in that municipality.

On the other hand, there are many unions in Hjørring with a different area basis. This often results in competing interests representing the union movement in the municipal council, the Association of Unions, and in the Social Democratic Party itself. At the same time, they have to compete with the unions of functionaries and civil servants (FTF), many of whom have local branches in Hjørring. It is obviously much easier for the party to represent the labour movement as a whole, though this of course would bring the conflict between public and private employees to a head much more openly. Nevertheless, political engagement in the local unions is increasing.

This development says something about the relations between party and unions, and the unions and local politics, where spatial structures are a mediating factor between economic structures, class interests and politics.

Another area where we can penetrate beneath the surface of things in order to shed more light on our three theoretical themes is to concentrate on the significance of the public sector to the local economy by examining the local economic effect of public employment.

From 1970-80 the share of public employees in the work force in Hjørring climbed from 21% to 33%, and has increased since to almost 35%. Amongst women in the work force, 46% are publicly employed, while men account for only 20%.

In Dronninglund between 1970 and 1980 the proportion grew from 14% to 27%, among women from 32% to 48%, and among men from 7% to 12%.

The proportion of women who work in the two municipalities is about 60% (close to the national average), and in Dronninglund 74% of all public employees are women, compared to 63% in Hjørring.

If we now adopt a "family perspective", and assume that both incomes in the household are "necessary", a rapid calculation will show that about half of all wage owner households depend directly on public employment. If further we add those that are indirectly dependent upon public construction and investments, public use of private services, together with the unemployed, the pensioners and those on public relief, we can see quite clearly then that more than half of the total population in these municipalities is economically wholly dependent on the public sector: far more than half of the voters. Even though the conditions for that dependence – and available resources – are certainly not controlled locally in all cases, nevertheless this means that the public sector plays a more significant role at the local level than at the national. Furthermore, the local state operates on different premises and has different functions from the central state. This difference becomes quite clear when we take into account the character of local services and infrastructure.

We can also illustrate the whole problem in another way by listing the main divisions of public employees according to number and total salary.

Table 6. Employees and salaries in the public sector in Hjørring 1982.

	Number employed	Salary (mill.kr) ca.
Municipal Jobs	2,253	270
County Jobs	1,495	225
Government Jobs	1,200	200
TOTAL	5,948	695

Sources: Budget for Hjørring, Dronninglund og Nordjyllands Amtskommune. 1983.

Around half of the municipal jobs are financed locally via municipal taxes. Expenses for county jobs are shared with the whole county and state on the basis of a relatively modest tax of about 6%. The same principle, but to a higher degree, holds for government jobs. For the municipality, half of their own jobs and almost all county and government jobs are financed from outside the locality. However, in terms of the local economy, municipal jobs are just as good "base-industries" as employment in industry, construction etc.

We can now make a comparison with industrial jobs. In Hjørring in 1982 there were 2,300 employed in industry, with salaries totalling around 300 mill.kr., which in terms of the local economy is somewhat lower than the value of local county and state employment. In Dronninglund in 1982 there were 500 industrial jobs with salaries of about 70 mill.kr., also somewhat below the local economic value of total public employment. If we then introduce state and county taxes, which leave the municipality again, and compare them to the municipal taxes which remain, we can see the difference between "well-to-do" Hjørring (with many public jobs) and "poor" Dronninglund (with fewer county and government institutions). Dronninglund pays more to the county of North Jutland and to central government than it gets back directly, taking refunds and block grants into account. On the other hand, there is a net surplus in Hjørring, which certainly contributes to the overall favourable financial situation in that municipality.

Differences such as these between municipalities and those between municipalities and the state lead to increased segmentation and divergence in the overall political-administrative system. Municipalities not only compete with each other, but have begun to "compete" with the central state.

The necessary conditions for single municipalities to fulfil the increasing number of functions of various kinds (infrastructure, service reproduction as well as service and production-oriented functions vis-a-vis the private sector) thrust upon them both by the centre and the private sector (child care, retraining, health etc.) are often jeopardised.

Today, Denmark is approaching a situation where the municipal sector, through the growth in functions, not least those directed towards local production activities, assumes such a strategic position in the local economy that the only logical and responsible policy - from a local point of view -would be to proceed further in this direction, that is to take a direct part in business. Such a policy occurs partly to obtain a share of the "private profits" (instead of only bearing the expenses) and partly to prevent the creation of still further ("unnecessary") service and repair functions such as unemployment, health and environmental problems.

This perspective is much closer and far more easy to handle on the municipal than at the national level. From a position of strength in reproduction municipalities can, and likely will, move into the production sphere. Furthermore, such a policy will certainly tend to bring the unions to the hub of local politics, contributing to the reintegration of production and reproduction, work and "free" time.

It seems probable that the central state, by steadily trying to monopolise business policy, support and activities etc., while pressing reproduction tasks and financing onto the local level and at the same time cutting down financial support, will create a growing conflict with wage earners in the long run, through the development of contradictions of interest between the central state and municipalities.

CONCLUSIONS

The results of our empirical research can be summarised according to our three main themes as follows:

First, the geographical variations in the conditions of unions, social democratic parties, and municipalities are considerable and important so that general categorisation on an empirical and theoretical basis is not particularly meaningful. The organisational-political relations vary with the material-economic structure in a direct but complex way. The economic structure, for example, acquires its specific local significance through the way the labour movement is actually organised and activated through that structure and tradition which the Danish labour movement has developed and strongly maintained. Had the Danish labour movement, for instance, developed unions organised around industries rather than around trades, then the trade-industrial structure would have had different consequences for organisations and politics than it actually has now, just as another distribution of resources and functions in the public sector would lead to new local problems and processes.

Rather than blurring the picture with local variation and detail, the introduction of spatial variety makes it possible, precisely through the same variations and details, to identify the fundamental and abstract relations that lie behind. Thus only by introducing the spatial dimension can we approach a simplified picture of these complex relations on a theoretical basis. Just as light dissolved by a spectrograph is yet resolved back again in simplified form, through the elements, the geographic-local dimension "de-mystifies" and brings clarity to our view of civil society as a mediating sphere between economy and the state.

Second, there are considerable and complex variations to be observed in the relationship between party and unions. Nonetheless this relation is relatively clear at its base. The traditional division of labour between party and unions, between the political and the economic struggle, finds its parallel in their respective fundamental bases: where you live - the reproduction unit, the municipality; and where you work - the production unit, the economic structure. But this division of labour is increasingly melting together at the local level and we can observe an increase in competition and conflict. The developing municipal "production activities" and local governments' role as employers attract to the political process increased attention from the unions. The Associations of Unions (the FOs), structured according to municipal boundaries, became active and spread to new municipalities, and the direct representation of the unions in local councils increases.

But in the party public functionaries dominate more and more. In a cutback situation as we have seen in recent years, it is quite natural for public employees to give priority to services (where they are employed), rather than to construction and capital investments (which "only" affect manual workers in the private sector primarily dependent on public activity). However, it is increasingly obvious to manual workers, the unemployed and unskilled workers in the public sector that it is they who are paying a higher price than their more privileged companions for the maintenance of social services, which are not always the most relevant or most necessary for them. They suffer from higher unemployment, fewer tax allowances and, at the same time pay relatively more in local income tax, while the priorities of the local council stand in the way of a more active and more just "business policy". The services that remain are used and, indeed, favour middle-class functionaries and the independent self-employed. This awareness has spread in spite of the differences which really exist between different unions. Even divisions between party and union within the labour movement tend to become subordinated to class conflicts. The front for the "class struggle" (if you will) seems to have moved towards the centre of the party as a result of the emergence of a new reformist faction, more concerned with obtaining votes, occasionally working with the Liberals, and on the whole more involved with the maintenance of public institutions than with the party's professed program - the statist faction.

There remains the state-municipal dimension, in so far as it can still be isolated as an independent dimension. Here the theory of divergences would appear to be well grounded. It almost seems as if the state has lost grip on its "decentralisation" policy, which it was forced to introduce in the seventies. The state has concentrated on the financial and general quantitative economic aspects, and undervalued the functional/political significance of reproduction as well as production, of concrete local functions within local autonomy, not least because of the way these local functions have developed in extent, in cost and political importance during the crisis and its subsequent cut-backs. Central state monopoly and recent expansion of the relatively general economic policy and support appear ineffective, and to an increasing degree provoke local interests, as local need and interest for a <u>local</u> economic policy begin to increase, borne by a constellation between workers and a <u>part of local trade</u> (Lindgaard et al. 1982, 1983 a-b). The perspective of municipal involvement in production moving against the grain of national policy would appear to be not that utopian, unless the state should instigate repressive legislation, in effect abolishing local autonomy, and thereby creating grave problems of political legitimation for itself.

The alliance between part of local business and their employees appears to weaken the thesis of a class-based local politics. One should note, however, that the resulting policy would probably favour local business life, structures and relations rather than the international-oriented, vertical structures which are characteristic of large, advanced, dynamic capital formations (Corporate Capital) (Maskell 1982).

It would instigate competition between municipalities as well as competition between local and international capital, which it would be precisely in the government's interest to avoid, since its policy is directed more towards dynamic, export-oriented big capital. The alliance between local capital and labour is, therefore, still marked by class dimensions and rivalries between class factions, and ought to be analysed as such, rather than by pluralistic consumption-oriented structures. In the longer view this trend might well crystallise into a specific form of "local corporatism" based on the growth of municipal trade councils and secretariats which have developed in Danish municipalities in recent years.

REFERENCES

von Beyme, Klaus (1978), "The Changing Relations between Trade Unions and the Social Democratic Party in West Germany", Government and Opposition, Vol.14, no.4.
Bild, Tage (1977), Ukviklingstendenser i forholdet mellem stat og arbejderklasse. Nordisk Tidsskrift for Politisk Økonomi, Nr.5, Lund.
Bild, Tage (1981), Socialdemokratiet og Fagbevaegelsen i Bild & Jørgensen (Red.), Fagbevaegelsen og Krisen, Samfundsvidenskabeligt Forlag, København.
Bogason, Peter (1978), Regional Planning in Denmark in K. Hanf and F. Scharpf (Eds), Intergovernmental Policy Making, Sage, London (215-243).
Castells, Manuel (1977), The Urban Question, Arnold, London.
Cawson, Alan and Peter Saunders (1983), "Corporatism, Competitive Politics and Class Struggle", in R. King (Ed.) Capital and Politics, Routledge and Kegan Paul, London.
Christensen, Erik (1977), Konflikter mellem faglaerte og ufaglaerte arbejdere, Aalborg Universitetsforlag. Aalborg.
Christensen, Erik (1981), Arbejderpartiernes faglige politik i 1970-erne, Aalborg Universitetsforlag, Aalborg.
Cooke, Philip (1983), The Spatial Dimension of Urban Politics. Local opposition to a regional coalition. Paper presented for the Seminar on Local State Research: Anglo-Danish Comparisons. University of Copenhagen. September.
Davidsen, Henrik (1981), Fagbevaegelsen og den decentrale politikformulering. Nordjyllandsundersøgelsen. Fagbevaegelsens Forskningsrad. København.
Dunleavy, Patrick (1979), "The Urban Basis of Political Alignment, British Journal of Political Science Vol.9, 409-43.
Finansministeriet (1983), Budgetredegørelse 1983, Budgetdepartementet. København.

Flynn, Rob (1983), The Value of Recent Urban Political Theory in Research on the Local State. Paper presented to the ANglo-Danish Seminar on Local State Research, Copenhagen.

Giddens, Anthony (1979), Central Problems in Social Theory, Macmillan, London.

Giddens, Anthony (1981), A Contemporary Critique of Historical Materialism, Macmillan, London.

Gouldner, Alvin (1980), The Two Marxisms, Macmillan Press, New York.

Gramsci, Antonio (1971), Selections from Prison Notebooks, Lawrence and Wishart, London.

Grümer, Herbert (1974), Zum Verhältnis vor Zentralstaat und Kommunen. Emenlauer et al., Die Kommunen in der Staatsorganisation, Frankfurt a.M.

Harloe, Michael, (ed.) (1977), Captive Cities, Wiley, London.

Harvey, David (1973): Social Justice and the City, Arnold, London.

Hirsh, Joachim (1974), Staatsapparat und Reproduktion des Kapitals, Frankfurt a.M.

Hjalager, Anne-Mette, Gert Lindgaard og Henning Snell (1982), Kommunale og amtskommunale erhvervsfremmende initiativer, AKF, København.

Hjalager, Ann-Mette, Gert Lindgaard og Henning Snell (1983a), Kommunale og amtskommunale erhvervsfremmende initiativer (en oversigt), AKF, København.

Hjalager, Anne-Mette, Gert Lindgaard og Henning Snell (1983b), Nogle Spaendende erhvervsfremmende initiativer i udvalgte danske kommuner, AKF, København.

Ibsen, Flemming og Henning Jørgensen (1979): Fagbevaegelse og stat 1+2. Gyldendal, København.

Ibsen, Flemming (1983), Organisationerne og arbejdsmarkedet, Samfundsfagsnyt, København.

Maskell, Peter (1982), Industriens regionale omlokalisering. 1970-80. Omfang, arsager, konsekvenser. TTF. Handelshøjskolen i København.

Minkin, Lewis (1978), The Party Connection. Divergence and Convergence in the British labour Movement. Government and Opposition. Vol.13, No.4.

Mouritzen, Poul Erik (1983a), The Resource Squeeze in Danish Local Government. The ambivalent role of the State. Odense University, Odense.

Mouritzen, Poul Erik (1983b), Background paper collected for the seminars on "Local Government Development Policy" og "Local State Research", Copenhagen. September.

Møller, Jørgen og Jens Chr. Tonboe (1983a), Levevilkar og civilforsvar. Plan og Arbeid, Nr.4, Oslo.

Møller, Jørgen og Jens Chr. Tonboe (1983b), Arbejderbevaegelse og lokalpolitik. Opposition eller samarbejde? Serien om offentlig planlaegning nr. 16. Aalborg Universitetsforlag. Aalborg.

Przeworski, Adam (1977), Proletariat into a Class. The process of class formation from Karl Kautsky's The Class Struggle to recent controversies. Politics and Society, Vol.7, no.4.

Przeworski, Adam (1980), Social Democracy: a Historical Phenomenon. New Left Review, (122). July/Aug.

Saunders, Peter (1979), Urban Politics - a Sociological Interpretation. Macmillan, London.

Saunders, Peter (1981), Social Theory and the Urban Question, Hutchinson, London.

Saunders, Peter (1982), Rejoinder to Hooper and Duncan & Goodwin. Political Geography Quarterly, Vol.1, no.2.

Skovsgaard, Carl Johan og Jørgen Søndergaard (1983), Danish Local Government. Recent trends in economy and administration. University of Arhus.

Tonboe, Jens Chr. (1981a), Fagbevaegelsen, lokalpolitikken og planlaegningen. Rasp, Vol.1, nr.2, Aalborg.

Tonboe, Jens Chr. (1981b), Divergenstendenser i det offentlige planleagningssystem. Aalborg Universitetscenter.

Tonboe, Jens Chr. (1983), Sociale krav og medbestemmelse i planlaegningen. Plan og Arbeid, no.3, Oslo.

Urry, John (1981a), The Anatomy of Capitalist Societies, Macmillan, London.

Urry, John (1981b), Localities, Regions and Social Class. International Journal of Urban and Regional Research. Vol.5, no.1.

Urry, John (1983), Deindustrialisation, Classes and Politics, R. King (ed), Capital and Politics, Routledge and Kegan Paul, London.

Valentin, Finn (1978), Corporatism and the Danish Welfare State. Acta Sociologica, vol.21, Supplement.

10 The local state and social movements in Denmark

KIRSTEN SIMONSEN
Copenhagen University

One of the major debates in both urban politics and sociology in the last decade has been concerned with what is called "social movements", "action groups", "grass root organisations", all characterising collective political action performed outside the institutionalised political system. Although social movements have been among the sources of social and urban change throughout history, the historical conditions of contemporary capitalism seem to create a basis for qualitatively new forms.

First, these movements mobilise around problems in the sphere of labour reproduction, thereby demonstrating that the uni-dimensional emphasis of the unions and the political left on working life is all too narrow. Such an emphasis omits half the individual's experience of exploitation in daily life, and it excludes all wageless people from the activities.

Second, many of the new social movements operate at the local political scene, indicating that in spite of the dissolution of the traditional community in modern society, the locality has a meaning in contemporary capitalism.

The aim of this chapter is to discuss the background and outlook of the new local or urban social movements, to explain them, and on this basis to evaluate this kind of political action as an agent for social change. The analysis remains at a general level, with an emphasis on the social development and qualitative content of the movements.

ON THE SPECIFICITY OF THE "LOCAL"

The problem of identifying and limiting the "local" has a close relation to the general geographical problem posed by the insertion of concepts of space, place, locale, or milieu into social theory. This problem which has permeated the literature on the urban question in the past decade (Hvey, 1973; Castells, 1977), and is central to the debate on social theory. (Soja 1984)

The reason why the locality has a special interest is that it is the point of intersection between the large social processes and people's everyday life and experiences. But the significance of the locality is <u>contingent</u> upon the historical social context, though here I shall suggest some important processes in contemporary capitalism which give the locality a new significance.

The increased concentration and centralisation of capital nationally and internationally leads to an increased mobility of capital as it seeks to redistribute its activities to take advantage of variations in the price, availability, skills and organisation of local labour. By contrast, labour remains relatively immobile. There are a number of reasons why this happens. First, the increased participation of married women in the labour force leads to the creation of two-job families; second, with a clear interest in their local economy, the increase of working-class people living in owner-occupied housing makes people generally less mobile, whilst the collective means of consumption is increasingly important in the process of labour reproduction. These are all trends which have strengthened the localised character of the consumption processes. Urry (1981) drives the implications of this contradiction even further in arguing that when, as locational studies demonstrate, the supply and cost of labour power is centrally important in determining industrial location, the locality and local class structures are of increased significance to capital and to the forms of social struggle.

These local class structures cannot be understood in terms of a general class analysis whose basic unit of investigation is the nation state. The local class structure derives from the organisation of the local labour market, its sectoral, occupational and gender changes, and thus to the specific history of the local community. General as well as locational changes affect local class structures and thereby local politics in contemporary capitalism. First, due to the internationalisation of capital there is an increased tendency for capitalist enterprise to be located outside local areas. Second, the intermediate classes have been growing, especially as a result of growing local authority employment, and they are to a large degree comprised of women. Third, the traditional working class has been diminishing, but at different rates in different localities. Last, there is a new and growing underclass outside the labour market, often highly concentrated in specific parts of cities, and particularly in what is generally known as the inner city.

Finally, the specificity of the local or the spatial aspect of social processes is due to political as well as economic factors. Institutional boundaries delimiting nation states, counties or municipalities produce specific local political, as well as economic and ideological, processes. In Denmark and other Western European countries, decentralisation reforms in the 1970s have transferred a number of services, particularly those concerning socialised consumption, from central to local government. These administrative changes have been an additional contribution to the significance of the locality in contemporary politics.

THE LOCAL STATE

An analysis of local political processes requires as its starting-point the functioning and organisation of the state apparatus as a whole. As Harvey as suggested, in order for the state to ensure an effective social reproduction, it must be able to internalise the conflicting interests of different classes, fractions, and geographical groups (Harvey 1978). A system which can simultaneously accommodate these various class and group interests must be pluralistic in structure, as can be seen in the internal organisation of the state apparatus. The administrative system has a segmented structure which can be identified along two dimensions.

> a sectoral organisation, composed partly of inherited elements of adminstration and partly of new institutions created to meet successive demands on the state, as a result of its increasing intervention into the process of social reproduction. One result is that the reproduction of labour power and its political treatment is increasingly split into isolated fractions. The result is that struggles around concrete problems of reproduction also risk being channelled into a segmented political system.

a hierarchical territorial organisation - i.e. a division into local political systems. These systems consist primarily (though not exclusively) of local authorities. Many locally administered public services are directly or indirectly controlled by the central state. The local municipal apparatus is thus only relatively independent of the central state, which sets strict limits to its possibilities of action. The various institutions which constitute the local political system must thus be seen as part of the overall state system. On the other hand local political systems are not simply passive branches of the central state system: they exert an independent influence on the development of urban organisations, and they develop their own activities and procedures in connection with collective consumption.

Interpreting the local municipal apparatus as part of the overall state apparatus led to the concept of the local state (Cockburn 1978), itself followed by a comprehensive debate on the relative autonomy of the local state. Is local power merely delegated power from the central state or is it formed by local political processes?

Early marxist contributions on urban policy suggested a functionalist relationship between central and local government (Castells, 1977; Cockburn, 1978). In reaction to this view, Saunders (1981,1982) recommends replacing the local state concept with a dualistic approach to the analysis of political processes. Using O'Connor's terminology (but not his theory), he argues that social investment policies are developed at national level and functions primarily in the interests on capital, while social consumption functions are local and functions primarily in the interests of other sections of the population.

This dual state approach rests upon an identification of three sets of social contradictions operating at different levels within the political system. First, the contradiction between capital and labour (or more diffusely expressed as "non-capital"); second, the contradiction between social investment and social consumption, and finally the contradiction between central and local government.

Saunders's argument not only emphasises the importance of these contradictions, it also assumes that they are coincident, an assumption which reduces the complexity of local political struggles. The contradiction between social investment and social consumption cuts across the problem of central-local relations and appears inside political levels as well as between them. Arguing that social consumption primarily functions in the interests of "non-capitalist" sections of the population ignores capitalist interests in the reproduction of labour power and in the production of the means of consumption. Thus, instead of abandoning the concept of the local state, we should seek to develop it in ways which can grasp the complexity of central-local relations. This implies an interpretation of the local state as a specific part of a non-monolithic state apparatus.

An approach to the theory of the capitalist state which renders such an interpretation possible is advanced by Poulantzas (1980). Here the state is perceived not as a monolithic bloc, but as a strategic field of struggle, where political struggle and domination are inscribed in the institutional structure of the state. Social contradictions are expressed within the state in the form of internal contradictions between, and at the heart of, its various branches and apparatuses, following both horizontal and vertical directions. These configurations are dependent on conflicts between and relationship of forces within the power bloc, that is, between different fractions of capital, and between that bloc and the popular masses.

One expression of these contradictions is the conflicts between the central and local levels of the state apparatus. As an example, the increasing economic role of the state seems to require the inclusion of municipal finances into state fiscal policy, while at the same time local authorities have to represent local production and reproduction interests in their policies. Thus, local politics are subject to different and contradictory pressures and tendencies.

On the one hand, local power cannot be seen solely as delegated power. Perceiving the concept of power in a relational manner, local power concerns the capacity of classes, fractions, genders and interest groups to realise their specific interests on the basis of their relationship to, and struggle against, opposite social groups. Local power must thus be seen as a political field of struggle influenced by social forces both within and outside the locality. It is determined partially by the total social class struggle (and as such must be seen as a delegated power from the central state), and partially by local political struggles. But the basis for local power is not exclusively a matter of class. First, many problems treated within the local political system are concerned with labour reproduction and, as we shall see later, are usually of a nature which involves large segments of the population. The foundation of local power is also to be found in the specific local social bases which are contingent upon local class structures and consciousness and can differ greatly from one locality to another.

In Denmark, the significance of local power was strengthened through a series of local government reforms during the 1970s. The main elements of these reforms were a reduction in the number of local authorities from almost 1400 to 275; a transfer of a number of functions, especially those concerning social welfare, from central to local government, and a change in financial relations, with a switch from matching to general grants based on so-called objective criteria. Last, there was a reform in physical planning, introducing greater local responsibility and the principle of citizen participation. Altogether, this legislation had the pronounced aim of decentralising power and functions from the centre to the locality.

On the other hand, local politics are subject to central control, and, despite the technical-administrative decentralisation reforms in Denmark (as elsewhere in Western Europe) the state system is increasingly characterised by political centralism (Poulantzas 1980). This development has taken place together with the emergence of monopoly capital, the increasing economic role of the state, and the appearance of structural crisis. Specifically, in Denmark, increased state control over local government has been achieved through cuts in social welfare: increased assignment of functions to the local level, together with reductions in the level of general grants; expanded budget co-operation with the aim of integrating local budgets into state fiscal planning; and increasing negotiation with the organisations of local authorities, which play an ambiguous role as instruments of control (Jensen and Simonsen, 1981). These tendencies restrict the possibilities for action by local authorities, and renders the local political scene problematic as a field of struggle for improving the standard of living of labour.

Central-local relations are a complex field, subject to contradictory historical tendencies. The extent to which objective contradictions between the central and local state result in open conflict, so that local autonomy is utilised and possibly expanded, depends upon the concrete political practice at the different levels. In Denmark where, in contrast to some French and Italian experience, central and local political leadership have generally been in agreement, the conflicts have been relative few and minor.

However, the major role of the state at the local level, and in particular of municipal activities, is to be found in the field of labour reproduction. Financing and planning social services, education, health services, housing and recreational facilities has increasingly become a local task. The central state determines the framework for these activities, but planning and executing them takes place at the local level. The nature of the problems involved necessitates finding solutions in co-operation with local people. Many of the functions of the local bureaucracy takes place in face-to-face contact with people (clients). The state thus often relates to the primary unit of labour reproduction – the family – and in practice often to the woman in the family (Cockburn 1978). In this way, women act as the standard-bearers of the welfare state. They do the work of running the social services, adapting them to the needs of the family and distributing them inside it, and they compensate for the gaps in state services through their invisible work at home.

In many localities, however, the state is leaning on an institution which is only partially present. The dissolution of the extended family networks of the working class, the changing family structure, and the "dual roles" of women render this expected co-operation difficult. In any case, the local state appears as the organiser of people's daily life, which is why resistance and protests around reproduction issues are often directed at that level.

SOCIALISATION OF CONSUMPTION AND SOCIAL MOVEMENTS

After the second world war, western capitalist countries experienced an explosive growth of state intervention into the reproduction of labour power, expressed in the growth of state activity in health, education, housing, social services, which constitute the major elements of the modern "welfare state". These services and their provision are often seen as being above the local state.

It was this state provision of consumption which gave rise to the concept of collective consumption (Castells 1977, 1978). Coinciding with this state intervention into the field of consumption is a continued expansion of capital, with the result that many of the requirements of reproduction earlier provided by the family have now been drawn into the circulation of capital. We have thus two partially contradictory forms of socialisation of consumption: commodification and state intervention.

However, socialisation of consumption not only concerns the provision of the means of consumption, but also the very process of consumption (or real appropriation relations) (Preteceille, 1977; Dunleavy, 1983). Collective consumption, therefore, is a theoretical concept grown out of this double process of the socialisation of consumption.

The growth of state intervention in collective consumption has its background both in economic-structural developments and in the development of class struggles (Pahl, 1977; Dunleavy 1979). Therefore a general explanation of the historical development, form and content of state intervention in a given nation cannot be given. This would require an analysis of the development of the national production structure, political systems and traditions, and levels of class struggle. In Denmark, as in other Scandinavian countries, the demands of labour have largely been channelled through the social democratic parties, which, as a result of social democratic welfare state projects, has resulted in an unusually well-developed provision of services in the field of labour reproduction.

The growth of state-provided collective consumption has undoubtedly improved the standard of living of labour. This gain, however, is an ambiguous one. As well as labour have an interest in receiving services, so capital also has an interest in seeing them serviced. Not only does capital need an efficient reproduction of the labour force, it also needs the welfare state to disarm social discontent. Furthermore, there is a general tendency for the capitalist state to displace and reshape the demands of the popular classes according to the dominant interests of capital, in terms of economic interests or in terms of the search for social control. It is important to understand this double character of collective consumption, and of the welfare state as a whole.

Coincident with the development of the welfare state we have seen an increasing political mobilisation at the grass-root level, especially in relation to the provision of collective consumption. State intervention in collective consumption can thus have the effect of increasing politicisation. This hypothesis, first advanced by Castells (1977,1978), has been under discussion for some time, but needs relating to three characteristics of collective consumption.

First, the welfare state operates in a very differential way. It provides nothing but a subsistence income for some, gives aid such as housing to others, and in some situations

213

throws in a whole apparatus of investigation, control and regulation. In this way, collective consumption creates new, but also reinforces existing, class differences. At the same time, however, the very nature of the problems involved mean that they concern broad segments of the population (housing problems, traffic congestion, lack of institutions and social facilities). Although the poor are hardest hit, other groups cannot entirely avoid problems. Moreover, there has been a general shift in the class structure and in the standard of living of all classes. As a result, the particular political form embodied in the idea of social movements seems to have arisen alongside the growth of the "new middle class". These classes also supply political resources to the movements. The involvement of the middle classes in these struggles should partly be seen in conjunction with the fact that these groups usually acquire their daily vocational experience in the area of reproduction and frequently in the public sector, thus establishing a connection between work and private life. Furthermore, increases in general living standards have tended to proletarianise the middle classes, while at the same time producing a considerable internal differentiation of the working class. On a more concrete level, we can thus expect to find growing common interests across class boundaries, making the establishment of broader alliances possible.

Last but not least the supply and content of collective consumption is determined by open parliamentary processes, in contrast to commodity consumption which is provided through the anonymous market and masked by the myth of equal exchange. This open politicisation creates the possibility of conscious understanding and action. However, there is nothing automatic in this process. The class nature of the state can be masked as well, by segmentation processes and by the ideology of the welfare state which sees it as representative of the common interest. Recognising that none of these effects produces mechanically greater political consciousness, they nevertheless have consequences, and tend to produce new types of struggles - urban social movements, ecological movements, struggles of people working in the public services and their growing links with the working class.

The broad social composition of social movements can be seen in data from a Danish investigation of participation in grass root activities:

Table 1 shows that grass-root participation in Denmark is a broad popular form of participation.

Table 1 Grass roots participation by sector (% Population)

Sector	Blue collar		White collar		self employed	students	pen-sioners
	unskill	skill	low	high			
Housing	3	6	8	7	2	14	4
Education	2	8	1	15	5	21	2
Other public service	4	6	11	15	5	21	2
Local actions	14	18	27	29	20	27	13
Environ-ments	4	8	10	10	7	14	8
At least one action	26	40	47	54	30	70	19

Source: Jørgen Goul Andersen (1981) table 2.

Struggles over collective consumption are very much concerned with the standard of living of labour, but in fact the causes in question are of a much more fundamental character. As Harvey points out:

> "The manner and form of this everyday, overt conflict
> are a reflection of a much deeper tension with less
> easily identifiable manifestations: a struggle over
> the definition and meaning of use values; the standard
> of living of labour; the quality of life;
> consciousness; and even human nature itself." (Harvey
> 1977, p.293)

Conflicts in the sphere of reproduction are seen as reflections of deeper structural contradictions in capitalism. Capital attempts to induce a quality of life which is conducive to the productivity of labour and to the expansion of commodity consumption. However, labour attempts to create its own life-style, derived partially from memories of earlier forms of production, and partially from the learning and consciousness which are created through the internal contradictions of the capitalist system. Such contradictions are between private appropriation and social production, between individualism and social dependency. The struggle in the area of reproduction is thus an expression of the fundamental contradiction between labour and capital.

This viewpoint helps us to expose the basic connection between struggles centred in production and those centred in the sphere of reproduction. One must not, however, conclude that contradictions found in the sphere of reproduction are simply direct reflections of contradictions in production. Such a view would ignore the cross-class character of the social movements related to the socialisation of consumption. It is important to emphasise that there is a cross-class, and not a non-class, base to such a social movement. Their subjects and their composition reflect changes in consumption relations and in the class structure. To suggest they are a non-class phenomena would imply that these consumption relations are independent of the relations of exploitation in capitalist society.

Another characteristic of social movements is based on the fact that collective consumption is mainly provided by the local state. Therefore, the new social movements have largely arisen at the local political level. Their importance rests upon the fact that, in contrast to political parties and organisations, they have their roots in the local social structure. This fact, however, emphasises two aspects of social movements which complicate their political perspectives: they are an expression of the struggle for reproduction and they are local. Both aspects result in a distortion and segmentation of the struggle when seen from a class perspective. As far as class consciousness is concerned, the struggle for reproduction is influenced by the ideological separation between production and reproduction in capitalist society, and by the segmented treatment given to reproduction by the state apparatus. The local nature of the struggle also creates the further risk of geographical segmentation.

Thus the increasing activity of urban social movements has its background partly in the socialisation of consumption and in growing state intervention, and partly in the fact that their struggles are often directed at the local level of the state. This leaves a paradox, in that the state has to tackle contradictions which itself helps to produce. Furthermore, social movements are not a phenomenon created by the economic crisis. They have developed in a period of economic growth against a background of the environmental and human consequences of capitalist accumulation and of state socialisation of consumption. However, the crisis has sharpened the contradictions involved.

THE CRISIS AND LOCAL SOCIAL MOVEMENTS

As we have seen, much of the interpretation of the politicisation of the urban question comes from the socialisation of production and consumption. It should also be emphasised that the extent and form of state intervention – and thereby of collective consumption – has to be understood, starting from its functional importance for capitalist accumulation as well as from the actual class struggle.

The development of collective consumption is both necessary for and helpful to capital accumulation. First, it ensures an efficient reproduction of labour power. For example, by training labour and repairing the harmful effects of the capitalist system, collective consumption lowers the value of the labour force, and by intervening in the built environment it facilitates the daily functioning of labour. Second, collective consumption has an integrative ideological effect; potential social discontent can be dampened by extended "welfare expenditures", thereby diverting and calming class struggles. Third, it seeks to reconcile labour demands for social services to the requirements of accumulation, thereby facilitating a process of "rational" consumption.

At the same time, however, there exist latent contradictions between capital accumulation and collective consumption which especially express themselves in the crisis. First, state provision of collective consumption involves a major part of public expenditure, which inhibits the direct process of capital accumulation, partly through taxation of profit, and partly because it is diverted from alternative uses more helpful to capital. The assumptions that all taxes are deductions from surplus value is a simplification, but still the overall tendency of contradiction is substantially correct (Gough 1979). State-provided collective consumption is also contradictory to capital accumulation by keeping sectors of the economy outside the control of the market, and therefore by inhibiting capital's movement into new spheres of accumulation. Finally, because its interests differ from those of capital, state organised consumption (such as education) is less inclined to follow changes in those interests.

These structural contradictions have deepened in the present crisis, and there is a general tendency in capitalist societies for public expenditures on collective consumption to be reduced and to switch to expenditures which are designed to maintain or improve industrial capability. Also there is a tendency to restructure the welfare services internally, by adopting policies designed to secure more efficient reproduction of the labour force; by shifting emphasis onto the social control of destabilising groups in society, by raising productivity within the social services, and possibly by reprivatising parts of the welfare state (Gough 1979).

Such a policy has consequences for the reproduction of labour power and political movements operating in this field. First, state provision of the means of consumption has contributed to an improvement in living conditions of labour. As a result of the economic crisis, people have experienced a deterioration in their living conditions, stagnating or decreasing real income, increasing unemployment, and increasing prices and rents. All these features place more demands on state services, but expenditures on collective consumption are being reduced. Thus, in addition to the social problems traditionally concentrated in particular parts of cities, there has been a general deterioration of living conditions amongst both the working class, the petty bourgeoisie and the "new middle class".

As well as these material aspects, increasing state intervention has ideological and political effects. Social services have changed from being assistance to the poor to becoming an obligation on the state to meet the social needs of the population. Needs, such as these, once created, are not completely convertible and cannot be reduced by the crisis, whereas cuts in collective consumption tend to undermine the ideological support for the capitalist system which the welfare state has provided.

As a result of these contradictions and the material and ideological consequences of cutbacks in welfare spending, authors like Preteceille recognise a possible background for the strengthening of social movements:

> "it seems that capitalist state policies react to the crises with a setback of socialisation of consumption which constitute a clear change in the evolution of the mode of consumption, and create objective conditions for the development of social movements on those issues, with potentiality for wide social alliances, political articulations with movements concerned with production". (Preteceille 1978, p.25).

However, none of these effects mechanically produce greater political consciousness and stronger popular struggles. At present opposite tendencies can be identified. On the one hand, ideologies of self-help and the constant process of displacement, reshaping and control over the welfare state have diverted and pacified popular movements. On the other hand, there has been a sharpening of conflicts in the urban context, a process underlined by other social contradictions.

SOCIAL MARGINALISATION

During the economic upswing of the fifties and sixties the scale of expansion was so strong that it necessitated a tapping of the labour surplus. The "industrial reserve army" of the traditional working class was exhausted, and other sources of labour power had to be drawn upon. New workers for expanding branches of industry and the rapidly growing service sector came from three main sources; small farmers and agricultural labourers, immigrant workers from less developed territories, and - in vastly increased numbers - women from the homes of the working class. These new entrants into the labour market did not join a homogenous labour force, but one stratified by skill and status, by ethnic group and by sex. During the present period of recession the same mechanisms are in operation. Looking at the composition of unemployment in capitalist societies, it is clear that disproportionately large numbers of women and ethnic minorities have become marginalised economically. Joining these previously employed people in the ranks of the unemployed are many young people entering the labour market for the first time during a decade marked by recession. Generally, these processes have resulted in an unprecedented division and marginalisation of the working class, and even of sections of the middle classes.

These marginalised groups - the old and chronically sick, single parents, long-term unemployed, low-paid workers, migrant families and unemployed youth - are most often concentrated in specific central or suburban working class areas. Further, as a high proportion of the population in these areas are dependent on all kinds of social services, the impact of the cuts and the restructuring of the welfare state becomes disproportionately severe in such places.

Now such a process at the economic level does not, of itself, produce resistance. In the last five years, however, confrontations between the police and urban youth have been experienced in London, Liverpool, Berlin, Zurich and Copenhagen amongst others. These confrontations can be seen as a refusal by sections of youth to bear the burden of economic change passively. Such a stand is made possible through the development of oppositional youth subcultures (most explicitly expressed in the West Indian youth culture in the great cities of Britain), and the demands of the youth movements often turn upon acquiring autonomous space to develop their own culture.

The most conspicuous Danish example of these youth movements - the "BZ's" - has been analysed by Madsen (1982). Their most important demands were for collective youth residences and youth-houses, where they could develop their own cultural life without any form of institutional control. The fact that these young people have grown up in a period dominated by state socialized consumption influences the movement in two ways. On the one hand, they react against any form of institutional authority. On the other hand, their demands are directed towards the state and specifically the local state apparatus.

Thus the problem for the study of urban movements is not that urban movements in Western Europe "have ceased to exist" (Pickvance, 1983), but that they have changed. Some movements disappear when the questions involved are institutionalized, but social development creates new kinds of interest and concern which are taken up by new types of movements.

PROBLEMS AND PERSPECTIVES

The state response to urban movements has generally been two-fold. One response is direct repression. However, the politicising effects of such a policy generally make it less attractive than other means of disorganising the resistance. Recent developments, however, have increased the methods of state coercion, but so far these operations have mainly been felt by the marginalised groups. The other kind of state response is based upon processes which either incorporate or fragment social movements and their struggles. The response embraces incorporation into a fragmented state apparatus, ideas of local democracy, deliberate attempts at diversion, as well as planning activities like community projects and public participation. Furthermore, the tendency towards the reduction of local state autonomy limits the possibilities for isolated local victories.

These processes could result in an evaluation of local social movements as being of minor importance and lacking political perspective. Why organize in local communities, when the problems are global and the possibilities of influence minor? To all appearances, such organisation occurs because there is no other choice. Growing sections of the popular masses have no entry to the basic defensive institutions of the working-class, namely the trade unions. And in these unions, moreover, the manual male worker has always been considered the main basis for organisation, leaving large parts of the population with poor, badly organised representation of their interests. The established political parties, on their side, have been historically produced by social movements and social interests different from those of people's everyday life, so that the two are mismatched.

By contrast, most recent social movements have developed on the basis ofthe daily life, experience and culture of their communities. They are products of new forms of social exploitation, and at the same time they are a means of social experience and learning. They have grown out of the local community and are concerned with the problems of socialized consumption, raising the possibility of developing a common consciousness in this sphere. The common consciousness of social movements is, however, a consciousness of interests broader than class alone. This broad organisational, ideological and social background gives rise to possible alliances across class barriers, but it is also a serious inherent weakness. First, such alliances often tend to narrow the movement's perspective to limited concrete cases. Alternatively, they reinforce the capitalist fragmentation of daily life into isolated spheres: work, commodity market, private life, political life, and so on. For that reason an increase in the struggles of social movements will not necessarily increase the political perspectives of conflicts in the non-work sphere. Such a development would depend upon the experience gained within the movements, and the extent to which the different interests try to cooperate. The development of a political perspective in the non-work sphere requires a fusion of the individual's segmented and contradictory experiences from the various spheres of daily life, including the workplace, and thereby it also requires cooperation with the unions. Furthermore, it requires a struggle in which the issue is not only the level of reproduction, but simultaneously concerns the nature, social organisation, ideological form and content of this reproduction. Tendencies towards such a holistic view of life can be found in qualitative movements like the women's and environmental movements, and in activities of self-management such as local resource centres, co-operative enterprises, and organised child-care networks.

The question of cooperation with the unions is a more ambiguous matter because of the cultural gap between the middle class influenced movements and the labour movement. But in various situations in Denmark there have been tendencies towards such coalitions of interests. During urban demonstrations, situations have occurred where the workers (in particular in the construction industry) have refused, while under police protection, to carry out work against the wishes of social movements.

Second, unions, pressed by dissatisfaction amongst their members, have been compelled to make demands on state policy concerning collective consumption. Within several groups of public employees, instances can be found where demands with respect to wages and working conditions have been coupled with demands concerning the quality of public services - an expression of a natural connection between the interests of "state employees" and "state clients", and a process also found in Britain.

As far as the struggle over collective consumption is concerned, this last issue is important. An alliance between public sector personnel and consumers of state services could mean an opening up of the institutions of the welfare state, as well as a discussion of the particular welfare needs of localities and how they can be met with existing resources.

Such a development seems unlikely, however, because of the continued segmentation of daily life forced by capital and state. Whether the struggles can be broadened quantitatively and qualitatively as a result of the undermining of welfare ideology, or whether they will be reduced to a simple defence of the status quo is still an open question. Nevertheless, it seems likely that, as Manuel Castells, has argued:

> "Without social movements, no challenge will emerge from civil society able to shake the institutions of the state through which norms are enforced, values preached, and properly preserved". (Castells 1983, p.294).

REFERENCES

Castells M (1977): The Urban Question, London, Edward Arnold.
Castells M (1978): City, Class and Power, London, MacMillan.
Castells M (1983): The City and the Grassroots, London, Edward Arnold.
Cockburn C (1978): The Local State, London, Pluto Press.
Dunleavy P (1983) : Socialised Consumption and Economic Development. Paper presented to Anglo-Danish Seminar, Copenhagen, September, 1983.

Gough I (1979): The Political Economy of the Welfare State, London, MacMillan.

Goul Andersen J (1981) Graesrodsbevaegelser -en indkredsning, Grus nr 3,   2.argang.

Harvey D (1973): Social Justice and the City, London, Edward Arnold.

Harvey D (1977):   Labour, capital and the class struggle around the built environment, Politics and Society, vol.7, pp.265-95.

Harvey D (1978):   On planning the ideology of planning, in Burchell and Sternlieb: Planning: challenge and response

Jensen J and Simonsen K: (1981): The local state, planning and social movements, Acta Sociologica, vol.24. no 4.

Nadsen T R, Nellergaard C and Thomsen L (1982): Ungdom 80, Copenhagen, Forlaget Politiske Studier

Pahl R (1977):   Collective consumption and the state in capitalist societies in R.Scase ed: Industrial Society: Aspects of Class, Cleavage and Control, London, Allen and Unwin.

Poulantzas N (1980): State, Power and Socialism, London, Verso.

Pickvance C (1983): What has become of social movements? Paper for I.S.A. conference, Nanterre, Paris, October 1983.

Preteceille E (1977): Equipements collectifs et consommation sociale, International Journal of Urban and Regional Research, vol.1, no 1.

Preteceille E (1978): Collective consumption, the state and the crisis of capitalist society, I.S.A. World Congress, Uppsala, August, 19778.

Saunders P (1979):   Urban Politics - a Sociological Interpretation, London, Hutchinson.

Saunders P (1981):   Social Theory and the Urban Question, London, Hutchinson.

Saunders P (1982):   Why study central-local relations? Local Government Studies, vol.8 no 2.

Simonsen K (1982):   Collective consumption, the state and the urban crisis. Paper for workshop on regional reconstruction and the urban crisis, Copenhagen, May 1982.

Soja E W (1984):   The spatiality of urban life: towards a transformative retheorization in Gregory and Urry eds: Social Relations and Spatial Structure, forthcoming, London, MacMillan.

Urry J (1981):   Localities, regions and social class, International Journal of Urban and Regional Research, vol.5 no.4.

11 The perceived impact of spending cuts in Britain, 1980-1984: social class life cycle and sectoral location influences

STEPHEN EDGELL AND VIC DUKE
Department of Sociology and Anthropology, University of Salford

INTRODUCTION

The first Conservative administration under Thatcher is widely regarded as marking a major quantitative and qualitative break with the post 1945 social democratic political consensus regarding the establishment of a welfare state and the maintenance of full employment (Bosanquet, 1983; Edgell and Duke, 1983; Glennerster, 1980; Gough, 1979 and 1983; Gough et al, 1984). The main grounds for arguing this are that between 1978/9 and 1980/1 for the first time the rise in social expenditure (defined as state spending on social security, health, education, housing and personal social services), was less than the overall increase in public expenditure (Walker, 1982:20). By contrast, in the post Second World War period to 1977 social expenditure had increased at a faster rate than the growth of GDP and also faster than public expenditure as a whole" (Gould and Roweth. 1980:357). Second, the 1979 Conservative administration "was the first government since the 1944 White Paper on Employment Policy not to make full employment one of its objectives" (Pliatzky, 1982: 171). Third, key assumptions, such as steady economic growth, Keynesian demand management and the interventionist role of the state, upon which the welfare state was founded and prospered, had lost much of their legitimacy by the end of the 1970s (Mishra, 1984). Fourth, the Conservatives have rejected the tripartite management of industrial relations (Hyman, 1984).

In opposition to the majority view that 1979 marks a watershed in the development of the welfare state in Britain, two alternative interpretations have been expressed that represent a critique of both sides of the watershed. First, it has been suggested that the nature and extent of the immediate post-war welfare consensus has been overstated (Deacon, 1984). Second, and more fundamentally, it has been claimed that the post-1979 restructuring of the welfare state in Britain and elsewhere is of "marginal significance beside the preceding growth" (Therborn, 1984:29). Therborn bases this claim on the achievement of labour movements in advanced capitalist societies. More specifically he suggests that "the record of advance in electoral support, union membership, strike activity, industrial relations and economic distribution disproves the thesis of a historical hiatus" (Therborn, 1984:18). On the basis of a combination of his own data and official statistics we would contend that this line of argument applies far less well to Britain than to the other twenty-two advanced capitalist societies discussed. First, Therborn notes that the Labour Party's electoral support in 1983 at 27.6% was more than 20% down on 1966 and its lowest since 1918. Second, his strike trend data for Britain shows that it peaked in 1979 and subsequently declined between 1980-2 to the mid-1970s level. Third, trade union membership has declined from a peak of 13.3 million in 1979 to 11.6 million in 1983 (Social Trends, 1984). Moreover, in work situations where trade union membership is a condition of employment, commitment to trade unionism is likely to be passively routine. Fourth, the power and legitimacy of trade unions has been considerably weakened by the 1980 and 1982 Employment Acts which removed many of the legal immunities enjoyed by trade unions, especially in conflict situations (Hyman, 1984). Fifth, the taxation system has become markedly more regressive since 1979. For example, "all those earning less than three times the average male wage" (95% of the population) were paying more in direct taxes in 1983 than in 1979, whilst the direct tax burden on high income earners and the owners of personal wealth actually declined during the same period (Pond, 1983:15). Thus the following analysis of the socio-economic implications of the political rise of the new right and the implementation of its anti-Keynesian monetarist policies is premised on the distinctiveness of the post-1979 policy to reverse the historical growth of the welfare state in Britain.

One of the major tasks of social policy analysis is to "evaluate the distributional impact of existing policies" (Walker, 1981:225). According to this view therefore, inequality is the central issue raised by the expansion of social expenditure that the term welfare state summarises. Although the basic structure of inequality in Britain has not been altered by the development of the welfare state (Wedderburn, 1974; Westergaard and Resler, 1975; Townsend, 1979), it is within this context that we will be considering the social impact of the cuts in public spending between 1980/1 and 1983/4.

Historically the distributional impact of the development of the welfare state has been analysed in terms of class, often in combination with need arising from the patterning of dependence over the family life cycle (Rowntree, 1901). Of these two dimensions, class inequality is by far the most dominant theme in the literature (George and Wilding, 1984; Le Grand, 1982; Tawney, 1952; Titmuss, 1962). Arguably, this dominance reflects its explanatory significance and the extent of its documentation in official statistics and social policy research. In this tradition, changes in welfare state services and benefits are usually examined with reference to occupational and/or income classes.

The recognition that need varies over the life cycle is a minor though persistent theme in the study of social policy outcomes (Taylor-Gooby, 1983; Titmuss, 1958; Whiteley, 1981). More recently, the gender dimension of the welfare state has belatedly attracted more attention, despite the limitations of available data (Edgell and Duke, 1983; Rose, 1981; Wilson, 1977).

Whereas there is considerable agreement regarding the social policy significance of class, life-cycle and gender inequalities, there is some controversy concerning the exact relationship between political-geographic areas and the patterning of social expenditure (Alt, 1971; Boaden, 1971; Davies et al, 1972; Oliver and Stanyer, 1969; Newton and Sharpe, 1977; Nicholson and Topham, 1972; Sharpe and Newton, 1984). Until quite recently this debate had, of necessity, been conducted solely in the context of the expansion of welfare state spending, rather than in the context of retrenchment (Duke and Edgell, 1985).

The racial and ethnic dimension of inequality and the welfare state has become a major social research specialism of great political importance in Britain, with particular emphasis on education and housing (Husband, 1982; Rex and Moore, 1967; Rex and Tomlinson, 1979).

Finally, it has been suggested that the distributive consequences of changes in public spending are best understood by a sectoral cleavage model (Cawson and Saunders, 1983; Duke and Edgell, 1984; Dunleavy, 1980; Saunders, 1981). Sectoral cleavages refer to divisions between those who are dependent upon the public or private sectors for their employment (i.e. as producers) or for certain services (i.e. as consumers). Production and consumption sectoral cleavages cut across class divisions and are thought to have become increasingly important in recent years in relation to both social inequality and political alignment.

Of these six possible sources of inequality and welfare state services (class, life-cycle stage, gender, political area, race/ethnicity and sector), our surveys on the social and political effects of the public expenditure cuts were designed to cover each of the dimensions except race/ethnicity, which was excluded to avoid the possibility of "contaminating" the class data (Edgell and Duke, 1981 and 1985). In the analysis that follows, gender is also excluded on the grounds that we have recently considered it in its own right (Edgell and Duke, 1983). Of the four dimensions that are examined below, political area has been discussed by us elsewhere at length and will only be referred to here where relevant (Duke and Edgell, 1985). The main focus of the analysis is to assess the relative merit and demerit of class, stage in the life cycle and sectoral dimensions of the perceived impact of the cuts in public spending between 1980/1 and 1983/4.[1]

GREATER MANCHESTER STUDY

The research design adopted involved a comparison of two socially similar urban wards in Greater Manchester, one in a district represented by a Conservative MP and controlled locally by the Conservative Party (Torytown) and the other in a district represented by a Labour MP and controlled locally by the Labour Party (Labourville). The decision to study more than one area was thus partly based on the wish to study variations in local authority policies (for a detailed appraisal, see Duke and Edgell, 1985).

At the time of the 1981 Census Torytown and Labourville were socially comparable in terms of age, sex, employment status (the official definition for neo-Marxist social class) and housing tenure. The selection of two matching socially mixed wards was a deliberate attempt to survey a cross-section of the population that excluded neighbourhoods at the extremes of the class structure.

The first interview survey was conducted between September 1980 and March 1981. The target was a 10% systematic sample selected from the electoral registers in each ward. A total of 948 were interviewed, which represents 63% of the initial sample and 76% of those who were known to be eligible. The follow-up survey was conducted between September 1983 and March 1984 and 685 of the original respondents were re-interviewed. This represents 72% of the original sample and 86% of those known to be eligible. For both stages the response rate in the two wards was almost identical and approximately 90% of all interviews were completed during the first three months of fieldwork.

TABLE 1a: Labourville and Torytown Comparisons: 1981 Census, First Interview Cross-Section (1981-82) and Second Interview Cross Section (1983-4)

	LV			TT		
	CENSUS %	GMS1 % (N=461)	GMS2 % (N=334)	CENSUS %	GMS1 % (N=487)	GMS2 % (N=351)
AGE						
16-29 (CENSUS)	27			29		
18-29 (GMS)		21	17		23	23
30-39	16	20	22	17	18	18
40-49	16	18	22	13	16	17
50-59	15	15	16	14	17	19
60-69	14	17	18	13	11	12
70-79	10	9	7	10	13	10
80+	3	1	.5	4	3	1
SEX						
male	47	49	48	48	49	53
female	53	51	52	52	51	47

TABLE 1b:Labourville and Torytown Comparisons: 1981 Census

Employment Status (Social Class)

	LV			TT		
	CENSUS %	GMS1 % (N=461)	GMS2 % (N=334)	CENSUS %	GMS1 % (N=487)	GMS2 % (N=351)
self-employed + employees i.e. employer	2	3	2	3	4	3
self-employed − employees i.e. petty bourgeois	4	5	8	5	4	10
supervisor of others, i.e. controller	22	29	30	24	32	30
employee i.e. worker	71	64	59	68	60	57
HOUSING TENURE						
owner-occupied	73	79	82	69	77	81
council rented	13	14	12	11	11	9

Table 1 shows that those interviewed at both the first and second stages of the project were broadly representative of the total population of the two wards. More specifically at the first and second stages, the youngest and oldest age groups were slightly under-represented; the former due mainly to the inclusion of 16-18 year olds in the Census but not in our surveys and the latter due to the lower response rate among older respondents. The over-representation of controllers of labour at both stages in both wards is due to the more restrictive operational definition of this social class adopted in the Census compared with our survey. The noticeable increase in petty bourgeois respondents at the second stage reflects the tendency for some redundant workers to become self-employed (Employment Gazette, 1983 and 1984). Finally, the high degree of owner occupation in the two wards was part of the research design in that several commentators attributed Conservative success in 1979 to the defection of manual worker house owners. The increase in owner occupiers at the second stage is partly due to local authority and housing association privatisation.

The interview survey data are but one of three main data sources; the other two are (a) official data on actual changes in public spending in the two districts and at central government level, and (b) local, regional and national press coverage of the spending cuts. In this chapter we will be concentrating on the survey data supplemented where relevant with official data.

Our survey data may be analysed in two forms, cross-sectional and panel. Cross-sectional results are based on the full samples at the first and second interviews (i.e. 948 and 685 respectively). Cross-sectional date is appropriate for comparing the relationship between variables at the two points in time. On the other hand, panel results are based only on those interviewed twice (i.e. 685) and they facilitate the measurement of individual changes over time. In the following discussion, the findings for Labourville and Torytown are combined for the analysis of social class, life-cycle and sectoral influences but are kept separate for knowledge and perceived impact, as there are significant differences between the two wards on these variables.

Prior to examining the perceived impact of the cuts it is necessary to establish the validity of our data. This will be done by presenting evidence of the levels of knowledge of changes in public spending displayed by our sample.

KNOWLEDGE OF THE SPENDING CUTS

At the time of the first interview 96% of the respondents had heard of the cuts in public spending. Of that 96%, only 7% failed to give a satisfactory explanation as to what they understood by the spending cuts. Subsequent questioning of the apparently nescient 11% (4% not heard and 7% unsatisfactory) about cuts in specific services left a residue of 4% of the sample who did not display any knowledge of the spending cuts during the first interview. This residue comprised only 2% of the panel sample (due to the disproportionate loss of the less knowledgeable old and frail) and of these only a quarter (or 0.5% of the panel sample) expressed no knowledge at the second interview. These high levels of knowledge suggest that the vast majority of our respondents were aware of public spending cuts at both stages of the research.

The extent of respondents' more detailed knowledge of changes in public spending was investigated in both surveys with reference to four services: education, health, transport and social services. This was achieved using an open-ended question on each of the four services and the answers were categorised into those with no knowledge of cuts, those with general knowledge only (i.e. there have been cuts but cannot give any specific details) and those with specific knowledge of the cuts in the service. Examples of the most frequent specific knowledge items mentioned are provided in Table 2 (over).

At the first interview the panel overall exhibited most knowledge on cuts in education (over two-thirds with specific knowledge cf. Table 2), though more emphatically in Torytown. The first stage followed a prolonged teachers' strike and school closures dispute in Torytown which accounts for education's relative prominence there. Of the other services, there were majorities with specific knowledge on transport and health but a distinct lack of knowledge of any cuts emerged for the personal social services. Indeed, there was evidence of considerable confusion among a minority of the sample as to what constituted these services.

Labourville displayed significantly greater knowledge on health and transport cuts than Torytown in 1980-1. These differences were maintained at the second interview and possible explanations for this will be taken up later after considering the impact data.

In both areas the proportion of respondents with no knowledge whatsoever declined in all four services at the second stage, the decline being quite substantial in the case of health and social services. Other changes over time were consistent in the two areas. Health was the only service whose level of specific knowledge increased in both areas, in fact taking over from education as the service with the most knowledge overall (though not quite in Torytown). Specific knowledge of cuts in education and transport decreased significantly for both areas at the second interview. These figures are explicable in terms of particular events prior to the first interview such as disputes over education cuts in 1980-81 and in the case of transport, a reduction in bus services and an increase in bus fares by Greater Manchester Transport during 1980. Personal social services remains the lowest on specific knowledge, though increasing slightly in Torytown.

Table 2: Specific Knowledge of Spending Cuts in Education, Health, Transport and Social Services by Area: Panel at First and Second Interviews

	LV (N=334)			TT (N=351)		
	GMS1	GMS2		GMS1	GMS2	
EDUCATION						
% specific knowledge	67	50	−17	70	52	−18
most frequent mentions at GMS2	fewer staff	72		fewer staff	91	
	school closures	36		school closures	69	
	universities	35		school books	47	
HEALTH						
% specific knowledge	61	66	+5	46	50	+4
most frequent mentions at GMS2	fewer staff	122		fewer staff	94	
	privatisation	74		hospital facilities	41	
	hospital closure	52		waiting lists	30	
TRANSPORT						
% specific knowledge	68	49	−19	59	32	−27
most frequent mentions at GMS2	fewer services	100		fewer services	78	
	increased fares	65		increased fares	40	
	fewer staff	34		fewer staff	15	
SOCIAL SERVICES						
% specific knowledge	31	26	−5	27	29	+2
most frequent mentions at GMS	home helps	23		home helps	59	
	elderly facilities	18		fewer staff	23	
	means on wheels	15		fewer visits	22	

At the second interview stage questions on four additional services were included: defence, police, housing and social security. Thus, in all, questions about changes in the patterning of public spending were directed at eight services. In 1983-4, not only the level of knowledge on each service was ascertained but also respondents' perceptions as to whether spending on the service had been cut, stayed the same or had increased.

Tables 3a and 3b show that Labourville respondents were generally more knowledgeable than Torytown respondents on six services in terms of the ability to mention specific service items. However, the percentage of respondents in Torytown who revealed no knowledge of specific services was higher for all the eight services investigated. Of the four additional services none matched the high levels of specific knowledge for health and education. Three of them were on a par with transport at just over 40% specific knowledge, whilst the police evoked low specific knowledge at around 30%, equivalent to the personal social services. The only significant difference between the two areas on these four services was the higher level of knowledge on welfare benefits in Labourville. This point will be taken up again later.

TABLE 3a:Perception of Spending Trends and Specific Knowledge of Spending Cuts and Proportion Local Specific Knowledge for Eight Services by Area: Second Interview Cross Section

LABOURVILLE (N=334)

Perception of spending trend

	% cut	% same	% increase	% specific	% of the specific knowledge which is explicitly local
Health	93	2	2	66	15
Education	84	1	1	50	37
Transport	66	14	2	49	80
Housing	50	14	6	44	29
Social Services	47	16	3	26	27
Welfare Benefits	49	14	20	47	0
Defence	19	11	57	44	1
Police	10	30	43	31	6

Table 3b:Perception of spending trends and specific knowledge of spending cuts and proportion local specific knowledge for eight services by area: 2nd interview cross-section (contd.)

TORYTOWN (N=351)

	% cut	% same	% increase	% specific knowledge	% of the specific knowledge which is explicitly local
Health	84	2	4	50	29
Education	83	4	2	52	52
Transport	52	15	2	32	70
Housing	54	10	3	40	26
Social services	52	9	4	29	32
Welfare benefits	36	14	19	38	0
Defence	20	9	52	40	1
Police	9	21	46	29	18

Respondents' perceptions of the direction of spending changes reveal some interesting patterns and a large degree of consensus. An overwhelming majority (in excess of 80%) are of the view that spending on health and education has been cut. These are of course also the two services with high levels of specific knowledge. For three other services (transport, housing and social services) there are marginal majorities (50% and just over) who perceive a reduction in spending. Slightly less than half of the sample (42%) state that welfare benefits have been cut but it is clearly the modal answer.

There are thus six services which our sample perceive as having been cut. In stark contrast the remaining two services are seen as experiencing increased expenditure; by a majority in the case of defence and by just under half (46%) in the case of the police. Given the clear patterning of relative spending perceptions it is instructive to compare these subjective appraisals with the "objective" statistics published by both central government and the two local authorities - see Tables 4 and 5. Prior to this comparison, however, it is necessary to consider briefly the definition of a "cut in spending".

There are basically three ways of measuring changes in public expenditure: (1) In cash terms which is the method favoured by the Conservative government since the Public Expenditure White Paper of 1982 on the grounds of cost (!). It is the least instructive for historical comparisons and recognised to be so by the Treasury and Civil Service Committee (Fifth Report Session 1981-2). (2) In cost terms controlling for the general level of inflation using the GDP deflator. This is the most commonly used definition and that employed in Table 4. (3) In relative cost terms within services which is the most difficult definition to operationalise but it has the virtue of taking into account relative price changes and the growth of demand for particular services (from for example increasing numbers of old people). This method formed the basis of the volume figures used in the Public Expenditure White Papers prior to 1982.

A further complication arises in that the subjective appraisals may be based on differing frames of reference. Thus it is perfectly possible for a service which has been increased nationally to have been cut in the local area. For many of our respondents local knowledge was paramount. Tables 3a/b list the proportion of specific knowledge which was explicitly local for both areas. This data should be interpreted as the minimum level of local knowledge, in that many respondents may have based their knowledge on local experience without explicitly stating a local example (which was our criterion for inclusion). The proportion of local knowledge is highest for transport and education and is also significantly higher in Torytown than Labourville for four of the services. Finally, even within overall programmes which may have experienced increased spending both nationally and locally, there can be specific cuts on particular items which may be of importance to the respondent.

Despite these problems there are clear links between the subjective perceptions in Tables 3a/b and the "objective" cuts in Tables 4 and 5. The perceptions of increased defence and police expenditure are clearly mirrored in the consistent upward trends in Table 4. Equally the perceived cuts in transport and housing can be located in the official data, although the extensive "objective" cuts in housing are not similarly outstanding in the subjective data. The local authority data (Table 5) provide evidence of actual cuts in both areas on all three services with the exception of personal social services in Labourville.

Table 4. Actual central government spending trends on eight services in cost terms at 1982-3 prices: Cmnd.9143 (1979-80)

(1979-80 = 100)

	1979-80	1980-1	1981-2	1982-3
Health	100	108.1	110.5	112.3
Education	100	102.7	101.5	102.0
Transport	100	102.7	100.00	96.4
Housing	100	83.1	53.1	42.0
Personal Social Services	100	104.4	104.8	107.1
Welfare Benefits	100	101.7	112.8	120.1
Defence	100	102.0	104.7	112.3
Police	100	100.3	110.5	115.0

The remaining four services, however, require closer examination in that there is a marked disjuncture between the perceived and actual patterns. In the case of education the discrepancy is readily explicable in terms of local cuts within the context of a slight national increase (although education spending did drop nationally between 1980-1 and 1981-2). There were real cuts in Torytown education spending during this period and specific items were cut in Labourville (see Duke and Edgell, 1985 and Table 5 over).

Health expenditure has increased consistently in cost terms according to Table 4 which sharply contrasts with the 89% perceived cuts in Tables 3a/b. The explanation here would appear to lie in a combination of: (1) adopting a relative costs framework which perceives volume cuts in the National Health Service (NHS); and (2) knowledge of local cuts in specific items. Both wards have large general hospitals on their boundaries and thus contain a substantial number of NHS producers (16% of households had one). The personal social services disparity between Tables 3a/b and 4 can also be accounted for by the application of a relative cost framework (particularly with regard to the increasing ranks of the elderly in need of such services) as well as by actual cuts in Torytown (see Table 5 over).

Table 5. Actual local authority spending trends on three services in cost terms

Labourville District Authority

Net Expenditure in Cost Terms* on Education, Personal Social Services and Housing 1978-9 to 1982-3: 1982-3 prices, 1978-9 = 100

	1978-9	1979-80	1980-1	1981-2	1982-3
Education	100	96.2	97.6	98.6	94.7
Personal Social Services	100	102.8	106.1	107.0	107.5
Housing	100	110.1	102.5	83.0	66.5

Torytown District Authority

Net Expenditure in Cost Terms* on Education, Personal Social Services and Housing 1978-9 to 1982-3: 1982-3 prices, 1978-9 = 100

	1978-9	1979-80	1980-1	1981-2	1982-3
Education	100	93.3	91.9	90.3	89.5
Personal Social Social	100	99.4	98.6	99.4	104.9
Housing	100	94.4	98.1	39.5	44.7

* Adjusted for inflation by the Gross Domestic Product deflator.
Adapted from Torytown Treasury Department figures.

The least consensus on the direction of spending changes in Tables 3a/b is over welfare benefits. This accurately reflects the reality of increased social security expenditure overall (because of rising unemployment) but at the same time the value of specific benefits has often not kept up with inflation (e.g. unemployment benefit) and some benefits have been abolished altogether (e.g. the earnings related supplement paid for the first six months of unemployment). Clearly, respondents varied as to which part of this paradox they emphasised.

On the basis of our survey data collected from the same respondents at two points in time we can confidently state that our Greater Manchester sample were clearly aware of cuts in 1980-1 and had become even more so by 1983-4.

PERCEIVED IMPACT OF THE PUBLIC SPENDING CUTS

Measuring the impact of the spending cuts is far from straightforward. For example, in objective terms it may be possible to document that hospital X has been cut and therefore argue that both NHS users of, and NHS workers in that hospital have been affected. However, it has already been suggested that the consumers and producers of state services may perceive the situation differently from this. Thus our strategy has been to measure the subjective impact of the cuts according to the respondents' definition of the situation.

Following on from the knowledge questions outlined above, we asked our respondents an open-ended question as to whether they or anyone else in the household had been affected by the spending cuts in the preceding period. Interviewers were instructed to probe fully on this question and record all details. The answers were coded according to who in the household was affected, whether this was as a consumer or producer of services, and which service or sector respectively was involved.

It is clear from Table 6 that the overall perceived impact of the cuts was quite similar in both areas and remained fairly constant over time at just over 50%. Moreover, a large minority (one-third) of panel respondents in both areas considered that they had been affected by the cuts in public spending in the period prior to both interviews. In fact, only 26% of the panel sample stated no impact at both interviews. The Torytown panel proclaimed a significantly higher level of multiple impacts on the household at both interviews, which squares with the picture obtained from local authority data of more substantial cuts in Torytown than in Labourville over this period (Duke and Edgell, 1985 and Table 5).

Table 6. Perceived impact of spending cuts on household as consumers and producers by area: panel at first and second interviews

	LV (N=334)			TT (N=351)		
GENERAL	GMS1	GMS2		GMS1	GMS2	
% reporting any impact	55	49	-6	55	55	0
CONSUMER						
% affected as consumer	35	27	-8	44	37	-7
% education	16	9	-7	24	17	-7
% transport	6.5	.5	-6	5	2	-3
% welfare	4	12	+8	2.5	9	+6.5
% health	3.5	2.5	-1	2.5	4	+1.5
%social services	1	.5	01.5	1.5	1	-.5
% housing	1	2.5	+1.5	1	.5	-.5
PRODUCER						
% affected as producer	23	28	+5	16	26	+10
% redundancy	7	17	+10	5	11	+6
% private sector	10	17	+10	5	11	+6
% local authority	9	6	-3	6	6	0
% education	6	2	-4	3	4	+1
% health	1.5	3	+1.5	2	5	+3
% central government	1.5	3	+1.5	2	2.5	+.5

There is considerable evidence to suggest that our subjective measure of impact is an understatement. Many respondents in both interviews responded to later questions on particular services by clearly outlining cuts which had affected them that they had not mentioned in response to the impact question. For instance, later in the second interview we obtained two indicators of understatement of education cuts impact: first, of those households resorting to private tuition (e.g. music lessons) specifically because of local cuts only 31% had mentioned it previously under impact; second, of those using private nursery facilities specifically because of local cuts, only 27% had given this answer earlier.

Reported impact on panel respondents as consumers declined by 7% between 1980-1 and 1983-4 in contrast to producer impact which increased by 8%. Nonetheless, quite high levels of consumer impact were reported at both interviews, especially in Torytown (i.e. fully 44% in 1980-1) which remained higher than Labourville despite the decline over time. Consumer impact remained significantly greater than producer impact in Torytown at the second interview, whereas in Labourville the level of producer impact surpassed that of consumer impact.

Education was clearly the main consumer impact at the first interview, accounting for over half of all such impacts. The distinctiveness of the impact of education cuts in Torytown is apparent at both interviews (24% and 17%). The proportion mentioning consumer impact in transport decreased substantially which matches the knowledge pattern described previously. The only consumer impact to increase significantly is welfare benefits which has trebled in both areas and indeed overtaken education as the leading consumer impact in Labourville. This finding is in line with the general tendency for producer impact to increase and for consumer impact to decrease over the three year period between the two interviews. In other words, it reflects the dramatic increase and concern over unemployment during the period of this study.

The level of reported household unemployment was almost identical in both areas at both interviews, doubling overall from 18% to 36% in three years. An incredible 43% of the panel claimed that someone in the household had been unemployed at some time and this in a socially mixed, not a deprived, milieu. Of those unemployed at the first interview, 65% of households remained so at the second interview.

Further confirmation of the steep rise in unemployment over the period of the research is indicated by the trebling of mentions of unemployment by panel respondents when questioned about the producer impact of the public spending cuts. Virtually all the increase in producer impact is accounted for by redundancy in the household. The level of redundancy impact reported in Labourville was significantly higher than in Torytown at both interviews.

Perceived producer impact of the cuts may be either direct in the form of public sector workers, or indirect in the form of private sector workers. Producer impact among those employed in the private sector increased by 7% in Labourville and by 6% in Torytown. Taken together this amounts to a doubling of reported producer impact among this sector. The level of private producer impact was significantly higher in Labourville throughout. Of the public sector producers, the only significant increase between the two interviews was the doubling of reported impacts by NHS workers. The overall level remained low however.

Having examined the changing profile of perceived impact with a marked shift towards producer impact, we turn now to an examination of the three theories of the impact of the cuts outlined in the introduction; namely social class, stage in the life cycle and sectoral location. As our dependent variable is perceived impact on the household, we have measured all three independent variables at the level of the household. A justification for utilising household social class is presented in our ESRC report (Edgell and Duke 1985).

THE INFLUENCE OF SOCIAL CLASS LOCATIONS ON THE PERCEIVED IMPACT OF THE PUBLIC SPENDING CUTS

The class impact of social policy is typically examined with reference to occupational class (Le Grand, 1982; George and Wilding, 1984). This type of classificatory scheme tends to assume that the key distinction in the class structure is between manual and non-manual occupational classes. The alternative operationalisation of social class is to adopt a neo-Marxian conceptualisation that emphasises the distinction between employers, controllers of labour and employees (Dunleavy and Husbands, 1985; Wright and Perrone, 1977). In Table 7 cross-sectional data on impact using social class is presented and an interesting class pattern emerges.

241

Table 7: Perceived impact of spending cuts on household by household social class: first interview cross-section and second interview cross-section

% reporting any impact	GMS1 (N)	GMS2 (N)	
employer household	62 (45)	43 (28)	-19
petty bourgeois household	54 (76)	44 (72)	-10
controller household	53 (380)	44 (721)	0
worker household	53 (436)	54 (299)	+1
% affected as consumer			
employer household	40	32	-8
petty bourgeois household	43	29	-14
controller household	37	32	-5
worker household	41	34	-7
% affected as producer			
employer household	27	18	-9
petty bourgeois household	13	21	+8
controller household	22	31	+9
worker household	17	26	+9

NB. The household is classified according to whichever of the respondent or spouse has the highest class location (in descending order employer, petty bourgeois, controller and worker). Thus we are employing Ericson's method of coding the highest family member, but applied to social class categories rather than the occupational class over that he suggests (Ericson, 1984).

Most revealing is the distinctiveness of the employers who reported a considerably greater decline in impact over the period of the study. At the time of the first interview this social class were the most affected, at the second interview stage three years later they were the least affected in terms of overall perceived impact. In 1980-1 the other three social classes were identical in perceived overall impact, whilst the employers' greater impact was largely due to a higher level of perceived producer impact (i.e. own business affected).

By 1983-4 however, a distinct pattern consistent with the class interpretation of the public expenditure cuts had emerged for overall impact; the employer and petty bourgeois classes were less affected than the controller and worker classes. Thus whereas our data at the first interview did not lend support to those theorists (e.g. Gough, 1979 and Hall, 1983) who argue that the spending cuts are intended to alter the balance of class forces in favour of capital, the second interview most certainly does.

THE INFLUENCE OF LIFE-CYCLE STAGE ON THE PERCEIVED IMPACT OF THE PUBLIC SPENDING CUTS

Four life-cycle stages were distinguished at the first and second interviews: (1) households with retired persons only, (2) households with a combination of retired persons and those in full-time employment, (3) households with non-retired adults and children, and (4) households with non-retired adults but no children.

At the first interview, the non-retired plus children group reported the highest level of perceived impact and this rank position was maintained over time, despite a small decline. The latter can be linked to the decline in salience of education cuts over the three years. The same explanation accounts for the drop in perceived consumer impact among this category.

The retired group reported the greatest increase in impact over the period of the study due partly to an increase in consumption impact (i.e. welfare benefits), but mainly to the incidence of unemployment impact (i.e. forced early retirement).

The overall pattern of impact in terms of the life-cycle did not basically change over time and confirmed that the two most vulnerable life-cycle stages are the ones identified by Rowntree at the end of the last century, namely "early middle life" before children begin to earn, and in old age following retirement (1901: 169-72).

Table 8: Perceived impact of spending cuts on household by life cycle stage: first interview cross-section and second interview cross-section

	GMS1	GMS2	
% reporting any impact			
retired household	38 (191)	46 (164)	+8
retired + full-time work household	52 (27)	57 (23)	+5
Non-retired + children household	65 (422)	60 (265)	−5
Non-retired − children household	48 (308)	49 (233)	+1
% affected as consumer			
retired household	36	38	+2
retired + full-time work household	44	39	−5
non-retired + children household	49	38	−11
non-retired − children household	27	22	−5
% affected as producer			
retired household	3	9	+6
retired + full-time work household	7	30	+23
non-retired + children household	24	31	+7
non-retired − children household	23	35	+12

Table 9: Perceived impact of spending cuts on household by life cycle stage and household social class: first interview cross-section and second interview cross-section

	GMS1 E/PB (N)	GMS1 C (N)	GMS1 W (N)	GMS2 E/PB (N)	GMS2 C (N)	GMS2 W (N)
% reporting any impact						
retired household	35 (17)	38 (76)	38 (94)	50 (16)	45 (69)	46 (79)
non-retired + children household	66 (61)	67 (161)	62 (197)	53 (51)	58 (107)	65 (107)
Non-retired – children household	53 (38)	45 (130)	51 (136)	23 (30)	53 (98)	51 (105)
%affected as consumer	E/PB	C	W	E/PB	C	W
retired household	35	34	37	44	36	39
non-retired + children household	51	51	47	39	33	42
non-retired household	29	20	35	3	26	23
% affected as producer	E/PB	C	W	E/PB	C	W
retired household	0	7	1	6	12	6
non-retired + children household	21	27	22	25	38	27
non-retired – children household	24	25	19	20	35	40

E/PB = employer/petty bourgeois household: C = controller household: W = worker household.
N.B. Retired + full-time work households have been excluded from the control table because of low Ns. For the same reason the employer and petty bourgeois categories have been merged.

When a control for household social class is introduced, the influence of life-cycle is largely confirmed (see Table 9). Perceived impact among the retired is remarkably stable across the three classes at both interviews. The non-retired with children consistently display the highest level of overall impact in all classes. There is, however, a hint of class influence within this category at the second interview in that fully 65% of worker households with children have been affected by the cuts as compared to 58% of similar controller households and 53% of employer/petty bourgeois households.

THE INFLUENCE OF CONSUMPTION AND PRODUCTION SECTORAL LOCATIONS ON THE PERCEIVED IMPACT OF THE PUBLIC SPENDING CUTS.

The government's affirmed policy of "rolling back the state" may be expected to affect public sector producers and consumers disproportionately. The point at issue here is to what extent do they feel themselves affected by the spending cuts? The analysis by sector is bifurcated into perceived consumer impact in different consumption locations and perceived producer impact in different producer locations.

The influence of overall consumption location on perceived consumer impact was slight at the first interview but 3 years later there was a clear pattern consistent with sectoral expectations (see Table 10). Indeed, the only consumption location to register an increase in perceived consumer impact was that of totally public households to fully 56%. Thus public spending cuts are increasingly affecting those consumers most reliant on state services.[2]

Perceived producer impact was significantly higher among public sector households at both interviews (see table 10). Moreover, the largest increase in producer impact over the three years was also in this category so that increasingly the spending cuts are affecting public sector producers rather than those working in other sectors.

In order to appraise the salience of the spending cuts to various specific consumer and producer locations we also examined what proportion of each location perceived themselves affected by cuts in their service/sector (rather than by any cuts), a measure we have labelled "cuts consciousness". By far the highest level of consumer cuts consciousness was associated with state education users. Overall at the first interview the level of cuts consciousness among state

246

Table 10: Perceived impact of spending cuts on household-by-household consumption and production sectoral locations: first interview cross-section and second interview cross-section.

	GMS	(N)	GMS	(N)	
% affected as consumer[3]					
totally private household	36	(61)	35	(60)	-1
predominantly private household	39	(519)	27	(400)	-12
predominantly public household	41	(209)	39	(133)	-2
totally public household	42	(65)	56	(41)	+14
% affected as producer[4]					
self-employed household	19	(98)	22	(77)	+3
private sector household	13	(462)	21	(329)	+8
public sector household	26	(351)	37	(255)	+11
self-employed and public sector household.	14	(22)	13	(23)	-1

education consumers was just under half (47%), largely due to the 63% of Torytown respondents who attributed changes in their educational provision to cuts in education spending. Education consumer cuts consciousness decreased at the second interview, but it was relatively high compared to all other services, with the area differential remaining as large as ever (Torytown 56% and Labourville 24%). Significantly, in Torytown the highest level of producer cuts consciousness at both interviews was among education producers, rising from 27% to 35% at the second interview. The persistent distinctiveness of education, where there was a lengthy industrial dispute during the first fieldwork stage, has been apparent since the start of this project (Edgell and Duke, 1982b).

When controlling for household social class, the relationship between overall consumption location and perceived consumer impact changes over time. At the first interview there is clear evidence of the sectoral effect among controller households but not among worker households (see Table 11). By the second stage of the research the sectoral effect is also apparent among workers, with public consumers markedly more affected than private consumers.

Table 11: Perceived impact of spending cuts on household-by-household consumption and production sectoral locations and household social class: first interview cross-section and second interview cross-section.

	GMS(N)		GMS(N)	
% affected as consumer[1]	C	W	C	W
totally private household	30 (33)	44 (18)	44 (32)	33 (15)
predominantly private household	36(228)	40(205)	28(174)	26(154)
predominantly public household	46 (72)	39(118)	33 (52)	44 (73)
totally public household./	46 (13)	44 (46)	67 (9)	50 (30)
% affected as producer[2]	C	W	C	W
private sector household	14	13	21	22
public sector household	31	22	40	34

[1] See Note 3 at end of this chapter

[2] if either the respondent or spouse works in the public sector, the household is classified as public.

N.B. The employer and petty bourgeois classes are excluded from the upper half of the table (consumer impact) because of low Ns in the public sector categories, and from the lower half (producer impact) because they are of course in the self-employed sector.

248

When the relationship between production sectoral location and perceived producer impact is re-examined controlling for household social class, two significant conclusions may be drawn. First, the sectoral effect is strongly evident among both controller and worker households at both interviews. Second, within public sector households it is controllers who are more likely to feel affected at both interviews. Thus both sectoral and class effects are in evidence here.

In concluding this section it is pertinent to return to the significant knowledge differences between the two areas with respect to health, transport and welfare benefits, and examine first whether these differences are repeated in terms of perceived impact and second, whether they may be due to significantly larger numbers of service users or producers in the area. Labourville's greater knowledge levels on health and transport are not reflected in higher perceived impact but in the case of welfare benefits the level of perceived impact, is markedly higher in Labourville.

Labourville's superior health knowledge cannot be attributed to having more state health consumers as the level of NHS usage is identical (i.e. 96% in both areas in 1980-1). Part of the explanation may lie however in a significantly larger proportion of households in Labourville containing NHS workers (19% compared with 13%).

On transport there is clear evidence of more frequent public transport usage in Labourville. At the second interview 49% used public transport in the previous week compared to only 29% in Torytown. The explanation here is clearly one of differential consumption of state services.

The greater knowledge and perceived impact of welfare cuts in Labourville cannot be linked to either high usage or more producers in the area, therefore the explanation must lie elsewhere. Similarly with redundancy and private sector producer perceived impacts, their greater frequency in Labourville cannot be accounted for by differential rates of household unemployment or private sector employment. In an earlier paper that was based partly on our press data, we tentatively suggested that the most likely explanation of these local differences was ideological (Edgell and Duke, 1982a).

CONCLUSIONS

1. Impressively high specific knowledge of the cuts in public expenditure is demonstrated at both interview stages.

2. Health has overtaken education as the specific service of greatest knowledge, although the distinctiveness of education in Torytown continued to be revealed over time. Interestingly both these services are predominantly public in their consumption and thus used by all social classes. By contrast, those state services used mainly by workers (e.g. housing, transport and means-tested welfare benefits) are less prominent in public perceptions notwithstanding greater cuts on some of these services.

3. Changes in the patterning of knowledge and perceived impact of the spending cuts were clearly linked to actual events, especially local ones, prior to the two interviews.

4. In 1980-1 the major perceived impact of the cuts in public spending was on respondents as consumers (especially education in Torytown). Corresponding to the steep rise in unemployment, there was a clear shift towards producer impact (especially unemployment in Labourville) at the second stage in 1983-4. Our panel data has shown the importance of distinguishing between perceived producer and consumer impact.

5. The dramatic rise in unemployment during the period of the study was clearly reflected in all the data however it was analysed and presented.

6. There was some empirical support for the relevance of all three theories of social inequality that were utilised to examine the perceived impact of the public spending cuts between 1980-1 and 1983-4.

(a) **Social Class Theories**   The class patterning of the perceived impact of the cuts became more marked over time to the relative disadvantage of employees (controller and worker households) compared to employer and petty bourgeois households.   In the case of producer impact, employers were especially distinctive, being the only social class to report a decline in this type of impact over time.

(b) **Life Cycle Theory**   At the first interview households with children reported the greatest impact and this pattern declined slightly over time.   Households with retired persons reported an increase in overall impact during the period of the study and were the only group to report an increase in consumer impact.

(c) **Sectoral Cleavage Theory**   Evidence of the increased importance of both production sectoral cleavages and consumption sectoral cleavages over time.   In other words, the cuts are increasingly affecting public sector producers and public sector consumers.

7.   The application of these theories of social inequality to our cross sectional and panel date on the cuts revealed in each case interesting changes in social impact over time, changes that may not have become apparent in a non-longitudinal research design. With the relentless advance of the policy to restructure public spending, social class and sectoral location influences appear to have grown stronger. Thus in addition to traditional social class inequalities, Britain in the 1980s is increasingly experiencing new inequalities based on sectoral cleavages.

8.   The perceived impact of the cuts has been fragmented and arguably this reflects the highly selective nature of the restructuring of public spending.   Thus different households have been affected in different ways at different times.   It may be that these two factors, the selective nature of the policy and the fragmentary experience of the cuts, together explain the lack of a successful opposition to the new right policy in Britain.

NOTES

[1] A rather different but very significant economic and ideological indicator of the cuts is privatisation (Hastings and Levie, 1983; Le Grand and Robinson, 1984).   Preliminary analysis of our survey data shows that support for the policy to privatise welfare state services and nationalised industries is related to respondents' social class and production sectoral location (Edgell and Duke, 1985). However, we have yet to relate our material on privatisation fully and systematically to the theories under consideration. This factor, plus the problem of doing justice to this topic in a brief manner, precludes discussion of it below, but we recognise its centrality to the New Right policy to restructure public spending.

[2] Our measure of overall consumption location is based on three universal services (housing, transport and health) which are more or less continuously consumed by most households in

either private or state mode. We are aware that other services are omitted, but these tend to be more selectively and discontinuously consumed. Furthermore, we have employed this composite index of overall consumption location successfully in an earlier article (Duke and Edgell, 1984).

[3] Overall consumption location is based on household consumption of housing, transport and health. Totally private or public indicates that all three services are consumed in that sector, whereas predominantly private or public indicates that two out of three are.

[4] Self-employed and public sector are the two polar defining characteristics of production sectoral location. Thus if either the respondent or spouse is employed in one of these sectors, the household is so classified. (This method produces a small category of contradictory locations, i.e. self-employed and public sector, which is included above in the interest of completeness.) The private sector household category is residual in the sense that it is private only, i.e. nobody is self-employed or public.

REFERENCES

Alt, J. (1971): Some social and political correlates of County Borough Expenditures. British Journal of Political Science 1, 49–62.
Boaden, N. (1971): Urban Policy Making, Cambridge: Cambridge University Press.
Bosanquet, N. (1983): After the New Right, London: Heinemann.
Cawson, A. and Saunders, P. (1983): Corporatism, competitive politics and class struggle, in King, R. (ed) Capital and Politics, London: Routledge and Kegan Paul.
Davies, B., Barton, A., and McMillan, I. (1972): Variations in Children's Services Among British Urban Authorities, London: Bell.
Deacon, A. (1984): Was there a Welfare Consensus? Social Policy in the 1940s. In Jones, C. and Stevenson, J. (eds) Yearbook of Social Policy in Britain 1983, London: Routledge and Kegan Paul.
Duke, V. and Edgell, S. (1984): Public expenditure cuts in Britain and consumption sectoral cleavages. International Journal of Urban and Regional Research 8, 177–201.
Duke, V. and Edgell, S. 1985: Local authority spending cuts and local political control. British Journal of Political Science, forthcoming.
Dunleavy, P. (1980): Urban Political Analysis, London: Macmillan.

Dunleavy, P. and Husbands, C. (1985): British Democracy at the Crossroads, London: Allen and Unwin.

Edgell, S. and Duke, V. 1981: The Social and Political Effects of the Public Expenditure Cuts, Social Science Research Council Report, HR 7315.

Edgell, S. and Duke, V. (1982a): Collective Resistance to the Expenditure Cuts. Paper presented at the University of Konstanz, mimeo.

Edgell, S. and Duke, V. (1982b): Reactions to the Public Expenditure Cuts: Occupational Class and Party Realignment. Sociology 16, 431-9.

Edgell, S. and Duke, V. (1983): Gender and Social Policy: the Impact of the Public Expenditure Cuts and Reactions to them. Journal of Social Policy 12, 357-78.

Edgell, S. and Duke, V. (1985): Changes in the Social and Political Effects of the Public Expenditure Cuts. Economic and Social Research Council Report G0023107.

Employment Gazette 91.1983: London: HMSO.

Employment Gazette 92.1984: London: HMSO.

Erikson, R. (1984): Social Class of Men, Women and Families, Sociology 18, 500-514.

George, V. and Wilding, P. (1983): The Impact of Social Policy, London: Routledge and Kegan Paul.

Glennerster, H. (1980): Public Spending and the Social Services: the End of an Era? In Brown, M. and Baldwin, S. (eds) Yearbook of Social Policy in Britain 1979. London: Routledge and Kegan Paul.

Gough, I. (1979): The Political Economy of the Welfare State. London: Macmillan.

Gough, I. (1983): Thatcherism and the Welfare State. In Hall, S. and Jacques, M. (eds) The Politics of Thatcherism, London: Lawrence and Wishart.

Gough, I. et al, (1984): Thatcherism and Social Policy: the First Four Years. In Jones, C. and Stevenson, J. (eds) Yearbook of Social Policy in Britain 1983, London: Routledge and Kegan Paul.

Gould, F. and Roweth, B. (1980): Public Spending and Social Policy: the United Kingdom 1950-1977. Journal of Social Policy 9, 337-57.

Hall, D. (1983): The Cuts Machine: the Politics of Public Expenditure. London: Pluto Press.

Hastings, S. and Levie, H. (1983): Privatisation. Nottingham: Spokesman.

Husband, C. (1982): Race in Britain. London: Hutchinson.

Hyman, R. (1984): Strikes, London: Fontana.

Le Grand, J. (1982): The Strategy of Equality. London: Allen and Unwin.

Le Grand, J. and Robinson, R. 1984: Privatisation and the Welfare State, London: Allen and Unwin.

Mishra, R. (1984): The Welfare State in Crisis. Brighton: Harvester Press.

Newton, K. and Sharpe, L. (1977): Local Outputs Research: Some Reflections and Proposals. Policy and Politics 5, 61-82.

Nicholson, R. and Topham, N. (1972): Investment Decisions and the Size of Local Authorities. Policy and Politics 1, 23-44.

Oliver, F. and Stanyer, J. (1969): Some Aspects of the Financial Behaviour of County Boroughs. Public Administration 47, 169-84 .

Pliatzky, L. (1982): Getting and Spending. Oxford: Blackwell.

Pond, C. (1983): Taxation. In Lee, P. et al. Banishing Dark Divisive Clouds: Welfare and the Conservative Government 1979-1983. Critical Social Policy 3, 6-44.

Rex, J. and Moore, R. (1967): Race, Community and Conflict, London: Oxford University Press.

Rex, J. and Tomlinson, S. (1979): Colonial Immigrants in a British City, London: Routledge and Kegan Paul.

Rose, H. (1981): Re-reading Titmuss: the Sexual Division of Welfare. Journal of Social Policy 10, 477-502.

Rowntree, B. S. (1901): Poverty: a Study of Town Life. London: Nelson.

Saunders, P. (1981): Social Theory and the Urban Question. London: Hutchinson.

Sharpe, L. and Newton, K. (1984): Does Politics Matter? The Determinants of Public Policy. Oxford: Clarendon Press.

Social Trends 15, (1984). London: HMSO.

Tawney, R. H. (1952): Equality: London: Allen and Unwin.

Taylor-Gooby, P. (1983): Legitimation Deficit, Public Opinion and the Welfare State. Sociology 17, 165-84.

Therborn, G. (1984): The Prospects of Labour and the Transformation of Advanced Capitalism. New Left Review, 145, 5-38.

Titmuss, R. (1958): Essays on the Welfare State. London: Allen and Unwin.

Titmuss, R. (1962): Income Distribution and Social Change. London: Allen and Unwin.

Townsend, P. (1979): Poverty in the United Kingdom. London: Allen Lane.

Walker, A. (1981): Social Policy, Social Administration and the Social Construction of Welfare. Sociology 15, 225-250.

Walker, A. (1982): Public Expenditure and Social Policy. London: Heinemann.

Wedderburn, D. (1974): Poverty, Inequality and Class Structure. Cambridge: Cambridge University Press.

Westergaard, J. and Resler, H. (1975): Class in a Capitalist Society. London: Heinemann.

Whiteley, P. (1981): Public Opinion and the Demand for Social Welfare in Britain. Journal of Social Policy 10, 453-76.

Wilson, E. (1977): Women and the Welfare State, London: Tavistock.

Wright, E. and Perrone, L. (1977): Marxist Class Categories and Income Inequality. American Sociological Review 42, 32-55.

12 Protecting the local welfare state: what can localities do? Some British examples

MICHAEL GOLDSMITH
University of Salford

This chapter is designed to raise questions about two issues. First the likely conditions which must pertain if local authorities are to be able to protect/promote the local welfare state in the face of the adoption of what might be called 'fiscal crisis' policies by central government towards services provided by local authorities, and second, what are local authorities and other local interests/social movements likely to be able to do to protect/develop welfare state services at the local level on their own.

It is important to recognise at the outset some of the assumptions which underlie such a brief. In the first place there is an assumptions that there is a common definition of what we mean by the local welfare state and that the kinds of goods and services (collective consumption) provided under welfare state systems are essentially similar cross nationally. There is also an assumption that local governments are the essential delivery agent for such services in different countries. But a quick examination of real world practice speedily reveals that both these assumptions are misleading. For example, in France local governments only have limited education responsibilities (they do not for example employ teachers), whereas in Britain local education authorities have responsibilities for education virtually from the cradle to the grave. In Denmark and Sweden local authorities have responsibilities for unemployment benefits and health, neither of which are allocated to local government in England. Furthermore, if we begin to break such services down into more detailed categories of functions, then comparison becomes extremely difficult, and it is quickly apparent that we are not necessarily comparing like with like.

A further assumption is that local government will want to protect (and if possible extend) the range of services and activities for which it is responsible, even under conditions of cutback and restriction imposed by the centre. British and some United States experience indicates that this is not necessarily the case. For example, many Conservative controlled authorities, especially in the more rural shire districts, actually spend less and provide fewer services than central government's own estimates of such authorities' expenditure would lead one to expect. Even in the English metropolitan areas and the GLC one finds authorities who are prepared to cut expenditure per head in real terms and reduce service levels, despite the fact that many such authorities can be shown to have high service needs. US data also suggests some similar patterns for expenditure levels for central city and suburban local governments (Goldsmith and Wolman, 1985). Putting this point in simple terms, it would be misleading to expect all municipalities to want even to protect existing service levels, let alone want to take local initiatives to promote new collective consumption.

Third, there is an assumption that the crisis (in so far as there is one) is a crisis of the welfare state. That is to say, it is a crisis of collective consumption and not of production. Yet there is evidence from a number of countries that the major focus of both central and local governments has been on economic regeneration. In particular, localities have sought to protect their workforces from the worst effects of changing technological and economic environments, and whilst most national governments have not resorted to a form of economic protectionism, they have all adopted strategies which they hope will be attractive to capital. In this sense, botyh centre and periphery see efforts at protecting the economy as the best way out of the crisis. As such the emphasis is on production rather than consumption. Indeed, it is the additional ideological belief in the value and virtue of market forms and self help which leads to a further attack on welfare state issues. Such a move has been pronounced in Britain, if not altogether successful, but less marked in Scandinavia, and strongly resisted in France.

Last, an assumption is made that services associated with the term welfare state are provided by the public sector, rather than by the private/voluntary sector, or in some mixed mode, as is the case with some services in France and parts of

Scandinavia. From the experience of Britain over the last few years, such assumptions are not necessarily valid. The Thatcher government has a minimalist, highly selective, safety net view of welfare, with a strong belief in private provision by individuals for such services as health, housing and even education: all services associated with the terms collective consumption or welfare state. It is worth noting in this context that even sectors of the organised working class have been prepared to accept deals which provide private health care as part of their pay settlement. Further the present British government sees the way in which people can be encouraged to accept these self-help ideas is by providing fiscal rather than social benefits: tax cuts and the removal of the lower paid from the tax net, together with an emphasis on indirect rather than direct taxation, instead of the provision of social wage benefits. Such policies may be very attractive, not only to the higher paid who have benefited most under the Thatcher government, but also initially to lower paid workers as well.

Whilst the Thatcher government is perhaps the best example of New Right (or is it a reversion to 19th century economic liberalism?) ideology currently available, there are echoes of it to be found in other parts of Europe, not least of all in Denmark. And whilst the Mitterand government in France adopted a radical Left approach to its problems in 1981, more recently it has adopted the retrenchment policies generally associated with more conservative regimes (Preteceille, 1983). Such policies are designed to meet the interests of capital in its various guises, in the hope that somehow each nation state can avoid the worst consequences of current economic and technological change, and protect itself from trends in the operations of multi-national capital.

All the examples concerning the assumptions on which much of this chapter is based indicate the kinds of constraints under which local governments cross nationally and in particular countries have to operate if they seek to protect the local welfare state or if they seek to redefine the economic relationship between labour and capital or between worker and employer. Not only must we make the assumption that individual localities can somehow compete with and even reverse the trends in international capital, but we must also make the assumption that localities will wish to do so are empowered to act in such a way, and have the discretion or autonomy to do so. Given this highly constrained situation, this chapter seeks to examine some of the conditions which seem necessary if localities are to be able to protect themselves, and to consider some of the strategies which such authorities are currently adopting in Britain.

CONDITIONS FOR LOCAL ACTION

In introducing these conditions, it is important to recognise their ideal typical nature. As a consequence, they may appear extreme, but in reality the scope for local initiatives and actions is heavily constrained, not only by the absence of many of the conditions set out here, but by other limiting factors. For example, in times of economic recession when national governments are hardly able to weather the storm, what localities can do must inevitably be marginal.

1. Functional Competence

If municipalities are to be able to promote or protect their welfare state services by their own actions and policies, then it follows that they can only act for those areas of activity for which they have responsibility. In those countries where local government is presumed to have general competence, scope for independent action is likely to be greater than in those countries where municipalities have only special competences. For example, British local authorities have only specific competences, these powers being determined by the doctrine of ultra vires. The doctrine states that local governments in Britain can only do those things for which Parliament has given them express powers.

But it is also clear that even in those countries where local government is presumed to have a general competence (as with Denmark), such competence itself may be limited by other central state action, legislation and policy. Thus being functionally responsible for a particular service, or being presumed competent to provide any service a locality likes is no guarantee that a municipality will be able to protect and promote that service in the face of considerable attack by the centre. Therefore, local government must not only be functionally competent and responsible for a particular service, it must also have the autonomy or the discretion to decide for itself the exact nature of provision for that service in its area.

2. Functional Autonomy/Discretion

Measuring the autonomy or discretion of a local government to undertake a function is fraught with difficulty, if only because the ways in which such autonomy/discretion may be limited are numerous. The autonomy/discretion of a local government will be greater, I suggest, under the following conditions, ceteris paribus:

First, where there is no general system of administrative regulation/control/approval for what municipalities do. A number of countries, including some in Scandinavia, have a system whereby local governments are subject to a process of administrative regulation and approval. Such a system can operate through the central state bureaucracy (as it does largely in Britain) or through some separate system of administrative tribunals. The more extensive and permeating such a system of administrative regulation becomes, the more likely it is that the autonomy/discretion of municipalities will be limited. There is some suggestion that in both Sweden and Denmark, for example, the process of administrative regulation is generally being weakened over recent years, but the reverse is more generally true of Britain, as policy planning systems and financial allocation processes have become more centralised (Goldsmith and Newton, 1983).

Second, local discretion will be greater where there is no State official charged with responsibility for the oversight of the affairs of a particular municipality or with approving its decisions. Put in more simple terms, the absence of a prefectoral/governor system is likely to increase local discretion. Clearly, as much French evidence suggests, the importance of such a system for overseeing the work of local authorities can vary over time, as does the extent to which such officials remain agents of the centre or become allies of the locality, but certainly the change in the role of the prefect after 1981 has been seen by a number of commentators in France as a significant development in forms of local discretion, even if the change had involved a formal recognition of an already existing informal practice. The inspectorates for particular services vary in their importance as agents for the centre in education; the inspectorate has been a major critic of falling educational standards in many authorities, but the criticism is by implication criticism of the centre, which has reduced finance available for education considerably over recent years.

Third, local discretion could be reduced if policy planning systems have been introduced for particular services at the behest of the centre, and which also require central approval for local proposals. For example, both Britain and Denmark have seen the introduction in recent years of such policy planning systems, and evidence from both countries suggests that they have led to increased evidence from both countries suggests that they have led to increased control by the centre over the localities for those service areas where such systems operate, such as housing, transport and land use planning in the U.K. (Malpass and Murie, 1983; Hambleton 1982).

By contrast, local discretion may be greater if technical resources (qualified professional staff for example) are locally rather than centrally based. For example, British local authorities employ large numbers of fully qualified professional staff, who are largely responsible for running the services provided by localities. The presence of such specialist staff gives the locality the (technical) resources to act independently of the centre, especially if such professionals are only weakly represented in the central bureaucracy. Compare the British example with French experience, however, where the centre has had (and maybe still does) a monopoly of such technical expertise. How professionals operate in practice, however, remains an open, debatable question: British experience suggests that in their own way and for their own reasons, such professionals have been a major centralising force at work in British urban policy (Dunleavy, 1981).

Last, the locality's financial dependence on the centre, for both current and capital expenditure should be minimal if local discretion is to be maximised. Access to a wide range of taxes, preferably of a naturally buoyant kind, is more likely to give localities the ability to fund services from own source revenues than (say) a system of local finance based on a narrow property tax. There is some evidence that those countries which have a local income tax as the basis for local finance (as is the case in Scandinavia largely) have been better able to maintain their discretion than is the case with those countries where the locality is dependent on property taxes (as is the U.K.) (Newton, 1980; Sharpe, 1981). Furthermore, local discretion is likely to be greater where a general/block/unhypothecated grant system is used than where grants are both specific and highly conditional. Despite the changes which have taken place in the grant system in Britain over recent years, authorities still should retain the freedom to decide how they will spend their money, although it may raise in local taxes may be further limited (via ratecapping or revision of the rating system), and that the use of specific grants has also increased in recent years.

All of the above seem to me to be conditions under which a locality may be able to retain its autonomy/discretion, that is to say to retain the capacity to act independently of the centre. Other factors which may also be important include a relatively weak role for the judiciary in deciding disputes between the centre and the locality, and the absence of some informal bureaucratic processes of regulation (government by circular or advice note). But if we assume that localities have both the functional capacity and the discretion to act independently of the centre, then they must also have the political will and the political access necessary to allow them to do so.

3. Political will and political access:

In some ways the ideas of political will and political access are the most difficult to operationalise. In simple terms I would suggest that two conditions have to be met if localities are to be able to act independently. First, local political elites must want to adopt political positions and policies which differ from those favoured by the centre. It also follows from this point that they must have some basis of local political support for doing so. In some cases this may mean a simple electoral mandate, though the problem is twofold. First, mandates may be reversed, as has been the case in some British localities. Second, the political elite (or the majority of them) may not remain firm/unified as a result of external pressure to conform with central guidelines also the case with some British authorities over expenditure guidelines and ratecapping.

More important it seems to me is the necessity for local elites to have strong local support if they are to oppose the centre, whether these be links with the ranks of organised labour (as is the case with some Left authorities in Britain, Denmark and France), both public and private sector; or be it with urban social movements (organised groups of service consumers/ the voluntary sector or whatever), or be it some sense of community solidarity (a manning of the community barricades – as with the miners' strike in some parts of Britain). Such a support building strategy is not simply the prerogative of the Left, however, and in many respects the Right has been at least as successful in some countries in securing local support for policies of tax cutting and service reduction.

The second condition which has to be met is that of political access. To put this point simply, the locality has to have the ability to put its view successfully to the centre: it has to be able to make the centre aware of its opposition in such a way that the centre will not accept the costs of confrontation. It is in this sense that such devices as the cumul des mandats in France and of party and proportional representation systems in Sweden and Denmark become important, for they allow political access, providing extra channels through which the locality may successfully express its opposition. The highly centralised nature of much bargaining between central government and the national representatives of local government (the local authority associations) in England means that it is difficult for localities to oppose the centre on anything other than a matter of relatively small importance, though the smaller, more personal networks of Wales, Scotland and Northern Ireland do sometimes produce substantial local victories (Goldsmith, 1985).

The Role of Capital Interests

It is perhaps obvious, but it also often overlooked in much British writing, that the nature of the local economy and of local capital is important to a locality's ability to operate independently of the centre. A strong, adaptable local economy, with sources of local capital (particularly finance capital) readily available to the locality is an ingredient making it possible for such a locality to oppose the centre. Not only do local political elites need to be able to build up support amongst local labour, local social movements and the community at large, but they also need the support of local capital interests, which themselves have to have the capacity to act independently. In my view, one of the major weaknesses of British localities is the absence of local/regional capital interests with strong local/regional ties, especially amongst finance capital. A similar situation may also exist in Denmark: it appears to be less true of France, where local/regional capital and finance interests remain with strong ties to their locality. To put this point crudely, national and multi-national firms and financial interests are rarely tied to a locality and thus have few reasons to support local fights against the centre.

WHAT CAN BE DONE: SOME BRITISH EXAMPLES

Assuming that the conditions I have suggested as necessary if localities are to have the capacity to act have been met, at least substantially, what can be done? In this section, discussion generally focuses on two developments associated with Left-wing municipalities in Britain. First there is the development of links with local capital interests, a move designed to protect and promote the local economy. Second there are the moves towards intra-authority decentralisation, designed to improve the planning and delivery of local welfare state services and to build up support for them amongst the local community. The first strategy tends to receive at least limited support amongst the Right: the second tends to be rejected, at least in part, by the Right.

Protecting/promoting the local economy

The problem of local economic decline is one faced by most British local governments, with few being able to contemplate measures designed to restrict growth. As a number of authors have noted (Mason and Young, 1983; Boddy and Fudge, 1984), most British local authorities now have some form of development programme; many employ officers whose sole responsibility is economic development or industrial policy, whilst in some cases both the programme and the strategy, as well as the staffing, is quite elaborate. At a very minimum all authorities will now have some sort of publicity outlining the opportunities for investment in their area; many will have building programmes which make industrial premises readily available to new industry. But it is the kind of programme adopted by the larger, frequently urban authorities, or their county counterparts in areas of severe economic decline (such as by Lancashire or the North East) which is of most interest for our purposes. Having first established some kind of development agency/board to promote this work (often one independent of the authority itself) such municipalities adopt two main strategies. The first kind involves a mixture of investment and incentive offering, at times in partnership with private capital. The strategy involves offering loans, or taking shares, to and in private firms, perhaps on favourable terms to the firm, but also involving some "commercial" basis to the operation. In this sense the municipality has to be prepared to call in its loans or sell off its shares if the risk proves overwhelming. In a number of cases (Sheffield is a good example) this kind of strategy has involved the authority becoming involved from the product identification stage through product development to marketing, as well as a preference for working with local, indigenous firms rather than national or multinational ones.

The involvement with private capital (banks, insurance companies, finance houses etc.) could be an important element in this strategy, but it is one which is often difficult to achieve. First, many of the firms involved will only have come to the municipality after they have failed to raise finance elsewhere. If they are such "bad risks", why should private capital agree to share them with the municipality? Second, private capital may seek a higher rate of return on its investment than might the municipality, though this is not

264

to say that municipalities should operate at low or negative rates of return on their investments. Third, and in some ways most critical, the highly nationalised and increasingly internationalised nature of much of British finance capital may make local investment unattractive to it, whilst their knowledge of local industry and its problems may be slim. Despite the fact that many banks advertise their willingness to assist small business, much finance capital is essentially footloose, and there is a case for introducing measures which would force some regionalisation of finance interests and obliging them to operate some kind of quota of investment on a regional level. Such a move would strengthen the ties between capital and the locality/region, perhaps putting the process of local economic development on a sounder basis.

A second element in this strategy is one designed essentially for small firms, either of the starter variety or for those who have reached what might be called take-off point. There is evidence first that many would-be entrepreneurs lack some essential business skills, may need cheap premises and/or some other ingredient, even if what they wish to do looks promising. May local authorities in Britain have introduced this kind of starter oriented activity, designed to help small businesses get off the ground. Training courses in running a business; special deals on small factory units etc. are all possible. If such firms are successful, they may well face a second collection of problems at a later stage, likely to occur after about four or five years after start up. At this stage, usually one of proposed expansion, the firm may well be faced with the need to find new premises, acquire large and more expensive machinery, add substantially to the labour force, or simply face a short term cash flow problem. A number of municipalities have learned to identify this stage of development in firms in their locality and have devised ways and means of offering assistance, sometimes in partnership with private capital, more frequently on their own account.

Both of these elements are concerned with the promotion of the economic development of the locality and essentially with the creation of new firms and new jobs. A further strategy is more concerned with job protection and involves reaching agreements with firms about labour conditions, rates of pay and no redundancy arrangements in return for financial assistance from the municipality. Such has been the strategy used by economic development agencies in such areas as the West Midlands, the GLC, Greater Manchester and Sheffield amongst others. Such a strategy must be relatively short term if it is not to become a longer term drain on local resources, and is obviously most usefully applied to those firms going through some temporary setback. In these cases firms can be protected along with jobs until the temporary difficulties have been overcome. In the longer terms such an approach is no guarantee that jobs will be permanently secured and means that municipalities' own resources are tied up and not either being renewed or released for use on some other activity. Partly for this reason, but obviously for more ideological ones, this strategy is not generally favoured by Conservative controlled authorities, even if they might accept the kind of strategies involving share holding or starter activity.

The area of economic development is one which is perhaps most favourable to local state activity, assuming that the climate of international capital and the state of the national economy are not such to dissuade the central state or private capital from allowing such local action. In a period of recession and high unemployment, it is unlikely that any central state will oppose such local activity too strongly, however opposed it might be to such local state intervention ideologically. In Britain, state aid to industry in a variety of guises has a long history, and whilst there have been and may well be further attempts to reduce the British central government involvement in such aid, it seems unlikely that local activity would be restricted, however, inefficient it may prove to be in the use of resources. To be seen as actively discouraging local policies which might create jobs during a period of high unemployment would have high costs for the centre, however symbolic in practice such local efforts prove to be in the national context. Whether private capital interests would regard such local activity favourably is slightly more difficult: clearly it would be well regarded by hard-pressed manufacturing interests, though perhaps it is less attractive to finance capital which is more likely to be attracted by the possible gains to be made from overseas investment. If the latter were to be restricted, then there might be another story.

But there remain two further difficulties: to what extent can such local activities be regarded as anything more than marginal in the face of world economic trends, and to what extent can municipalities avoid being exploited by major international/multi-national capital interests? Taking the money and running (albeit five or ten years later) is a well-known tactic adopted in Britain by many a national and multinational firm (as Merseyside could testify). Furthermore, if national governments have difficulty facing and weathering the economic storm, then how much more successful can municipalities be? Whilst reporting municipal job creation at a rate 1-2000 per annum, British cities such as Liverpool and Sheffield have lost jobs at a rate nearer to 10,000 per annum

266

in the last three or four years. However successful such areas as Silicon Glen in Central Scotland or Swindon in the South's Golden Triangle might be, they pall into insignificance when measured along current unemployment levels formally in excess of 3 million.

Promoting/protecting the Local Welfare State:

For those countries experiencing severe attempts at cutback in expenditure and service provision, protecting and promoting the welfare state has become a major national as well as local issue. In Britain it seems as if the whole concept of the welfare state is under attack and that it is undergoing a none too subtle redefinition from universal umbrella to a highly selective safety net. Given the importance of local government as the service-providing agency in many social democratic countries (its role in Britain is large, but perhaps not as big as that of local government in Scandinavia), then clearly it is at the centre of any attack which seeks to redefine the scope and nature of those services. It is in this context that the issues of functional allocation, local discretion and political will become paramount if municipalities are to be able to protect what they do in the name of the local welfare state.

In this context, it is the alliance of municipalities with local social movements, voluntary groups, local unions (particularly those representing the public sector) which is crucial if local welfare state policies are to be protected. In Britain again, a number of left-wing Labour authorities have begun to build such an alliance and have sought to consolidate it by the decentralisation of a number of services (Hambleton, 1978). Though there were a number of attempts at decentralisation/area management in the post reform period of the mid-70s and after, in places like Newcastle and Stockport, these attempts were generally few and far between. The real move towards a more committed intra-authority decentralisation policy did not really start until the early 80s, when some left-wing Labour authorities who came to power after the 1981 local elections saw decentralisation as they way in which they could oppose Thatcherism and also defend local government against some of the worst attacks by the centre. But decentralisation was also seen as a means by which other objectives close to the heart of some local Labour politicians could also be achieved. First it was seen as a means by which local political power (that of the elected official) could be re-established against that of professional/bureaucratic power, something which many local left-wing politicians disliked and distrusted. Second, decentralisation was also seen by some as a means by which power could be "returned" to the people - the introduction of community/participatory democracy popular amongst many community activists since the mid/late 60s. Third, decentralisation has also been seen by some as a means by which welfare state services might be provided more efficiently and more in line with "client/consumer" needs, and it is interesting to note that most of the decentralisation schemes so far in operation tend to focus on a service like housing, with tenant participation in housing management as a good example of a decentralised service. Furthermore most schemes (actual and proposed) have some kind of community development as an objective.

Decentralisation schemes of this kind were first introduced in Walsall in the West Midlands and have since spread to a number of inner London authorities (such as Hackney, Islington, Lambeth and Camden) and to cities outside London such as Manchester, Birmingham and Bradford.

What experience to date would suggest is that progress towards decentralisation has been slow, limited in terms of the kind of services it embraces (frequently housing; education hardly ever), and that for most of the politicians involved the commitment is largely a symbolic one. Certainly there is some slight evidence to suggest that if "decentralisation" has allowed local left-wing politicians to re-assert their power over that of their paid· professional officials (in some cases this has led to a more overt politicisation of paid officials), then it has served its purpose, and there is then seen to be little need to proceed very much further on anything more than a symbolic level.

The other kind of realignment one can see in a small number of Labour controlled authorities is a closer alliance between local councillors and local public sector unions in a move to protect jobs and to maintain service levels. In places like Liverpool and Manchester, such alliances helped bring the Left to power in in the early 80s, but has subsequently involved local councillors in demonstrating considerable skill as they walk the tightrope between centrally imposed expenditure targets and tax limits on the one hand and their agreement with local public sector unions not to make cuts which result in lower services and job loss.

There is some evidence, both from Denmark and France, that similar alliances have been established, for example, over day care services in Denmark as well as alliances with local labour interests. Whether such alliances can persist in the long run seems doubtful, if only because there are many interests involved, none of which are likely to give up power enthusiastically. Nevertheless, some fundamental realignment of local political forces, which would involve a far greater recognition of local consumer, producer and community interests, is necessary if local government (in Britain at least if not elsewhere) is to have any real future as something more than a mere service delivery agent for the centre. Unfortunately what seems more likely to emerge in Britain is a much diminished local government in which the individualistic, selective market forces of the Right with an emphasis on low taxes, low services and individual self help are dominant. Whilst such a development will probably lead to a far greater role for the voluntary sector in the provision of welfare services, such provision will be on the basis of volunteerism and charity rather than on the basis of a universalistic welfare state. And whilst the ideologues of the Left continue to preach decentralisation and the importance of forging new local alliances, it is the forces of the Right who have to date been prepared to practise such a policy: in so doing they devalue and reduce both the character of the local welfare state and of local government, something which the unclear result of recent local elections in Britain, which resulted in a large number of "hung" authorities, is unlikely to change in the immediate future.

REFERENCES

Boddy and Fudge (eds) (1984): Local Socialism, London, Macmillan

Dunleavy, P. (1980): "Professions and Policy Change: Notes Towards a Model of Technological Corporation". Public Administration Bulletin no.36, August, pp.3-16

Goldsmith M. and Wolman H. (1985): "Changes in Grant and their consequences for metropolitan areas". Paper for ECPR Workshop on Metropolitan Government, Barcelona, March.

Hambleton, R. (1978): Policy Planning and Local Government, London, Hutchinson.

Hambleton, R. (1982): "The Housing Investment Planning System". Paper to SAUS Seminar on Planning Systems and Policy Implementation, Bristol.

Malpass P. and Murie, A. (1982): Housing Policy and Practice, London, Macmillan

Mason T. and Young K. (1983): Urban Economic Development, London, Macmillan.

Newton K. (1980): Balancing the Books, London, Sage.

Preteceille, E. (1983): "Economic Crisis, Urban Crisis, Hegemonic Crisis and the Territorial Reorganisation of the State". Paper prepared for ESRC Conference on Comparative Central-Local Government Relations, Nuffield College, Oxford, October.